GIBBS·SMITH
P
PUBLISHER
SALT LAKE CITY

AN ARCHITECTURAL
GUIDEBOOK TO
PHILADELPHIA

FRANCIS MORRONE ▾ PHOTOGRAPHY BY JAMES ISKA

TO VICTOR AND MARY RAINSFORD,
PHILADELPHIANS BORN AND BRED.
"PHILADELPHIA ARCHITECTURE"

04 03 02 01   5 4 3 2

Text copyright © 1999 by Francis Morrone
Photographs copyright © 1999 by James Iska

Published by
Gibbs Smith, Publisher
P.O. Box 667
Layton, Utah 84041

Orders: (1-800) 748-5439
Web site: www.gibbs-smith.com

Book design and production by Leesha Jones, Moon and the Stars Design

Printed and bound in the U. S. A.

LIBRARY OF CONGRESS CATALOGING-IN-PUBLICATION DATA

Morrone, Francis, 1958–
An architectural guidebook to Philadelphia / Francis Morrone; photography by James Iska.— 1st ed.
p. cm.
Includes bibliographical references and index.
ISBN 0-87905-890-0
1. Architecture—Pennsylvania—Philadelphia—Guidebooks.
2. Philadelphia (Pa.)—Buildings and Structures—Guidebooks.
3. Philadelphia (Pa.)—Guidebooks. I. Iska, James. II. Title.
NA735.P5M67   1999
720'.9748'11—dc21
                                                                98-50531
                                                                CIP

CONTENTS

INTRODUCTION

I am not now nor have I ever been a Philadelphian.

I am, however, married to a native Philadelphian. My wife's family has deep and varied roots in the city and its hinterland, and over the last fifteen years I have been privileged to observe certain aspects of certain habits of thought and action that have been shaped by (and that in turn helped to shape) Philadelphia, its history, topography, architecture, food, neighborhoods, and livelihoods.

I first visited Philadelphia on business trips before I married into the city. I stayed at the Bellevue-Stratford Hotel. I loved the hotel then and love it in its renovated form as Hotel Atop the Bellevue. I have stayed in many hotels around the world, but I have never enjoyed a hotel more than I have this Philadelphia classic on Broad Street. My wife's maternal grandmother, of Irish emigrant stock, was a maid at the Bellevue-Stratford.

My father-in-law's family was of a slightly different background. He grew up in Rittenhouse Square, a place with which I first became familiar, before visiting it, through the seminal writings of the great urbanist Jane Jacobs. When I first went to Philadelphia, I made a beeline for the square. I was not then and am not now disappointed by it, even though my father-in-law now prefers to live some distance from it.

Some readers or potential readers of this book may find me presumptuous for commenting upon and criticizing so many aspects of Philadelphia, since after all I do not live there. Perhaps I am presumptuous. But what I say is heartfelt. I do love Philadelphia, or I should say there is a Philadelphia that I love. It is not in all cases the Philadelphia that many residents of that city profess to love.

I am hardly the first to note a curious duality in the historical character of the place, a duality symbolized by the sharply contrasting characters of the city's two most famous sons (auslanders both): William Penn, who founded the city, and Benjamin Franklin, who founded or helped to found many of the city's leading institutions. I love William Penn. I suppose I love Benjamin Franklin, too, though I love little of what we may, with justification, count among his influences. The distinction is limned with artistry by Philadelphia's greatest writer, the historian John Lukacs. Penn, writes Lukacs, "was the contemplative humanitarian." Franklin was "the utilitarian eager beaver":

> Penn was the essential English (or, rather, Anglo-Celtic) case of the Rich Young Man Turned Humanist; Franklin was the more Germanic (and essentially Bostonian) ideal of the Poor Apprentice who became a Famous Scientist. . . . It is easy to fancy Franklin addressing the assembled ironmongers in the elephantine vault of the Masonic Temple in 1875, inaugurating the first nickelodeon movie in Philadelphia in 1900, judging the Miss America contest in Atlantic City in

1925, or introducing someone like Buckminster Fuller at the American Philosophical Society in 1975; it is difficult to imagine Penn doing anything of the sort. The shy, the gentle, the introverted, the myrtle-and-brick Philadelphia, where houses were named "Strawberry Mansion" and "Solitude," was that of William Penn. The city of the first utilitarian prison (a failure), of anthropological institutes, of the first national advertising agency (N. W. Ayer, founded in 1901), of the Curtis Publishing Company, was that of Benjamin Franklin. Franklin represented a certain inclination of the Philadelphia mind; Penn gave what was best to the Philadelphia heart. And by 1900 most Americans associated Philadelphia with Franklin as much as, if not more than, with Penn: in their minds *The Saturday Evening Post* and the *Ladies' Home Journal* were vaguely but indissolubly connected with images such as Independence Hall. Still, within Philadelphia the tolerant spirit of Penn continued to prevail. His peculiar mixture of pallid purposefulness, of deep-seated melancholy hidden behind the beneficent vigor of action has been his mysterious legacy to this day. (*Philadelphia: Patricians & Philistines, 1900–1950,* New York: Farrar Straus Giroux, 1981, pp. 43-44)

It is the quest for this "mysterious legacy" that informs (never with anything approaching the sparkle of Lukacs' prose) my ruminations on Philadelphia architecture and its associated realm. I prefer Penn to Franklin; I, after all, prefer (and here I speak only for myself) Maria Theresa to Frederick the Great (sorry, residents of King of Prussia).

I am not saying that Penn was perfect. He was not. Nor am I saying that Franklin did not do much good and does not have much to teach us. He did and does. But in the case of Penn, I think it can be said that never was a great city founded by so mild a man. And of Franklin, I think it can be said that much of what most disturbs in the evolution of the American character, the huckstering nature of our commercial civilization, the steady drumbeat of publicity, was, if not invented by him, cast by him in the pious light of duty, thus to obviate much of what was best in the American project.

One of the most touching and significant examples of Penn's "mysterious legacy," to turn now to architecture, was the "gentlemen's agreement" that kept all the city's buildings lower than the top of Alexander Milne Calder's statue of Penn surmounting City Hall. This, one of those things Philadelphians could know in their hearts made their city unique in America and better than other American cities, was killed by a combination of thoughtlessness, greed, and fashion in the 1980s. Even the ghastly "Penn Center" (it should have been called "Franklin Center") redevelopment of the heart of Center City, begun in the 1950s, had observed the gentlemen's agreement. By the 1980s, Philadelphia was losing her soul. And it is not so much that people seemed not to care that it is so upsetting, as that there were those, denizens of Center City and contributors to glossy magazines, who celebrated this turn of events, who felt that the towering Liberty Plaza by Chicago's Helmut Jahn conferred upon their city a certain *chic*. Little did these trend-mongers realize at the time that Helmut Jahn skyscrapers would soon be seen as ridiculous a *cliché* of the 1980s as, say, bell-bottom pants are of the 1970s.

This sort of thinking did not begin in the 1980s, of course. In 1974, Philadelphian John Francis Marion published his *Bicentennial City: Walking Tours of Historic Philadelphia,* one of the most genial, thorough, and informative guidebooks I know, and a book with which I have spent many happy hours. Yet, here is Marion on page nineteen: "It is generally accepted that Louis Sullivan, who preceded Frank Lloyd Wright as America's greatest architect, was influenced by the Leland Building when he designed some of the country's first tall buildings." Why does John Francis Marion, an exceptionally cultivated man who knows Philadelphia as few others do, fail or refuse to acknowledge that Philadelphia has produced a handful of architects *superior* to Sullivan and Wright? Even more bridling is how, in their eminently useful book *Architecture in Philadelphia: A Guide,* published in 1974, the academic architectural historians Edward Teitelman and Richard W. Longstreth, in their juxtaposed commentaries on the Cathedral of Saints Peter and Paul and on Mitchell/Giurgola's United Fund Building, both on the Benjamin Franklin Parkway, so obviously regard the latter as the superior example of architectural art, when everything that has been bequeathed us by the great tradition of Western civilization tells us this is not so, that, indeed, one of the very greatest treasures Philadelphians have in their midst is the Catholic cathedral on Logan Square.

There is, as the reader will note, much about Philadelphia today that I find distasteful: Penn Center, Penn's Landing, South Street, Independence Park, and so on. It seems, indeed, that it is many of the city's most heavily promoted attractions that I disdain. Yet there is another, an alternative Philadelphia redolent of bygone graces, that I love. Architecturally, Philadelphia, not Chicago or New York, is in my opinion the greatest American city. From Thomas U. Walter to Horace Trumbauer to Paul Cret, Philadelphia has been home to many of my favorite architects. No other American city can compete with Philadelphia in painting, from Charles Willson Peale through Thomas Eakins to Andrew Wyeth and Patrick Connors. Philadelphia is a great city for antiquarian books, for indigenous gastronomy, for museums and libraries. No other city has anything quite like Fairmount Park and the Wissahickon Valley, obtruded right in the densely populated metropolis: *rus in urbe.*

Thus my eagerness to celebrate Philadelphia even as I disparage its shibboleths.

This book concentrates solely on the city proper, and even then on only those areas that might reasonably be expected on visitors' itineraries. There is much more to Philadelphia, including the Barnes Foundation in Merion and the Brandywine River Museum in Chadds Ford.

I could not have written this book without the aid and example of many other books, including, especially, John Francis Marion's wonderful book mentioned above. Also of note is the informative *Philadelphia Architecture: A Guide to the City,* edited by the redoubtable John Andrew Gallery for the important and enterprising Foundation for Architecture. I hope that my book may complement Gallery's as well as the walking tours offered by the foundation. Three interpreters of Philadelphia stand, for me, above all others, as quotes from their works in the pages that follow will attest: John Lukacs, mentioned above; Agnes Repplier, one of the greatest American essayists, though her works are little read today; and the sociologist E. Digby Baltzell, who wrote with a grace and geniality that is exceedingly rare in works of academic sociology, and whose encyclopedic books on Philadelphia society are the essential starting points for anyone who wishes to write about this city. In many, though not all, matters of architecture I defer to the great Henry Hope Reed, descended from an old Philadelphia clan, though he himself was born in Greenwich Village and lives in New York. I might also mention the tutelary presence in these pages of Professor William H. Pierson Jr., whom I have never met, of Williams College, which I never attended: had I had perfect foresight, I would have gone to Williams to study under Pierson. I did not, but his writings have meant much to me.

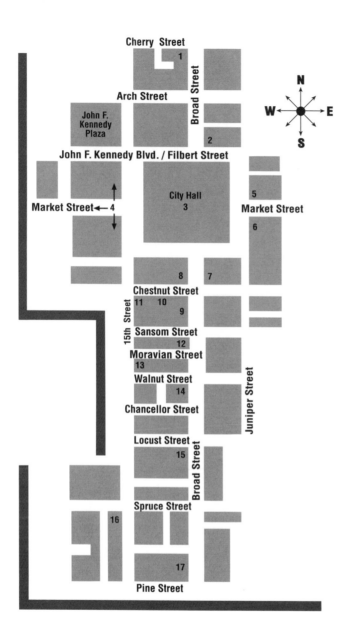

Cherry Street

1

Broad Street

Arch Street

John F. Kennedy Plaza

2

John F. Kennedy Blvd. / Filbert Street

City Hall
3

Market Street ←— 4

Market Street

5

6

7 8

Chestnut Street

15th Street

11   10

9

Sansom Street

12

Moravian Street

13

Walnut Street

14

Chancellor Street

Locust Street

15

Broad Street

Juniper Street

Spruce Street

16

17

Pine Street

N
W ← → E
S

AROUND CITY HALL

1 *Pennsylvania Academy of the Fine Arts*

AROUND CITY HALL

This chapter focuses on Broad Street just north and south of City Hall at Market Street. For Market Street west of City Hall, see "Market West." For Market Street east of City Hall, see "Market East/Convention." The area south of Market and west of Broad is covered largely in "Rittenhouse Square," while south of Market and east of Broad is covered largely in "Washington Square."

1 PENNSYLVANIA ACADEMY OF THE FINE ARTS

Broad Street, southwest corner of Cherry Street
1872–76, Furness & Hewitt
Restored in 1976, Day & Zimmermann Associates

Founded in 1805, the Academy actually had its origin in 1794, when Charles Willson Peale ("the Benjamin Franklin of Philadelphia art," said E. Digby Baltzell) established his Columbianum—an art gallery and a museum of natural history inspired by his mentor Benjamin West's Royal Academy in London—in the then recently built Philosophical Hall on South 5th Street. Peale's operation moved into Independence Hall, thence metamorphosing into the Pennsylvania Academy of the Fine Arts (PAFA) that would, throughout the nineteenth century, serve as one of the most important artistic institutions not only in Philadelphia but in the nation. Indeed, the PAFA was the first art school and museum established in the United States and had, for about the first three-quarters of the nineteenth century, what was probably the best and most extensive art collection in the country. (Remember, New York's Metropolitan Museum, Boston's Museum of Fine Arts, and Philadelphia's Museum of Art were not founded until the 1870s.) Nicholas Biddle, only eighteen and Secretary of Legation in Paris, secured one of the first groups of the all-important antique casts for the PAFA's new home, a domed classical building on Chestnut and 10th that opened in 1807. The casts were exhibited along with some large canvases by Benjamin West.

The PAFA has long been known for its Annual Exhibition, which when it began was dominated by the Peales—father Charles Willson and sons Raphaelle (the most gifted painter of the brood) and Rembrandt. By 1904 the exhibition had attained such status that its entrants read like a who's who of American art: Sargent, Whistler, Hassam, Cassatt, Eakins, Homer, Chase, Anshutz, Beaux, Henri, Sloan, La Farge, Saint-Gaudens—New York produced no assembly of talents greater than this.

CHARLES WILLSON PEALE (1741–1827)

Charles Willson Peale was not only the driving force behind the Columbianum and the Academy but the progenitor of perhaps the most distinguished and certainly the largest artistic family in American history. Born in Maryland, he studied painting under John Hesselius (another progenitor of an artistic family) in Annapolis, then went to London to study under Benjamin West. In London, Peale saw West's copies of Italian masters (some of which Peale in turn copied from West) and acquired some Italian drawings that served as references throughout his career. But he never went to Italy and knew little firsthand of Italian painting. A deist, Peale became deeply indebted to the writings of the sixteenth-century Italian Giovanni Paolo Lomazzo, who said that the imitation of nature was the imitation of God. He also met Benjamin Franklin, who became a good friend, in London. Peale served in the Continental army and was with Washington at Valley Forge, where miniature portraits of the general and of about forty other officers were painted by Peale. Over the years, he painted Washington from life sixteen times, while Gilbert Stuart painted Washington from life only twice; yet Stuart's portraits have become the "official" ones. This is not surprising since, judging from Peale's painting of Washington that is in the Metropolitan Museum in New York, Peale depicted the general as a fat and slightly slovenly man, which is not how most people like to remember the father of our country. But Peale, a jack-of-all-trades, also made a set of wooden teeth for Washington, something I do not think Gilbert Stuart ever did.

Peale developed into a fine portrait painter with an outstanding command of lighting effects. After his service, he settled in Philadelphia in 1778, already thirty-seven years old. He opened his first picture gallery in 1782, followed by a natural history museum in 1786, and the Columbianum in 1794; he was as much an artistic entrepreneur as an artist. A nonbeliever in

God-given talent, Peale said that anyone, with enough work and the right training, could be a good artist. He tried to prove this in his own work by continually tackling difficult technical problems, a famous example being the trompe l'oeil painting *The Staircase Group* (1795) in the Philadelphia Museum of Art. George Washington was apparently so fooled by the illusion in this life-size painting of two of Peale's sons climbing a curving staircase that the then president bowed in greeting to the figure of Raphaelle Peale. (Imagine the media furor had Dan Quayle done that!)

By the time of *The Staircase Group,* Peale's interest in natural history had superseded his interest in fine art. He began to design elaborate exhibits on natural history, including a display of a stuffed bird against a painted backdrop of its natural habitat. He also exhibited a mastodon skeleton, exhumed in upstate New York under his supervision. (His 1806 painting of the event is in Baltimore's Peale Museum.)

The most impressive of Peale's productions: he fathered seventeen children by three wives, naming most of them after great artists—Rembrandt, Raphaelle, Titian, Rubens, even Angelica Kauffmann. The last two sons, though, were Linnaeus and Benjamin Franklin.

The excellent portraitist Thomas Sully succeeded Peale as the Academy's star attraction, followed by Thomas Eakins, thence by Thomas Anshutz. (Anshutz taught William Glackens, John Sloan, John Marin, and Alexander Stirling Calder. Glackens and Sloan had been classmates at Philadelphia's Central High. They were later championed by another Central High alumnus, Albert C. Barnes. Eakins was also a Central High alumnus.) Thanks to the PAFA and its succession of brilliant instructors, Philadelphia had as significant a role in the evolution of American painting as did New York. Indeed, a surprisingly direct line can be drawn from Charles Willson Peale to 1913's Armory Show in New York, which was organized in part by William Glackens.

THOMAS SULLY (1783–1872)

Sully was born in England and moved to Charleston, South Carolina, in 1792. His training was sporadic, as he sought the advice of John Trumbull in New York, of Gilbert Stuart in Boston, and of Benjamin West and Thomas Lawrence in London. He came to Philadelphia in 1808, equipped with a letter of introduction from Washington Irving to the Sephardic beauty Rebecca Gratz, whose portrait Sully later painted. He became Philadelphia's—and the nation's— leading portrait painter, painting some two thousand portraits and some five hundred other paintings. Among his portraits of Philadelphians, by E. Digby Baltzell's enumeration, were twenty-nine Biddles, twenty-three Wetherills, fourteen Rushes, twelve Fishers, ten Ingersolls, seven Gratzes, and six Cadwaladers. He painted a dozen portraits of Fanny Kemble, and in 1837 a young Queen Victoria sat for Sully.

Sully had a long career. In 1821 he painted Thomas Jefferson (the painting resides in the American Philosophical Society Building) and in 1869 he painted Lincoln. The most Philadelphian thing about Sully is that all six of his surviving children became painters.

With the Museum of Art and the University of the Arts having usurped or eclipsed many of the Academy's longtime functions, it is today valued above all for its Furness building.

Its wild profusion of stylistic elements was typical of what we call the High Victorian Gothic. This style is sometimes loosely referred to as "Ruskinian Gothic," which is tricky. Ruskin hated most of what was done in his name, but his influence, however bowdlerized or diluted, is evident in the Gothic decorations of Furness's building. The classical elements— for example, the symmetry of the composition and the mansard—are more in the spirit of the "Queen Anne" of Richard Norman Shaw, a largely classical though picturesque style that might not have emerged but for Ruskin.

As it happens, Furness's father, the Reverend William Henry Furness, a famous Unitarian minister in Philadelphia, was an advocate of Ruskin's ideas about architecture and preached against the Quaker plainness of Philadelphia's streets. Following Ruskin, the elder Furness campaigned for a richer public architecture, where a building would be "a great work of public instruction." The architect son took off from this point. Yet he would combine Ruskin with Owen Jones, Viollet-le-Duc, and the Beaux-Arts classicism of Richard Morris Hunt (in whose New York office Furness came up) to create startlingly original and fecund concoctions.

FRANK FURNESS (1839–1912)

Right now, Frank Furness ranks just below (the vastly overrated) Frank Lloyd Wright, Louis Sullivan, and Henry Hobson Richardson in the pantheon of American architects. (I prefer Leon Krier's alternative pantheon of John Russell Pope, Henry Bacon, and Horace Trumbauer, but we won't get into that now.) But Furness's reputation has had some wild ups and downs.

He was born and raised in Philadelphia, son of a prominent Unitarian minister and brother of Horace Howard Furness, the great Shakespearean scholar. Frank began his career in the office of John Fraser, architect of the Union League Club on Broad Street. But at the age of twenty, Furness went to New York to work for America's first École des Beaux-Arts–trained architect, Richard Morris Hunt. After serving in the Civil War as a cavalryman, he returned to Philadelphia where he became Fraser's and then George W. Hewitt's partner. (The young Louis Sullivan came up in Furness & Hewitt's office.) From 1875 Furness worked alone for six years, then elevated his assistant Allen Evans to partnership, and until century's end they were a prominent firm. But, perhaps because of the taste for Beaux-Arts classicism ushered in by the Worlds' Columbian Exposition, Furness's commissions declined, and his works fell distinctly out of fashion, at least until the 1920s when Lewis Mumford and others "rediscovered" and praised Furness (along with Louis Sullivan) as an American Original.

It is well to note, by the way, that the PAFA was designed by the *partners* Furness and (George W.) Hewitt, the latter of whom would soon form a new firm with his brother, William D. Hewitt. G. W. Hewitt was himself a gifted architect, and undoubtedly contributed much to this building. Today, some historians maintain that the interior stair hall is largely Hewitt's and the exterior largely Furness's.

What is ultimately most impressive about the Academy building, though, is not its picturesqueness but its stateliness. Furness was a classicist at heart, I think, and his buildings are nothing if not logical. He just liked to dress them up, always very carefully, in a rich panoply of decorations and materials, ultimately as un-Unitarian as it is un-Quaker.

2 *Masonic Temple*

2 MASONIC TEMPLE
1 North Broad Street, northeast corner of Filbert Street
1868–73, James Hamilton Windrim
1880s–1890s, George Herzog

Freemasons everywhere are nutty for architectural stage sets, and, as a result, Masonic temples are virtually theme parks of architectural history. This has something to do with the Freemasons' origin in stonemasons' guilds, and the consequent notion that architectural history is in some measure the history of the works of Freemasons.

Philadelphia's Freemasons were the first in the colonies, dating from 1732. The Romanesque Revival building on Broad Street was designed by Brother (as Masons identify themselves) Windrim, a real pooh-bah among the city's architects (director of Public Works in Philadelphia, president of the Philadelphia Chapter of the A.I.A., and so on). Of note here are the interiors, by the German George Herzog. There's a room inspired by the Alhambra, another based on the temples of Luxor, another . . . well, you get the idea. There are seven such "lodge halls." Masonic temples in other cities are much the same, though in this particular one you have George Washington's own Masonic apron! (The Mason Washington is commemorated in our nation's capital by the obelisk of the Washington Monument on the Mall; obelisks are frequently used to commemorate Freemasons.)

3 CITY HALL
Broad and Market Streets
1871–1901, John McArthur Jr. (d. 1879), with Thomas Ustick Walter

The basic exterior form of the building is McArthur's from the sixties (when he started work on it) and seventies (when construction commenced), a remarkably monumental and lavish interpretation of Second Empire motifs and principles. City Hall holds its space with all the authority of Garnier's Opera, and with a high finish in its carvings and materials (Maine granite, Massachusetts marble, and limestone). This is, more than any of Furness's works, one of the great American buildings of the Victorian era.

Ground was broken for City Hall in 1871. The first mayor to occupy the building was Edwin Henry Fitler in 1889, even though the building was not declared complete until 1901. In the thirty years it was under construction, Philadelphia had eight different mayors. (One, William Stokely, was elected to three successive terms in the 1870s.) The building was in the midst of construction again in 1903–8, when the Market Street subway was built, and yet again in 1915–20 when the Broad Street subway was built; the lines intersect directly beneath City Hall.

"Silent, weird, beautiful," is what Walt Whitman, of all people, called this mountain of colonnettes, pediments, and mansards. Agnes Repplier called it "that perfected miracle of ugliness and inconvenience, that really remarkable combination of bulk and insignificance." I will almost always take Agnes Repplier's word over Walt Whitman's: not in this case. Amazingly, the site originally proposed for McArthur's City Hall was not Penn Square but Independence Square, adjacent to Independence Hall—a site sensibly rejected as inappropriate for so monumental an edifice. (The previous City Hall was located in the old Supreme Court wing of Independence Hall.) When construction began at Penn Square in 1871, the French Second Empire style was at the height of architectural fashion in America; by the time City Hall was completed thirty-one years later, the style was regarded as a *retardataire*. Still, the French influence remained strong in American architecture (witness Trumbauer's Philadelphia buildings from around this time), including elements of the Second Empire style, though

3a   *City Hall from South Broad Street*

3b   *City Hall*

the mansarded galoots of the seventies had given way to sleek and sophisticated interpretations with a high finish both in their Beaux-Arts command of spatial arrangements and in their superb craftsmanship. City Hall does not bear all the hallmarks of constructional quality we associate with Beaux-Arts buildings; nonetheless, it rose high above the standards of the seventies and was not, after all, so out of place in its milieu by 1901. It was considerably out of place when in the early 1950s came the last of a series of official recommendations that the thing be knocked down, presumably to be replaced by a Vincent Kling shoe box betokening "progress." (At times the only thing that kept McArthur's wonder standing was that it would be so costly to demolish something so gigantic.)

JOHN McARTHUR JR. (1823–90)

McArthur was a Scotsman who came up in Thomas Walter's office, and whose career was understandably dominated by the City Hall commission. References to other buildings of his design are hard to find but include the fine Romanesque Revival Tenth Presbyterian Church on 17th and Spruce, 1854, and the less fine Romanesque Revival First Presbyterian Church of Frankford, 1859. McArthur the Scot was, unsurprisingly, a Presbyterian and, I think, a parishioner at the church at 17th and Spruce. He also once worked for Alfred B. Mullett, the panjandrum of the Second Empire style in America (as at the Post Office and Court House built in the 1870s at 9th and Market, on which McArthur worked; it was demolished in 1935).

Philadelphians like to claim that this is the largest municipal building in the country, though I am not sure how this is calculated. In square feet of floor space it is only about half the size of New York's Municipal Building—indeed only half the size of many municipal office buildings around the country. City Hall looms enormous over its city, it is true, but its 630,000 square feet of floor area is simply not that large for a modern office building.

ALEXANDER MILNE CALDER (1846–1923)

The thing that gives City Hall its considerable frisson, however, is its sculptural program, perhaps the most extensive ever undertaken by one man for a single building. That man was yet another of the remarkably many Scots who built so much of Philadelphia: Alexander Milne Calder. Born in Aberdeen, he came to Philadelphia at the age of eighteen and enrolled in the Pennsylvania Academy of the Fine Arts. Calder was only twenty-seven in 1873 when he was hired by his countryman McArthur to carry out City Hall's sculptural embellishment. If we think of little else that Calder ever accomplished (besides begetting a family of famous sculptors), it is because his life was fairly consumed in his work at City Hall. He set up his basement studio in the recently begun building in 1875, thereby laying claim to being City Hall's first occupant. And the sculpture is not a load of conventional doodads: it's largely figurative work. There are portrait figures ranging from Moses to Horace Binney (not to mention John McArthur Jr.); allegorical figures of continents, arts, sciences, virtues, and so on; and a panoply of animal and plant forms. Atop the tower is the monumental figure of William Penn. Calder completed the Penn statue in 1892, and for two years it stood in the courtyard while a means of hoisting it in place could be devised. Perhaps the most astonishing things here are in the north pavilion: Calder's "capitals" composed of writhing human and animal forms.

While all the architectural sculpture here is Calder's, there are a couple of freestanding pieces on the north side that vividly demonstrate the approaches of two distinct generations of American sculptors. The equestrian statue of General John Fulton Reynolds is by John Rogers and dates from 1884, and the statue of Matthias William Baldwin (1795–1866, the Baldwin locomotive man) is by Herbert Adams and dates from 1906. Rogers (1829–1904) may have been the most commercially successful sculptor in America around the time of the Civil War. Trained in Paris and Rome, he came to specialize in small, intricately detailed plaster sculptural groups that were aggressively marketed through mail-order catalogues as inexpensive statuary for middle-class homes. These included Civil War scenes, vignettes of small-town life, and literary scenes. Adams (1858–1945) was quite different. He was trained at the École des Beaux-Arts. Influenced by the fifteenth-century Italian sculptors Francesco da Laurana and Desiderio da Settignano, Adams, unlike Rogers, specialized in monumental public commissions, as did his Beaux-Arts confreres Saint-Gaudens and MacMonnies.

The tower of City Hall is 511 feet high and the statue of Penn adds another thirty-seven feet for a total of 548 feet. For many years there was a "gentlemen's agreement" that no building in Philadelphia would rise higher than the top of William Penn. Today this agreement has been shot to hell, perhaps because there are no longer gentlemen.

4 PENN CENTER

Bounded by 15th, 18th, and Market Streets
and John F. Kennedy Boulevard
1953–82

It's hard to believe today how much excitement was generated when Penn Center was first developed back in the fifties. In 1953 the old Broad Street Station and its "Chinese wall" were taken down, and the people cheered, unlike when a mere ten years later New York's Penn Station was similarly demolished. Broad Street Station was designed by the Wilson Brothers and built in 1881 across 15th Street from City Hall. The station was enlarged in 1893 by Furness, Evans & Company, and it had the largest single-span train shed ever built. The "Chinese wall" was the massive viaduct carrying the tracks from the station west to the Schuylkill along Filbert Street (now John F. Kennedy Boulevard), effectively cutting west Center City in half. In the shadow of the wall, all was dank, depressing, and dirty; it was an enormous hindrance to traffic circulation and to the good cheer of the populace. Then came the plan to replace Broad Street Station with two new stations: Suburban Station in Center City for commuters and 30th Street Station for long-distance passengers. Suburban Station was built in 1924–29 at 16th and Filbert Streets; 30th Street Station was built in 1927–34. Both were designed by Chicago's Graham, Anderson, Probst & White. For a variety of reasons, however, it was not possible to knock down the old Broad Street Station until 1953. (The Philadelphia Orchestra, in a lovely sentimental gesture, played "Auld Lang Syne" from a platform in the station as its last train pulled out.) This means that for twenty-five or so years Broad Street Station operated simultaneously with Suburban Station and 30th Street Station.

What's lost in the saga is that the Broad Street Station itself was a remarkable High Victorian Gothic structure, at least from what I can gather from photos (it was taken down before I was born). Another bit that's lost is that Penn Center, touted as the Rockefeller Center of the postwar years (down to its skating rink and up to its rooftop restaurant) and masterminded by an urban planner who claimed his greatest influence was the painter Paul Klee, is one of the colossal failures of vision and nerve in American planning history, owing largely to the banal design of its buildings.

No one thought or would have thought in 1953 that some portion of Broad Street Station might be saved and rehabilitated; the baby was thrown out with the bathwater. Why? Because Philadelphia's planners, architects, politicians, and business leaders, among them such undeniably fine men as Mayor Richardson Dilworth, indulged a "progressive" vision of urban renewal that has, in the decades since, been thoroughly discredited. But perhaps we should not cavil overmuch: after all, the Penn Center planners also proposed knocking down City Hall, an eventuality that was eluded only because of the daunting cost of demolishing so humongous a masonry structure. (By the way, Paul Cret, right about most things, had in 1924 suggested tearing down City Hall, leaving only its tower but with new and modern facing.)

In 1947, the whole shebang was presented to an enthused public in the *Better Philadelphia* exhibition put on by the modernist architect Oskar Stonorov at Gimbel's department store on Market Street. Philadelphians were eager for the enlightened future, in which there would be no blue laws and Center City would gleam with new corporate towers. And, as so often happens in the histories of cities, the people got exactly what they wanted.

5 ONE EAST PENN SQUARE BUILDING

1 Juniper Street, northeast corner of Market Street
1930, Ritter & Shay

Every city seems to have had one firm that dominated the skyline in the Art Deco era of the 1920s and 1930s. In Chicago there was Holabird & Root, in New York Buchman & Kahn. In Philadelphia, it was Ritter & Shay,

5 *One East Penn Square Building*

whose distinctive "modernistic" towers have, in contrast to their Chicago or New York brethren, boxier silhouettes in conformance with Philadelphia zoning. Ritter & Shay's towers tend to rise their twenty or so stories in a minutely sculptured mass and become winsomely variegated at their tops. The One East Penn Square tower is one of their best and most characteristic efforts. Its use of polychrome terra-cotta tiles is reminiscent of Ely Jacques Kahn's famous Park Avenue Building in New York. Originally, this was the Market Street National Bank, and it prefigured several of the innovations that have been credited to Howe and Lescaze's nearby PSFS Building.

Howell Lewis Shay (1885–1975) graduated from the architectural school at Penn in 1913, then went to work in New York for McKim, Mead & White (White and McKim were both dead, but the firm was still very prominent). Moving back to Philadelphia, he entered the office of John T. Windrim and then Horace Trumbauer, for whom Shay worked on the design of the Philadelphia Museum of Art. He then formed a partnership with Verus T. Ritter (1883–1942) that lasted for over a decade, during which time they designed several of Philadelphia's most noteworthy tall (but still shorter than William Penn!) buildings, including One East Penn Square, the Drake Tower, and the Packard Building.

6 JOHN WANAMAKER'S

1300 Market Street, between Juniper and 13th Streets
1902–11, D. H. Burnham & Co.
Renovated in 1991, Ewing Cole Cherry Brott

Another of the many sad fates to befall this beautiful city is the recent bowdlerization of what had been second only to Chicago's Marshall Field's as the most beautiful department store in America. And Marshall Field's and John Wanamaker's were designed by the same firm—Chicago's D. H. Burnham & Co., which also designed Broad Street's fine Land Title Buildings. (The Burnham firm also designed London's greatest department store, Selfridge's of Oxford Street.)

In 1991 the building was extensively remodeled, and given the exigencies of the situation (namely, that Center City has been replaced by King of Prussia as Philadelphians' shopping mecca), I think it was carried out as well as it could have been. A neat space was carved out for the department store (it is now a branch of New York's Lord & Taylor), with the atrium that was the heart of the old Wanamaker's still largely intact. The remainder of the enormous building has been made over into office space.

6 *John Wanamaker's*

The exterior is a restrained (if outsized) Renaissance palazzo of lime-stone and granite. The glory is within: the five-story-high central atrium with a vaulted mosaic ceiling. On the second level is the legendary Wanamaker's pipe organ, reputedly the largest such instrument in the na-tion (the world?—it has 30,000 pipes), where the time-honored Wanamaker's Christmas sound-and-light show takes place. Another level up is what is now Lord & Taylor's restaurant; it has been redesigned since its Wanamaker's days so that it is no longer possible to sit at a table at the marble railing in the afternoon, nursing a drink while watching the passing pageant below: it was one of Philadelphia's finest experiences. From that vantage, one might well feel, one's spirits gently lifted by the alcohol, that the scene spread out before one is the reminder of the highest stage American civilization has ever attained: the polished marble surfaces, the mosaic of the ceiling, the soaring space, the majestic columns, the crisscrossing paths of shoppers below,

6b *John Wanamaker's central atrium*

the peculiar and magical sounds and sights and sensations of a great store. I think of such scenes from early in the century whenever someone tries to tell me that the PSFS Building is Philadelphia's greatest twentieth-century building. Maybe it is, but this is Philadelphia's greatest twentieth-century *scene*. And for all the adjustments that have been made to the picture, it's still enough to make one cry. Daniel H. Burnham himself claimed, "The building as a whole, both inside and outside, is the most monumental commercial structure ever erected anywhere in the world" (quoted in Thomas S. Hines, *Burnham of Chicago: Architect and Planner,* 1974). President William Howard Taft attended the grand opening of the store on December 30, 1911.

The Wanamaker's building contains some two million square feet of floor space, making it, I believe, the largest building in Philadelphia. The Philadelphia-born Wanamaker (1838–1922) opened his first men's clothing store in 1861 and within a few years built it into a true department store, one of the largest retailing enterprises in the world. In 1896 he moved in on the New York market by buying the great store that had once been A. T. Stewart's (depending upon one's definition of "department store," Stewart's at Broadway and 10th Street, opened in 1864, may have been the first true one as opposed to being a very large dry-goods store, like Paris's Au Bon Marché) and vastly expanding it with the annex that is still standing on Broadway between 8th and 9th Streets (and in part of which there is now a K-Mart). Wanamaker, a remarkable man, also served as postmaster general of the United States from 1889 to 1893 under President Benjamin Harrison. A 1923 statue, *John Wanamaker, Citizen,* by the fine sculptor John Massey Rhind, stands on the east side of City Hall.

7 WIDENER BUILDING
Chestnut Street, between Broad and Juniper Streets
1914, Horace Trumbauer

This is a luscious and beautifully restored office building, designed by the man who designed everything Widener. There are exuberant Corinthian pilasters and superb vaulted entries on both the south (Chestnut Street) and north (Penn Square) ends of the building, their coffers picked out with glazed terra-cotta, and an exciting vaulted and galleried lobby.

The lobby gives upon:

J. E. CALDWELL & CO.
1339 Chestnut Street, between Juniper and Broad Streets
1916, Horace Trumbauer

A gorgeous retail space with black-and-gold floors and Baccarat chandeliers. How long will it last?

SOUTH BROAD STREET

"No other street in America quite compares with Broad Street," wrote E. Digby Baltzell. By what peculiar providence did Broad Street in the blocks south from City Hall become one of the most beautiful commercial streets in the United States? And how did it achieve such beauty by such variegated forms? It is not the Philadelphia of red brick, nor indeed are there works by any of the most touted of Philadelphia's architects (excepting the minor work by Furness at the southern end of the stretch at the University of the Arts). It is utterly *sui generis*.

8 GIRARD TRUST COMPANY
34–36 South Broad Street, northwest corner of Chestnut Street
1905–8, McKim, Mead & White

It is no secret that I regard McKim, Mead & White as America's greatest architectural firm. There is, unfortunately, little of their work to be seen in Philadelphia, though there is this marble temple right on Broad Street, a

7 *Widener Building*

8   *Girard Trust Company*

component in that spine-tingling parade of buildings extending south from City Hall. Completed two years after Stanford White's death and a year before McKim's, it was designed by the latter in concert with the local architect Allen Evans of Furness, Evans & Company (the bank's president had specifically requested that Furness himself be allowed nowhere near the project) and McKim, Mead & White's William Symmes Richardson, who was at this time McKim's factotum, but who would shortly become one of the firm's principal designers (he did the Racquet Club on Park Avenue in New York). The stately Ionic temple, with a large and beautifully proportioned dome, is finished in the most gleaming white Georgia marble you'll ever see.

9 LAND TITLE BUILDINGS

Broad Street, between Chestnut and Sansom Streets
North building: 1897, D. H. Burnham & Co.
South building: 1902, D. H. Burnham & Co., with Horace Trumbauer

These buildings are as though a bit of Chicago's South Michigan Avenue was transplanted to Broad Street, though in fact both buildings are a bit earlier than their Windy City brethren (for example, the Railway Exchange

Building, 1904, and the People's Gas Building, 1910) or their New York brethren (Flatiron Building, 1901–3).

The north building is much in the mode of 1890s Chicago School classicism, and features a modest Ionic granite base, a rusticated shaft with intaglio brickwork, shallow oriels in alternating bays rising to an arcade with another arcade above that, and a strong cornice. The south building is similarly tripartite, with an austere granite base rising to a shaft of rusticated limestone, the whole crowned by a bravura Corinthian colonnade.

Burnham and his designers seemed to believe that it was the skyscraper's proper fate to be a towering cliff of rustication. I think they were right. By the way, the Burnham firm (once believed to be the largest in the world), which also gave us John Wanamaker's, metamorphosed into another Chicago firm, Graham, Anderson, Probst & White, whose contributions to the Philadelphia scene include 30th Street Station and Suburban Station.

10 JACOB REED'S SONS STORE
1424–26 Chestnut Street, between 15th and Broad Streets
1903–4, Price & McLanahan

Diamond in the rough: On increasingly tawdry Chestnut can be found one of the finest retail façades and interiors in the country. The big Palladian

9 *Land Title Buildings*

entryway gives on a long, barrel-vaulted sales floor separated by columns from side aisles, above which are artificially backlit clerestory windows. On the façade, note the top-story loggia and, above it and beneath the cornice, the handmade tiles from Henry Chapman Mercer's Moravian Pottery and Tile Works, established in 1897 in Doylestown, Pennsylvania.

In the 1980s, this building was briefly a Barnes & Noble bookstore at a time when that chain, which has since become chic, deliberately indulged a déclassé—indeed a tawdry—standard of design (they were then known as specialists in the sale of "bargain books"). This style clashed mightily with the space of what had once been an elegant haberdashery. B&N has since moved out, but I cannot help thinking that in its newly classy guise it wouldn't yet make a suitable tenant for this otherwise languishing space. Right now it is being ill-used by a chain drugstore.

The architect of Jacob Reed's Sons was William L. Price (1861–1916). Philadelphia-born, he attended the Orthodox Quaker Westtown School before going to work in the office of the Quaker architect Addison Hutton. Price teamed with M. Hawley McLanahan from 1903 to 1916, and was largely responsible (with funding from Edward W. Bok) for the design and development of the quasi-Utopian planned community of Rose Valley (1901–11) near Media in Montgomery County. McLanahan, who was also deeply involved in Rose Valley, later teamed with Ralph Bencker, the Automat architect.

10 *Jacob Reed's Sons Store*

11 *Packard Building*

11 PACKARD BUILDING

Chestnut Street, southeast corner of 15th Street
1924, Ritter & Shay

The most notable feature here is the ironwork of the ten-ton gates and the lighting fixtures of the Chestnut Street façade. It is by the great Philadelphian Samuel Yellin.

SAMUEL YELLIN (1885–1940)

Yellin's brilliant ironwork can be seen throughout the country. Good examples in Philadelphia are the following: the ornamental iron screens in the chapel of Zantzinger, Borie & Medary's Philadelphia Divinity School, built in 1925–26 at 42nd and Spruce; gates and doors at the Lea & Febiger Building (*see* chapter two) on South Washington Square between Walnut and Spruce; the University Museum (*see* chapter ten) on South Street between 33rd and 34th; St. Mark's Church (*see* chapter eight) on Locust Street between 16th and

17th; the Rosenbach Museum (*see* chapter eight) on Delancey Place between 20th and 21st; the Curtis Institute of Music (*see* chapter eight) at Locust and 18th; St. Clement's Church (*see* chapter nine) at 20th and Cherry; and the Samuel S. Fleisher Art Memorial (*see* chapter six) on Catharine Street between 7th and 8th.

Yellin is regarded as one of the foremost craftsmen contributing to the buildings of the 1920s and 1930s. Born in Poland, he was apprenticed to a blacksmith at the age of seven. At seventeen he set out on his journeyman years, in which, traditionally, the artisan travels from place to place working for various masters. At the end of the journeyman years, the artisan produces his "master piece," demonstrating that he has himself become a master. (This is actually the proper use of the term *masterpiece*.) When Yellin became a master at age twenty, he decided to immigrate to the United States, and in 1905 he came to Philadelphia. In order to learn American practices, he enrolled in classes at the Pennsylvania Museum and School of Industrial Art (forerunner to the Philadelphia Museum of Art), where he was quickly made an instructor. In 1910 he opened his studio on Arch Street, and in 1915 his new workshop and offices at 5520 Arch Street were designed by Mellor & Meigs. By the early 1920s, he employed over two hundred craftsmen.

He profoundly believed that the craftsman's works must be informed by tradition, and to that end he became a scholar as well as an artisan. In 1929 Yellin wrote the article on ironwork for the fourteenth edition of the *Encyclopaedia Britannica*. And he not only created the greatest body of ornamental ironwork of modern times, but he amassed America's greatest collection of historical ironwork, which he kept at his studio and which later ended up at New York's Metropolitan Museum of Art. Edward W. Bok had planned to donate a wing to the Philadelphia Museum of Art that would be devoted to ironwork and would include a working studio. He wanted Yellin to be in charge of it all. In effect, this would have been to move the Arch Street studio to the Museum of Art, which would maintain it in perpetuity. But Bok died before the plans could be finalized, and when Yellin died in 1940, modernist architecture had all but made ornamental ironwork a thing of the past. Still, Yellin's reputation rose in the 1960s when, as part of that decade's handicraft revival, blacksmith work once again became popular, after arc welding threatened to doom it permanently. It was then that Yellin was readily and rightly acknowledged as the modern master of hand-wrought ironwork.

Of Ritter & Shay's building, Teitelman and Longstreth's assessment cannot be improved upon: such buildings "formed much of the core of what most remember as 'downtown,' its effectiveness cannot be dismissed as anything less than successful in generating the concept of the city as a place of importance."

12 UNION LEAGUE CLUB

140 South Broad Street, southwest corner of Sansom Street
1864–65, John Fraser
Addition to W. in 1909–11, Horace Trumbauer

Since the Union League split from the Union Club over Civil War policy, it needed to establish its own digs during the war. It was a curious moment in American history that produced Fraser's curious brownstone clubhouse on Broad Street, as distinctive a building as its decade can show in America. New York has nothing to show for the sixties, let alone anything so fine as this.

Trumbauer's annex on 15th Street is limestone Beaux-Arts, very different indeed from Fraser's building. Yet, in that peculiar and magical way that is characteristic of this stretch of Broad, the two parts work together, owing largely to their shared classical vocabulary.

12 *Union League Club*

13a   *Drexel Building*

Across Moravian Street to the south is the:

13 DREXEL BUILDING

135–43 South 15th Street, southeast corner of Moravian Street
1925–27, Day & Klauder

This Florentine palazzo is a fine essay in rusticated granite. Note how the bottom two stories are designed to look like one story. While some architects go to great lengths to increase the apparent height of their buildings, other architects go to similar lengths to *decrease* the apparent height. Also note how the top of the two-story base is ringed by a lovely sequence of carved stone panels illustrating zodiac figures. The Drexel Building has lately been disfigured by the fitness club placed in the base, filling its street windows with prancing yuppies. The Day of Day & Klauder, by the way, was Frank Miles Day, but since he died in 1918 it's safe to infer he did not design this building. Rather, we might credit the other partner, Charles Zeller Klauder (1872–1938).

On the next block of 15th Street is:

BOOKBINDERS SEAFOOD HOUSE
215 South 15th Street, between Walnut and Locust Streets

There could not conceivably be a less chichi or a more Philadelphian restaurant than this, the *real* Bookbinders. (Forget that joint on 2nd and Walnut that calls itself "Old Original Bookbinders." The seafood they serve is
fresh enough, but it is basically an overpriced tourist trap that trades on the
venerable Bookbinders name. The reason they can call themselves "Old
Original Bookbinders" is that, if I have the story right, they bought what
was in fact the original Bookbinders from the family that owns Bookbinders Seafood House on 15th Street.) All the fish and seafood served here is
fresh and good, but this is the place to go to savor Old Philadelphia's traditional cuisine: snapper soup, Philadelphia pepper pot, and fried oysters served
with chicken salad.

Bookbinders' snapper soup is made from turtle meat, hard-boiled egg,
and sherry. The pepper pot is made from cream, tripe, dumplings, and
pimiento. And it is to Bookbinders that Old Philadelphians repair when
they crave that traditional—odd only to non-Philadelphians—combination of big fried oysters served side-by-side with a mound of cold chicken
salad.

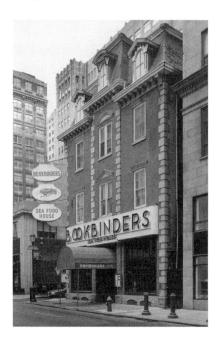

13b   *Bookbinders Seafood House*

As the peripatetic gourmands Jane and Michael Stern put it so well, "Bookbinders is Philadelphia before nouvelle cuisine swept into town, before purveyors of preciousness turned the city's head with their dubious 'new Philadelphia cuisine,' which really isn't any different from what's served in trendy bistros in a dozen self-renovating American cities." Since they wrote this way back in 1983, it's probably safe to say "two dozen self-renovating American cities"—or more. By the way, Richard Saul Wurman's *Access* guide to Philadelphia says Bookbinders' cuisine is "a bit dull by today's nouvelle standards." Don't look for this restaurant to get raves from the restaurant reviewers, any more than you'd expect an Edgar Seeler building to get raves from an architectural critic. Just try to use your own judgment, informed by a sense of tradition.

14 THE BELLEVUE

Broad Street, southwest corner of Walnut Street
1902–13, G. W. and W. D. Hewitt
Renovated in 1980, 1989, Day & Zimmermann

Is there a more beautiful hotel in America? I've been privileged to stay here twice. The first time was when they slashed prices following the Legionnaires' Disease debacle; the second was when they slashed prices during that golden moment when Philadelphia built a slew of luxury hotels in anticipation of the opening of the new convention center that, as it happened, was delayed, leaving all these fabulous hotel rooms going for a song. Alas, it's not that way any longer, and a stay in a Center City hotel will set you back as much as in any other city. At any rate, my first post-Legionnaires' Disease stay at the Bellevue was back when the whole building was still the Bellevue-Stratford Hotel. (In 1976, the deaths of twenty-nine members of the American Legion were attributed to bacteria borne by the hotel's ventilation system.) By the time of the second visit, the building had been renovated and the hotel had become Hotel Atop the Bellevue—occupying the top seven stories of the skyscraper with offices and stores below. The spectacular Grand Ballroom was retained and continues to serve as the setting of Philadelphia society's galas (in particular, the venerable Assembly). Sad as the loss of the old grand hotel was, I must say that the reworking by Day & Zimmermann was more sensitive than anyone imagined it could be. The main floor of the mixed-use building retains much of the grandeur it possessed when it was the lobby of the hotel. (Among the new retailers is an excellent Rizzoli Bookstore.) The ornate plasterwork, the marble columns, the chandeliers, and the Cosmati floor are all restorations of original features.

The Bellevue-Stratford was designed by the brothers Hewitt. George was the elder, and the one who paired with Furness; William was the kid brother. They designed the Bourse, the Wissahickon Inn, numerous houses and churches (especially for Henry Howard Houston in Chestnut Hill), and deserve a more honored place in the history of American architecture.

The building's Broad Street façade retains all its original splendor, with its lovely oriels, rustication, balconies, cornices, terra-cotta decorations, and what I consider to be Philadelphia's biggest and baddest mansard roof. The Bellevue is the most beautiful hotel in America, and as good a twentieth-century building as the PSFS over on Market.

That absolutely hideous building with the faceted façade and the sloping glass atrium on the southeast corner of Broad and Locust is the Hershey Hotel, built in 1983. It replaced a parking lot that in its turn had replaced the old Walton Hotel, which opened in 1896. Designed by Angus "Anxious" Wade, the Walton was a big High Victorian (a bit late for that sort of thing) galoot of a building that nonetheless was a characterful presence and an infinitely more pleasant neighbor than the present monstrosity. It came down in 1966. Speaking of good neighbors, just to the south of the Bellevue across Chancellor Street once stood the Art Club, one of Frank Miles Day's best buildings. It was demolished in 1975 so the Bellevue-Stratford could build a parking lot.

15 ACADEMY OF MUSIC

232–46 South Broad Street, southwest corner of Locust Street
1855–57, Napoleon LeBrun and Gustave Runge

When it was built in the 1850s, the Academy of Music was one of the country's best opera houses, and it still is. LeBrun's firm became Napoleon LeBrun & Sons of New York. But the elder LeBrun concentrated his energies in his home city of Philadelphia, designing two of the town's best buildings of the immediate antebellum years—the Catholic cathedral at Logan Circle and the Academy of Music.

The great Philadelphia Orchestra was founded in 1900. Its conductors have been Fritz Sheel (1900–1907), Carl Pohlig (1907–12), Leopold Stokowski (1912–36), Eugene Ormandy (1936–80), Riccardo Muti (1980–92), and Wolfgang Sawallisch (since 1993).

15 *South Broad Street, Academy of Music on left*

LEOPOLD STOKOWSKI (1882–1977)

Brought to the city from Cincinnati in 1912, Stokowski built the Philadelphia Orchestra into the finest in the world by the time of his retirement in 1936.
—E. Digby Baltzell

One of the famously flamboyant conductors ("an exhibitionist and genius," in Baltzell's words), Stokowski conducted all the way up to three months prior to his death, when he was ninety-four. In spite of his name—Leopold Antoni Stanislaw Boleslawowicz Stokowski—he was born in London (he is honored by a plaque on the side of Marylebone Parish Church) and educated at London's Royal College of Music as well as at Oxford. In 1905 he moved to New York to be the organist of St. Bartholomew's Church (that was before it moved to its present location on Park Avenue) and by 1909 was directing the Cincinnati Symphony Orchestra, defecting to Philadelphia three years later. From 1946 to 1950 he was the conductor of the New York Philharmonic and held numerous other posts, including that of music director of the 1940 Walt Disney film *Fantasia* (with the Philadelphia Orchestra). He was devoted to modern music (not such an oddity in Philadelphia, it turns out, as one might think), and he premiered works by such living composers as Stravinsky, Mahler, Schoenberg, and Berg.

By the way, many Philadelphians believe that the Academy of Music is an acoustical marvel. Stokowski—and every other conductor, for that matter—felt that for orchestral music the Academy was (and is) dreadful. It has long been a truism in the musical world that if you want to hear the Philadelphia Orchestra at its best, you have to go to New York for their performances at Carnegie Hall.

Leo L. Beranek, in his *Music, Acoustics and Architecture* (1962), said the Academy of Music was "unquestionably the finest opera house in the United States." LeBrun reputedly traveled to Milan to study the Scala, designed by Giuseppe Piermarini and built in 1776–78, and this is apparent in the similarity of the plans of the Scala and the Academy. But the Academy, for all its charm and history and though it is acoustically felicitous for opera, is inadequate for orchestral music, which is why a new concert hall, at Broad and Spruce Streets, is being built. The architect of the new facility is New York's Rafael Viñoly. The old Academy will still be used for visiting performers.

NAPOLEON LeBRUN (1821–1901)

The architect LeBrun was born in Philadelphia to a former French diplomat. Like McArthur who designed City Hall, LeBrun came up in Thomas Walter's office. (Walter in his turn had come up in the office of Strickland, who came up in Latrobe's office.) LeBrun established his own firm in 1841 and worked with Notman on the design of the Catholic cathedral. Part of what qualified LeBrun to design the Academy of Music was his musical sensitivity: he was an accomplished organist. He later moved to New York where he established the firm of Napoleon LeBrun & Sons, which might more accurately have been called Napoleon LeBrun's Sons when they designed the world's tallest building—New York's Met Life Tower—in 1909. (Credit for that building is generally given to Napoleon's son, Pierre LeBrun.)

The exterior was never finished to plan. Apparently LeBrun wanted it revetted in marble in the Corinthian order. This is odd, given that the building as it emerged is so different from that and, as it stands, a very handsome thing with its strong arcades and, not least, its still-operating gas lamps. When Martin Scorsese made his film of Edith Wharton's *The Age of Innocence,* with its scenes that take place in New York's long-demolished Academy of Music on 14th Street, he used Philadelphia's Academy—a relic of bygone elegance.

E. Digby Baltzell, writing in 1979:

> Both the Boston Symphony and the Philadelphia Orchestra have always stood for Society and Culture, especially among Proper Women in both cities. Every Friday afternoon in season, year after year, Boston women, after an uplift lecture and a simple lunch at the Chilton Club, arrive at their hereditary seats at Symphony Hall; rarely early, they are never late. At the same time on Fridays, year in and year out, slightly more stylishly dressed Philadelphia ladies, after a delicious lunch at the Acorn Club, walk three blocks down Locust Street and take their customary seats at the Academy of Music; some are always late and some always leave early to catch the Paoli or Chestnut Hill locals. (*Puritan Boston and Quaker Philadelphia,* New York: Free Press, 1979)

Still? And, if so, could it possibly be the same when they all start going to Rafael Viñoly's new concert hall?

16 DRAKE TOWER

1512–14 Spruce Street, between 15th and 16th Streets
1929, Ritter & Shay

There are Ritter & Shay towers on both the northern outskirts (One East Penn Square) and southern outskirts (this) of the marvelous Broad Street stretch—appropriately so, for these are Philadelphia's excellent background buildings. This one, when viewed from 15th Street, seems like one of the biggest buildings in the city. The narrow front of the slab is on Spruce. It's as fully realized an example of the slab skyscraper, designed to allow maximum penetration of natural light, as was Raymond Hood's RCA Building at Rockefeller Center, completed three years later in New York. When Lewis Mumford taught at Penn in 1952–53, he and his wife, Sophia, lived in the Drake.

16 *Drake Tower*

17 UNIVERSITY OF THE ARTS

(ORIGINALLY PENNSYLVANIA INSTITUTION FOR THE DEAF AND DUMB)

320 South Broad Street, northwest corner of Pine Street
1824–26, John Haviland
Additions: 1875, Furness & Hewitt
Renovated in 1983, F. Daniel Cathers & Associates

Until the 1980s there were two separate schools: the Philadelphia College of Art and Design and the Philadelphia College of Performing Arts. They were merged into the pretentiously named University of the Arts. Its most famous faculty member is not any of its teachers in the fine or the performing arts but the literary scholar-cum-media celebrity Camille Paglia.

The University of the Arts's Broad Street building began life as the Pennsylvania Institution for the Deaf and Dumb, built in the 1820s by John Haviland during the same period as his Eastern State Penitentiary. Though the two structures are equally imposing, the styles are quite different. The penitentiary is picturesque, castellated Gothic, where the asylum is painfully austere Doric revival. The wings, with their late-Georgian blind arches, were added in 1838 by Strickland. Round 15th Street is a large addition from the 1870s by Furness, in his characteristic Gothic-inflected manner. In the 1870s this was still the Institution for the Deaf and Dumb; the College of Art moved here in 1893. The building was renovated in 1983 when it became the University of the Arts.

CHAPTER

2

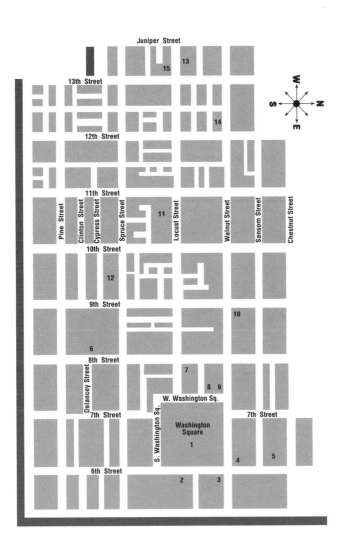

Juniper Street

13th Street

12th Street

11th Street

10th Street

9th Street

8th Street

7th Street

6th Street

Pine Street

Clinton Street

Cypress Street

Spruce Street

Locust Street

Walnut Street

Sansom Street

Chestnut Street

Delancey Street

S. Washington Sq.

W. Washington Sq.

Washington
Square

7th Street

WASHINGTON SQUARE

FREEDOM IS A LIGHT
FOR WHICH MANY MEN HAVE DIED IN DARKNESS

IN UNMARKED GRAVES WITHIN
THIS SQUARE LIE THOUSANDS
OF UNKNOWN SOLDIERS OF
WASHINGTONS ARMY WHO DIED
OF WOUNDS AND SICKNESS DURING
THE REVOLUTIONARY WAR

THE INDEPENDENCE AND LIBERTY
YOU POSSESS ARE THE WORK OF
JOINT COUNCILS AND JOINT
EFFORTS OF COMMON DANGERS
SUFFERINGS AND SUCCESS
WASHINGTON'S FAREWELL ADDRESS APRIL 1789

1 *Washington Square,
Statue of George Washington*

CHAPTER 2

WASHINGTON SQUARE

1 WASHINGTON SQUARE

Bounded by Walnut Street on the north, 6th Street on the east, South Washington Square on the south, and West Washington Square (just west of 7th Street) on the west

Washington Square had become a troublesome place when Jane Jacobs wrote about it in her book *The Death and Life of Great American Cities* in 1961. In her frontal assault on the orthodoxies of city planning, Ms. Jacobs set out, using her considerable powers of inductive reasoning, to determine if the laws of urban decline ought to be rewritten. Her book rocked the world of city planning and changed how many people viewed their urban environment. Washington Square was her example of decline. It was, she wrote, "Philadelphia's pervert park." The square and its neighboring area suffered from insufficient diversity of uses. By contrast, Rittenhouse Square was the very model, in her eyes, of everything a city neighborhood should be.

Four years later, the English architectural critic Ian Nairn toured the United States to study its cities. Though in many ways a kindred spirit to Jane Jacobs, Nairn looked at Washington Square and liked what he saw. After remarking on the "pointless and formless variety" of Rittenhouse Square, Nairn noted that at Washington Square "the buildings are about the same height, the enclosure is preserved, the square remains a square. There may be less light and fewer trees, but it remains more of an oasis."

Today Washington Square "reads" both as part of Independence Park (boring) and as the anchor of a neighborhood that, Jane Jacobs might be surprised to discover, possesses many of the virtues we associate with Rittenhouse Square.

Washington Square was one of the five squares laid out by Penn in 1682 and received its present name in 1833. (It had previously been called the Southeast Square.) Like its New York namesake, and like public squares

37

all over, it served at one time as a potter's field, which means that today there are numerous bodies buried beneath the square, including bodies of Revolutionary War soldiers who died in the Walnut Street Prison that was located on the northeast corner of 6th and Walnut. (As a debtors' prison after the war, it was where Robert Morris was incarcerated and visited by his friend Washington.) Also interred here are victims of 1793's yellow-fever epidemic, during which the man for whom the square was later named repaired to the Deshler-Morris house in Germantown.

Within the square, note the bronze cast of the marble original of the statue of George Washington by Jean-Antoine Houdon (1741–1828). The original, created in 1788–91, has stood majestically in the State Capitol of Richmond, Virginia, since 1796. This is one of only three castings and dates from the early 1920s. It was originally placed in the Philadelphia Museum of Art and was then relocated to Washington Square in 1954.

2 ATHENAEUM OF PHILADELPHIA
219 South 6th Street, between Walnut Street and
South Washington Square
1845–47, John Notman

Notman was a wonder. He could do a St. Mark's in exacting Ecclesiological manner, then turn right around and do as convincing an Italianate palazzo as this. The immediate inspiration for Notman's design would appear to be a pair of London clubs: Decimus Burton's Athenaeum Club of 1828–30

2 *Athenaeum of Philadelphia*

2   *Penn Mutual Building*

and Sir Charles Barry's Reform Club of 1837–41. Though Notman's building is of brownstone, he wanted, like Barry in his Pall Mall clubhouses, to use marble. Economy prevailed.

Founded in 1814, the Athenaeum is a private library that, in 1818, made its home in Philosophical Hall on South 5th Street. In addition to the Athenaeum, the present building has housed the Historical Society of Pennsylvania, the Philadelphia Chapter of the American Institute of Architects (in a room remodeled by Furness in 1870), the American Catholic Historical Society, the Philadelphia Law Library, and the Victorian Society of America.

3   PENN MUTUAL BUILDING
510 Walnut Street, between 5th and 6th Streets
1969–70, Mitchell/Giurgola Associates

Our country's pioneer of *façadisme:* The façade of Haviland's **Pennsylvania Fire Insurance Company** from 1838 is incorporated into the base of the new skyscraper. There used to be an observation deck at the top, but it's been closed. (Why? It's hard to believe it wasn't popular.) As for the new tower, it has all the hallmarks for which Mitchell/Giurgola are renowned:

4   *Curtis Center*

"the firm's responsiveness to the urban context," concrete sunscreens, "indentations responding to the older building" (Penn Mutual's 1931 skyscraper to the west), blah-blah-blah. It's all a lot of mumbo jumbo to obscure the fact that this *façadisme* just does not work, and the building, whatever its (largely theoretical) urbanistic bows, is vastly overscaled for its surroundings.

4   CURTIS CENTER
6th Street, between Walnut and Sansom Streets
1910, Edgar V. Seeler
Renovated in 1990, Oldham & Seltz and John Milner Associates

If I had to choose the most underappreciated Philadelphia architect, it would be Edwin Durang. Edgar Seeler would be second. His works get short shrift in every account of the city's architecture, yet the École des Beaux-Arts–trained Seeler was a careful and versatile designer, capable both of this office building and of the fine First Baptist Church on 17th and Sansom. In three years in the atelier of the great Victor Laloux (architect of the Gare d'Orsay) at the École des Beaux-Arts, Seeler earned a reputation as a brilliant student. And if he never quite fulfilled his promise, he certainly deserves better than the casually dismissive comments, at best, or complete absence, at worst, in books about Philadelphia architecture. The Beaux-Arts tends to be undertreated by Philadelphia's architectural historians. This is in part, I am sure, because the city is so rich in other kinds of architecture, but regarding Beaux-Arts, it cannot hope to compete with New York or Washington. When Philadelphia Beaux-Arts is treated, naturally it is Trumbauer and Cret who get (as they should) the greater attention than Seeler, who fades into the stonework. But it is precisely the historian's job to rectify such imbalances, and Seeler, who among other things was a public-spirited man, deserves better.

Of special note here is the gleaming marble lobby, with a spectacular forty-nine-foot-high by fifteen-foot-long mosaic, *The Dream Garden,* by the Philadelphia-born Maxfield Parrish, executed by the Tiffany Studios in 1914–16. The mosaic consists of some 100,000 pieces of favrile glass and uses 260 colors. Its use of perspective makes it one of the most complex mosaics you'll ever see, and though it may not be to everyone's taste (it is to mine), the craft of the thing is at a very high level indeed.

The Curtis Center was once the Curtis Building, home of *The Saturday Evening Post, Ladies' Home Journal,* and other publications that defined Philadelphia as the center of middlebrow publishing in the United States. Cyrus Hermann Kotzschmar Curtis (1850–1933) founded the Curtis Publishing Company in 1883. His daughter (and only child), Mary Louise Curtis, married Edward William Bok (1863–1930), the huckstering editor of *Ladies' Home Journal* (from 1889 to 1919) and author of the super-bestselling autobiography *The Americanization of Edward Bok* (1920). (Edward and Mary Louise's grandson, Derek Bok, became president of Harvard University.) Mary Louise founded the renowned Curtis Institute of Music in 1924, and, following Bok's death, she married the famous violinist Efrem Zimbalist. While Bok turned *Ladies' Home Journal* (the name had been supplied by Cyrus H. K. Curtis's wife, Louisa Knapp, for whom the Curtis Institute's Knapp Hall was named), Curtis hired George Horace Lorimer (1867–1937) to turn *The Saturday Evening Post* into the huge success that it became. Lorimer ran the magazine from 1899 until 1937, and it was he who, among other things, brought Norman Rockwell to the magazine. (Today there is a "museum" of Norman Rockwell reproductions in the Curtis Center.) Though *The Saturday Evening Post* is remembered for its sentimental Americanism and Rockwell covers, and though Ezra Pound, in his *Guide to Kulchur* (1938), remarked that "Lorimer honestly didn't know that there ever had been a civilization," it should still be remembered that the magazine published such writers as Stephen Crane, Theodore Dreiser, Willa

Cather, Joseph Conrad, F. Scott Fitzgerald, and Sinclair Lewis. With these and other magazines, Curtis Publishing Company was at one time the undisputed king among American magazine publishers. For all intents and purposes, it had ceased to exist by 1970.

PUBLISHING IN PHILADELPHIA

Washington Square was the center of Philadelphia's surprisingly thriving publishing industry through the nineteenth century and well into the twentieth. In addition to the Curtis empire and its extremely popular magazines, there were at least four other major publishing businesses that operated (and in some cases still do) in buildings still standing around Washington Square.

Lea & Febiger was located in the building at 600 South Washington Square, between Walnut and Spruce Streets, that is now occupied by the Marion Locks art gallery. The building was designed by Earle Nelson Edwards and built in 1923 for Lea & Febiger, already an ancient concern. The company was founded by Matthew Carey in 1785 and is the oldest continuously operating publisher in the United States. It was the most important publishing house of the young republic, and among its many books was Mason Locke Weems's fanciful *The Life and Memorable Actions of George Washington* of 1800. Under Matthew Carey's son Henry Charles Carey (1793–1879), the renowned economist (and leading advocate of protectionism), the firm of Carey, Lea & Carey became the nation's leading fiction publisher. Later, as Lea & Febiger, it was a major medical-book publisher whose titles included *Gray's Anatomy.*

Henry Charles Lea, who ran the family publishing business for many years, was one of the most interesting Philadelphians of his time. A patrician civic reformer, he was also an important historian whose *History of the Inquisition of the Middle Ages* (1888) was praised by (the Roman Catholic) Lord Acton and is still consulted today. Lea is the only Proper Philadelphian ever to be elected president of the American Historical Association.

The story of Lea & Febiger is told in the book *Two Hundred Years of Publishing: A History of the Oldest Publishing Company in the United States—Lea & Febiger, 1785–1985,* by R. Kenneth Bussy, published in 1985 by (who else?) Lea & Febiger.

Another major medical-book publisher was W. B. Saunders Publishing Company, located at the corner of 7th and Locust in a building erected in 1910. Saunders, long known in the medical community for its technical works, became famous (or infamous) in 1948 when it published *Sexual Behavior in the Human Male* by Alfred C. Kinsey, the now largely discredited "scientific" study of human sexual practices.

Perhaps the best-known of Philadelphia's trade publishers was **J. B. Lippincott & Company,** long located in the building at 227–231 South 6th Street. Erected in 1900, this building was designed by William B. Pritchett. Lippincott was founded in 1792 and merged into New York's Harper & Row (now Harper Collins) in 1978. In addition to being a major book publisher, the company also issued the well-known *Lippincott's* magazine, which has an honored place in the history of English literature for having published Oscar Wilde's *Picture of Dorian Gray* in 1890 and in the history of American architecture for having published Louis Sullivan's famous essay "The Tall Building Artistically Considered" in 1896.

Finally, *Farm Journal* originated in Philadelphia in 1827 and since 1912 has been published out of the building at 230 West Washington Square. The building, designed by Morgan Bunting and Arthur Shrigley, was built in 1912. This is the largest magazine of farm news in the country—something one would expect to be published in Chicago, not Philadelphia.

5 PUBLIC LEDGER BUILDING

6th Street, between Sansom and Chestnut Streets
1924, Horace Trumbauer

Speaking of Trumbauer, here's a good (not great) one by him, which with Seeler's Curtis Building makes a superb street wall for Independence Square. What's nice is that the Georgian and Federal of the Independence Square buildings find their classical mates of nearly two centuries hence across 6th Street.

The *Public Ledger* was Philadelphia's highest-circulation daily almost from its inception in 1836 as the city's first penny paper. In 1864 the *Public Ledger* started to become a national political force when it was purchased by George W. Childs (1829–94) and Anthony Joseph Drexel (1826–93). Childs ran the paper and moved it to this site in 1867. When Childs died, the paper passed to Anthony J. Drexel's son, George Childs Drexel, who in 1903 sold the paper to Adolph S. Ochs, owner of *The New York Times*. In 1913 the *Public Ledger* was purchased by Cyrus H. K. Curtis, the magazine tycoon whose office building (now called the Curtis Center) was right next door. Thus, the present, Trumbauer's, building was erected by Curtis. In 1934 the *Public Ledger* merged into the *Philadelphia Inquirer*.

6 PENNSYLVANIA HOSPITAL

8th Street, between Spruce and Pine Streets
East and west wings: 1750s, Samuel Rhoads
Central section: c. 1800, David Evans Jr.

The central section of the hospital by Evans is superb. Unlike the grouping at Independence Hall, where the center is an earlier Wren-Georgian while the wings are Federal, here it's the center, oddly, that's Federal, while the wings are earlier. Rhoads's east wing went up first, I guess, followed some years later by Evans's central section, then by the west wing—built to Rhoads's original design. Is this right? It seems they did the same thing that was done almost two centuries later at the Philadelphia Museum of Art: built the outer wings first as a way of ensuring that funds would be raised for the central section.

It is the most beautiful hospital in the country, built at a time when a person wouldn't have wished surgery on his worst enemy.

It is the oldest hospital in the United States, founded in 1751 by Dr. Thomas Bond (with the public relations help of Benjamin Franklin). Inside can be found the oldest surgical theater in the country, under the skylight drum where a dome had been proposed atop the central section. It was here that the first appendectomy and the first gall bladder operation in the U.S. were performed—without anesthesia, of course (general anesthesia was not introduced until the 1840s). Also inside can be found one of Benjamin West's most famous paintings, *Christ Healing the Sick,* from 1817.

SOME WASHINGTON SQUARE WORTHIES
Agnes Repplier
Agnes Repplier (1855–1950), "the Jane Austen of the essay" (John Lukacs), lived in the house at 920 Clinton Street, between 9th and 10th Streets, from 1921 until her death—twenty-nine years.

Nicholas Biddle
The house at **715 Spruce Street** was built in 1820, and Nicholas Biddle lived there from 1828 to 1839, which is to say during the last eight years of his fourteen-year presidency at the Second Bank of the United States (Chestnut between 4th and 5th). The bank was put out of commission by President Jackson in 1836, and the ensuing national financial crisis was (unfairly)

6 *Pennsylvania Hospital*

blamed in part on Biddle, who in his last years in this house was one of the most unpopular men in America. This was his last city house: from here he retired to his country estate, Andalusia, in Bucks County, where he died five years later.

Joseph Bonaparte

Since before the Marquis de Lafayette was the dinner guest of Samuel and Elizabeth Willing Powel on South 3rd Street to Julian Francis Abele's design of Penn's Irvine Auditorium, based on the church of the monastery of Mont Saint Michel, in 1929, there has been a surprising and vital connection between Philadelphia and France. One of the most famous episodes of this "special relationship" occurred in 1815 when Joseph Bonaparte, King of Naples and of Spain and elder brother of Napoléon, lived in the house at **260 South 9th Street** after fleeing to the United States in the wake of the Waterloo debacle. Bonaparte shortly vacated the city for Bordentown, New Jersey, but this house, built in the 1810s, still stands as a reminder of his brief Philadelphian transit.

Richardson Dilworth

Richardson Dilworth (1898–1974) was mayor of Philadelphia from 1956 to 1962—crucial years in Philadelphia's attempted self-renewal, of which he was one of the principal promoters, from long before he became mayor. In order to convince middle-class Philadelphians that Society Hill/Washington Square had become a decent place to live, Dilworth decided to take up residence there himself. But the house he chose proved structurally unsound, and so a copy of a Georgian house was erected on the site, at **223–25 South 6th Street**, in 1957. The house is now the headquarters of the Philadelphia County Dental Society.

7 REYNOLDS-MORRIS HOUSE

225 South 8th Street, between Walnut and Locust Streets
1786–87

Built by a physician named John Reynolds, the house was sold to Luke Wistar Morris in 1817, and his descendants occupied it for 120 years. It resides on a double lot and has a central-hall plan, which is unusual for a city house. The Georgian style was somewhat old-fashioned when the house was built, which is why it is not inaccurate to say that the Hill-Physick-

Keith house in Society Hill is the only freestanding Federal-*style* town house left in Philadelphia, but one of two such Federal-*era* houses left in the city.

8 N. W. AYER BUILDING

210 West Washington Square, between Walnut and Locust Streets
1927–29, Ralph Bencker

N. W. Ayer, founded in 1869, was Philadelphia's largest advertising firm until its defection to New York in 1973. The Art Deco building that was long the firm's headquarters features all kinds of ornament extolling the virtues of advertising, including its truth telling. The bronze doors of the entrance, designed by J. Wallace Kelly (1894–1976), depict advertising workers mysteriously clothed in what look like ancient Egyptian costumes. It has been noted that this was inspired by the Tutmania following the opening of the king's tomb in 1922. The architect, Bencker, is most famous for his Automat designs for Horn & Hardart.

8 *N. W. Ayer Building*

9 *Philadelphia Saving Fund Society*

9 PHILADELPHIA SAVING FUND SOCIETY
700–710 Walnut Street, corner of 7th Street
1868–69, 1885–86, 1897–98, Addison Hutton
1917, Furness, Evans & Co.

This Italianate palazzo, revetted in marble, was the Philadelphia Saving Fund Society's second of three headquarters. The first was the building at 306 Walnut Street, designed by Thomas Walter and built in 1839–40. The third was the famous Howe and Lescaze skyscraper of 1930–32. The earliest part of the building here went up at the corner in 1868–69, to the Quaker Hutton's designs—it was his first major success. Hutton added the rear addition around 1885–86 and the western addition in 1897–98, and Furness, Evans & Company added to the western addition in 1919. (These dates are approximate.) Howe and Lescaze then had a go at remodeling in 1929–31.

10 WALNUT STREET THEATER

829–33 Walnut Street, northeast corner of 9th Street
1808–9, 1827–28, all, apparently, by John Haviland

When Haviland wasn't designing Quaker prisons, he did, of all things, the-aters. The Walnut Street Theater is the oldest continuously used theater in the country. Edwin Forrest, who is buried in the churchyard of Old St. Paul's on 3rd Street, made his acting debut here, and the roster of those who have trod the Walnut's boards—from Edmund Kean to Edwin Booth to Ethel Barrymore—reads like a who's who of the acting profession in the English language.

11 EAKINS GALLERY, THOMAS JEFFERSON UNIVERSITY

1020 Locust Street, between 10th and 11th Streets

Within Jefferson Alumni Hall, if you look hard, you will find one of Philadelphia's most unexpected treasures: the Eakins Gallery, set up in 1982

10   *Walnut Street Theater*

to display three extraordinary paintings owned by Thomas Jefferson University. All three are, of course, works by Thomas Eakins (1844–1916), one of Philadelphia's greatest painters.

The most famous of the three by far is *The Gross Clinic,* often reproduced and generally regarded as one of the greatest American paintings and as perhaps Eakins's greatest work. It is a mesmerizing picture of Dr. Samuel David Gross (1805–84) at work in the surgical amphitheater of Jefferson Medical College in 1875. Gross was one of the most renowned American physicians of the nineteenth century. Born on a farm in Pennsylvania Dutch country, he earned a medical degree from Jefferson in 1828. He held the chair of surgery there from 1856 to 1882, and as teacher and author (*A System of Surgery: Pathological, Diagnostic, Therapeutic, and Operative,* 1859) was known as the "Nestor of American surgery." He also wrote an autobiography that is said to possess true literary value. (I have not read it.) Gross received honorary degrees from Oxford, Cambridge, and Edinburgh—and from Penn, to whose famous medical school Jefferson has always played second fiddle. In addition to being the subject of a great painting by Eakins, Gross is the only physician to be honored with a statue in our nation's capital: standing at the Army Medical Museum, it was the work of Eakins's student, Alexander Stirling Calder. (A cast of the same statue stands here at the Jefferson campus.)

An interesting bit of trivia is that Gross's mentor, and the founder of Jefferson Medical College, was Dr. George McClellan. (Jefferson graduated its first doctor in 1826, two years before Gross.) McClellan's son was General George Brinton McClellan, whom Lincoln named to head the Army of the Potomac. The general's son, McClellan's grandson, also named George McClellan, was professor of anatomy at the Pennsylvania Academy of the Fine Arts during the time Thomas Eakins taught there.

In the painting, the group gathered around the patient consists of Gross, his assistants, and the patient's mother. Behind Gross is a clerk recording notes, and in the background is an audience of students observing the surgery. Of the two figures visible in the tunnel, the one on the right is Gross's son, Samuel W. Gross, who also was a surgeon. The first of the figures to the right of the tunnel is a self-portrait of Eakins, who appears to be sketching. Gross is explaining to his students the removal of a bone from the leg of the patient, who is a teenage boy suffering from osteomyelitis. (Today, osteomyelitis is commonly treated with antibiotics, but this was not an option for Gross in 1875.) The patient's head is buried in a chloroform-soaked towel, and Gross's assistants hold a retractor, an instrument used to hold back the edges of an incision. The patient's mother is turning away from the scene, covering her eyes with her clenched hands. Note that Gross wears an ordinary business suit, which was typical of surgeons in their clinics at that time.

Eakins insisted that *The Gross Clinic* was not a genre picture but a new kind of naturalistic portrait. He had wanted it to be displayed at the Centennial Exposition's art exhibit, but the picture was rejected for being rather too grittily realistic. (Five other Eakins paintings were accepted for the exhibit, however.) But *The Gross Clinic* made it to the fair anyway: it wound up being exhibited at the model hospital sponsored by the U.S. Army. It is believed that Gross himself intervened to find an exhibitor for the painting at the fair. In 1878 Jefferson Medical College purchased the picture for two hundred dollars. Eakins, noted as a master of anatomy, had taken courses to that end at Jefferson, where he became aware of Gross. The painter was only thirty-one when he portrayed the seventy-year-old surgeon.

Also on exhibit in the Eakins Gallery are two other excellent portraits by Eakins. One is of Dr. Benjamin Howard Rand, a chemist, and was painted in 1874. Rand was chair of chemistry at Jefferson Medical College from 1864 to 1877 (he was dean of Jefferson from 1869 to 1877) but had earlier been a teacher of chemistry at Philadelphia's renowned Central High School, where one of his students was . . . Thomas Eakins. Rand is believed to be the first sitter for a portrait by Eakins outside the painter's family and friends. Note how Eakins portrays Rand at work—engrossed in his studies, unposed, apparently oblivious of his portraitist. This is the same kind of naturalism that Augustus Saint-Gaudens was introducing into American sculpture around the same time (as in his *Admiral Farragut* statue in New York). Rand commissioned this portrait from Eakins, and it was accepted for the art exhibit at the Centennial Exposition, after which Rand donated the painting to Jefferson Medical College.

The other portrait, and more similar to *The Gross Clinic,* is of Dr. William Smith Forbes and is much later than the other two paintings: 1905. Forbes became chair of anatomy at Jefferson Medical College in 1886 and is best known for his work toward legalizing the dissection of human corpses for medical-research purposes. (Dissection had long been illegal, and medical researchers had had to pay grave robbers for bodies. Forbes, as an advocate of dissection, was subjected to public condemnation, and in 1882 was even arrested for grave robbing. He was of course acquitted but at great personal cost.) In Eakins's portrait, Forbes is shown in his clinical theater. Hanging over the edge of the dissecting table is a parchment copy of the Pennsylvania Anatomy Act (which legalized dissection). The Latin inscription on the wall credits Forbes's efforts on behalf of the act. The picture was commissioned by Jefferson students, who donated it to the College at its eightieth annual commencement.

THOMAS EAKINS (1844–1916)

Eakins was born and died in Philadelphia (in the same house). All told, he spent sixty-eight of his seventy-two years in the city of his birth. He attended Central High, the Pennsylvania Academy of the Fine Arts, and, for three years (1866–69), the École des Beaux-Arts in Paris, where he studied painting with Jean-Léon Gérôme and sculpture with Alexandre Dumont. He attended anatomy lectures at Jefferson Medical College in 1864–65 and again upon his return from Europe in 1870, at which time he began to paint portraits of his family members. *Max Schmitt in a Single Scull,* a rowing picture of his old Central High classmate, now in the Philadelphia Museum of Art, was exhibited at the Union League Club on Broad Street in 1871. Eakins continued to send his works to Paris to be criticized by Gérôme, and he exhibited at the Salon of 1875. He started teaching at the Pennsylvania Academy of the Fine Arts in 1876 and became director of the Academy schools in 1882. But he was forced to resign from the Academy because of his insistence on the use of nude models. Among the board members who objected to the use of nude male models in classes that included female students, and who supported Eakins's ouster, was the famous lawyer and collector John G. Johnson. In protest, several of Eakins's students, including Charles Grafly and Alexander Stirling Calder, formed the Art Students League of Philadelphia, where Eakins taught until 1892. In 1888 he started to commute regularly to New York City, where from that year until 1895 he taught at the Art Students League and at the National Academy of Design. From 1891 to 1898 he also taught at Cooper Union. Thus, in 1891–92, Eakins taught at four different schools in Philadelphia and New York, all the while working on his own commissions. Sounds like a pretty heavy workload to me. In 1884 he married Hannah Susan Macdowell, who had studied at the Academy from 1876 to 1882.

The gallery also contains a couple of other interesting items. There is a Roman Imperial marble *Minerva,* forty-eight inches high, from the second century. And note *Portrait of a Soldier,* a 1917 painting by Hannah Susan Macdowell (Mrs. Thomas) Eakins, herself a gifted painter whose emotional support was crucial to her husband during the later years of his career when his work had fallen out of fashion and he did not always find it easy to enlist exhibitors for his paintings.

Before leaving Jefferson Medical College, it is interesting to note another remarkable family with a connection to that institution: the Mitchells. Dr. John Kearsley Mitchell, son of a Scottish-born physician who settled in Virginia, came to Philadelphia, where he took his medical degree at Penn in 1819. He became a professor at Jefferson, where his son, Silas Weir Mitchell, took his medical degree. S. Weir Mitchell would become, in Digby Baltzell's words, "Philadelphia's first citizen as no one before him had been since the death of Franklin." S. Weir Mitchell was a brilliant and internationally renowned physician, and his paper on shell shock, written in 1864 and based on his experience treating Civil War soldiers, is, so I have read, still the standard work on the subject. His pioneering work in neurology influenced, among others, the young Freud. Then, when he was in his sixties, Mitchell became a novelist, one of the few of any stature that Philadelphia has ever produced, even if his books are virtually unread today. *Hugh Wynne, Free Quaker,* published in 1896, was one of the best-selling American novels of the turn-of-the-century period.

12 PORTICO ROW

900–930 Spruce Street, between 9th and 10th Streets
1831–32, Thomas Ustick Walter

Walter's street of sixteen red-brick row houses, featuring marble porches with Ionic columns, is one of the most beautiful residential streets in Philadelphia.

13 CLARENCE MOORE HOUSE

1321 Locust Street, between 13th and Juniper Streets
1890, Wilson Eyre

Anglecot in Chestnut Hill shows Eyre's country-house style at its best. His town-house style is best exemplified here in this powerful romantic composition of pointed arches, deep window reveals, high chimneys, steep gables, contrasting materials, and château towers. The base is rusticated limestone; above that is Roman brick. As with many of Eyre's designs, it's all very carefully controlled—in spite of all the wild and crazy elements, the composition is actually very tidy. It is as though Eyre were an eclectic collector of bric-a-brac but with each item kept in its discrete compartment and neatly labeled.

14 ST. JAMES APARTMENTS
1226–32 Walnut Street, between 12th and 13th Streets
1900–1904, Horace Trumbauer

Apartment living came later to Philadelphia than to New York, and it is no surprise that the best of the city's earlier attempts at a luxury apartment house was the work of the Francophile Trumbauer. The Beaux-Arts excelled at large apartment buildings, and this is a beauty, with its sweepingly rusticated base, profusion of balconies, and big, rich dormered mansard. It is a contemporary of the Bellevue-Stratford and nearly its equal in quality.

15 HISTORICAL SOCIETY OF PENNSYLVANIA
1300 Locust Street, between 13th and 14th Streets
1910, Addison Hutton

The Historical Society was founded in 1824. It is primarily a research library, with outstanding collections of books, manuscripts, prints, and ephemera. But it is also a museum, with displays on Philadelphia history. There's furniture, portrait paintings, clothing, dishes, life casts, and so on. There's stuff that belonged to George Washington, William Penn, Benjamin Franklin, Robert Morris, George Fox, Abraham Lincoln, Joseph Bonaparte, Stephen Girard, and others. Among the paintings are works by the Peales, the Hesseliuses, Sully, Gilbert Stuart, Benjamin West, and John Singleton Copley. The treasures include the first two drafts of the Constitution and the largest collection of William Penn's letters.

Open Tuesday and Thursday to Saturday from 10:00 A.M. to 5:00 P.M., and Wednesday from 1:00 to 9:00 P.M. Admission is free. (215) 732–6200.

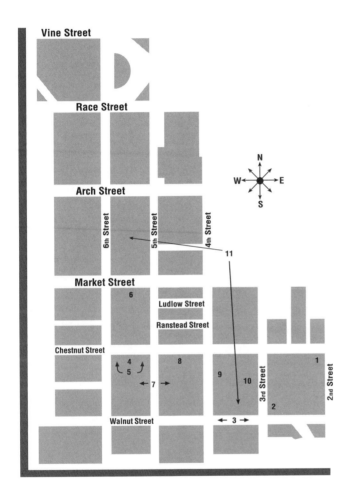

Vine Street

Race Street

Arch Street

6th Street

5th Street

4th Street

11

Market Street

6

Ludlow Street

Ranstead Street

Chestnut Street

4

5

8

7

9

10

3rd Street

2nd Street

1

2

Walnut Street

← 3 →

N
W ← → E
S

CHAPTER 3

INDEPENDENCE

1 *Customs House, with Merchants' Exchange on left*

CHAPTER 3

INDEPENDENCE

1 CUSTOMS HOUSE

100 South 2nd Street, southwest corner of Chestnut Street
1933, Ritter & Shay

It is odd what gets neglected: here's one of the most prominent buildings on the Philadelphia skyline, designed by a firm that enjoys a pretty good reputation. Yet one looks in vain in books about Philadelphia architecture for so much as a mention of the Customs House. It's a boxy, setback skyscraper decked out in quasi-Georgian details. Its silhouette on the Old City skyline is distinctive but out of scale with its Independence Park neighbors.

2 MERCHANTS' EXCHANGE

143 South 3rd Street, northeast corner of Walnut Street
1832–33, William Strickland

The semicircular "bow front" or "apse"—there's some confusion on the matter—negotiates, with a graceful sweep of the arm, a difficult triangular site and the tricky passage of Dock Street past Walnut Street.

The semicircular, octastyle Corinthian portico, let us call it, is at the apex of the triangle, a daring and exuberant manner of negotiating the space, and is nothing Strickland found in a pattern book. Its twin flanking— hugging—stairs, leading each to its own entrance in the main rectangular block of the building, are the perfect *appoggiaturi* to the portico. They are testament to Strickland's genuine artistry, as opposed to skill in exploiting pattern-book designs.

One thing he *did* get from a pattern book—Stuart and Revett's *Antiquities of Athens*—was the Choragic Monument that surmounts the portico.

2 *Merchants' Exchange*

This is based on a third-century B.C. Athenian form named for the *choragus* Lysicrates.

Prior to the construction of this building, Philadelphia's exchange activities took place in coffeehouses and taverns. This is the oldest standing stock-exchange building in the country. It was converted in 1922 into the city's produce market when Dock Street was the city's bustling wholesale market district. Strickland's building remained the produce market until it was incorporated into Independence Park in 1952.

3 WALNUT STREET, 3RD TO 4TH STREETS

On the south side of Walnut are a couple of interesting commercial buildings: the first headquarters of the **Philadelphia Saving Fund Society,** at 306 Walnut, and the **American Fire Insurance Company,** next door at 308 Walnut. The former is a Greek Revival job from 1839–40, designed by the great Thomas Ustick Walter. It is revetted in Chester County marble and has a two-story Ionic portico. The pediment was added in the 1880s. Founded in 1816, the Saving Fund Society was the first savings bank in the United States. The latter structure is from 1840 but was remodeled by Furness, Evans & Company in 1881.

On the north side of the street, to the west of the Merchants' Exchange and backing onto the park, are several late-Georgian houses, including a couple that are open to the public under the direction of the National Park Service: the **Bishop William White house,** at 309 Walnut, and the **Dilworth-Todd-Moylan house,** at 343 Walnut.

The Bishop William White (1748–1836) house, built in 1787, was the home of the first Episcopal bishop of Pennsylvania, who was the rector of Christ Church and St. Peter's. (In the National Portrait Gallery in the Second Bank of the United States is a portrait of White by Charles Willson Peale.) White was also the brother-in-law of Robert Morris. The Episcopal diocese of Pennsylvania was formed at Christ Church in 1787 with William White as its founding bishop, a position he held until his death in 1836 at the age of eighty-nine. Born in Philadelphia, White was graduated from the College of Philadelphia (the forerunner to the University of Pennsylvania). He is the only native Philadelphian to serve as bishop of the Pennsylvania diocese.

The Dilworth-Todd-Moylan house, built in 1775, was the home from 1791 to 1793 of a lawyer named John Todd and his wife Dolley Payne Todd (1768–1849). John died in the yellow-fever epidemic of 1793. His

widow was then introduced by Aaron Burr to a Virginian named James Madison, who would become our fourth president (serving two terms, from 1809 to 1817). In 1794 Dolley Payne Todd became Dolley Madison, later becoming one of our most famous first ladies. (Before becoming first lady she served as White House hostess for the unmarried Thomas Jefferson from 1801 to 1809, during which time her husband was secretary of state.) The next occupant of the house, from 1796 to 1807, was the Revolutionary General Stephen Moylan. Today the house has been restored to the way it looked when the Todds lived there.

The twin houses at Nos. 323 and 325, from around 1810, served until recently as the headquarters of the august **Pennsylvania Horticultural Society,** founded in 1827, which sponsors the annual Philadelphia Flower Show, now held in March at the new Convention Center. (The Society's new headquarters is at 100 North 20th Street.) The Society continues to maintain the excellent small eighteenth-century formal garden adjacent to its former headquarters on Walnut Street.

Right around the corner to the south at 212 South 4th Street, between Walnut Street and Willing's Alley, is the **Philadelphia Contributionship for Insuring Houses from Loss by Fire,** built for the insurance company founded by Benjamin Franklin in 1752. (*See* chapter four.)

According to Teitelman and Longstreth in their *Architecture in Philadelphia* (1974), this is "the only segment of the National Park that relates to the former urban landscape," i.e., the urban landscape prior to the scorched-earth creation of Independence Park.

3 *Walnut Street, 3rd to 4th Streets*

4   *Independence Hall*

4 INDEPENDENCE HALL

Chestnut Street, between 5th and 6th Streets
1731–53*, Andrew Hamilton with Edmund Wooley

This is the most famous Palladian window and Wren tower in America. It's early Wren-Georgian, shading into Gibbs' Palladianism, pure pattern-book stuff and not so outside the then English mainstream. The architectural historian William H. Pierson Jr. called it one of America's "most authentic English buildings surviving from the eighteenth century." Built over the same years as Christ Church, it is a little more Wren, a little less Gibbs than the church. Note the rather bulky and squat proportions and the rather heavy feeling of much of the interior ornamentation, quite different from

* The dates are Pierson's which, being Pierson's, I'd put my money on; the Foundation for Architecture's Philadelphia Architecture *says 1732–48, Wurman and Gallery's* Man-Made Philadelphia *says 1734–54, and Teitelman and Longstreth's* Architecture in Philadelphia *says 1730–48.*

the later Federal styles based on Adam, with their slender forms and graceful decorations.

Viewed from Independence Mall to the north, the rectangular main block is domestic in character but for two features: its length, and the marble panels set between the upper and lower rows of windows, a decorative device found in English civic buildings of the early Georgian period. Viewed from Independence Square to the south, the dominant feature is the tower, with the prominent Palladian window in its base. This treatment is almost ecclesiastical, except that the tower is in the center of the long side rather than at the west end.

This of course is where the Declaration of Independence was gestated and born, where the Second Continental Congress concocted the Articles of Confederation, and where the Constitutional Convention was held in 1787. There is, in short, no building in the country more closely or accurately identified with our nation's founding—and well should its design evoke the American nation's cultural debt to England.

Independence Hall has been altered and "restored" so many times (Strickland, Robert Mills, and John Haviland all had goes at it)—not the least of which was the "archaeological" phase begun in the 1950s—that it is in large measure a reconstruction of the original structure, rather as at Colonial Williamsburg.

Independence Square, the open space to the south of Independence Hall, has always been there (it's where the Declaration of Independence was first read to the public). Independence Mall stretches for two blocks to the north, and Independence Park stretches for three blocks to the east. Both were created from scorched earth beginning in 1948, the year after Oskar Stonorov's *Better Philadelphia* exhibit at Gimbel's.

In front of Independence Hall, don't miss the bronze cast, dating from 1908, of the marble statue of George Washington, dating from 1869, by one of Philadelphia's best sculptors, Joseph Alexis Bailly. (The original is in Conversation Hall in City Hall.) Bailly (1825–83) was born in Paris, and fled to England when he was conscripted against his will in 1848. He came to Philadelphia in 1850, another link in the remarkable chain of relation between that city and his native land. Although he started out in the city as a wood-carver, his evident skill was such that he was soon being frequently hired to carry out public commissions, such as the ornamental sculpture at the Academy of Music on Broad Street. He was as adept in bronze and stone as in wood, and created several memorials for Laurel Hill Cemetery, contributed works to the Centennial Exposition, and taught at the Pennsylvania Academy of the Fine Arts. His students included the gifted Howard

Roberts and Alexander Milne Calder, the latter of whom beat out Bailly for the commission to design the statue of William Penn atop City Hall.

5 CONGRESS HALL

Chestnut Street, southeast corner of 6th Street
1787–89

U.S. SUPREME COURT

Chestnut Street, southwest corner of 5th Street
1790–91

The late-Georgian (or Federal) west wing of Independence Hall housed the U.S. Congress from 1790 to 1800, when Philadelphia was the nation's capital. It has been restored to its appearance at that time. This is where the Bill of Rights was added to the Constitution, and where George Washington took his second-term oath of office. (His first oath was administered at Federal Hall on Wall Street in New York City.) John Adams was inaugurated here in 1797.

The east wing of Independence Hall is the original home of the U.S. Supreme Court. (The first chief justice was New York's John Jay.) After the

5 *Congress Hall,*
Public Ledger Building

capital moved to Washington in 1800, this served as City Hall until the present one on Broad Street was completed in 1901. Note the differences between the Wren-Palladian Independence Hall in the center and the later, more elegant and effete, Federal-style wings.

6 LIBERTY BELL PAVILION
Market Street, between 5th and 6th Streets
1976, Mitchell/Giurgola Associates

The cracked bell is Philadelphia's most popular tourist attraction, and, as such, it is rather touching that it is this relic of American independence, and not a branch of the Hard Rock Cafe, that holds that honor.

The bell once hung in the cupola of Independence Hall. The pavilion is a banal glass cube, lit up at night so that it displays the bell as a totemic object, which it was for the abolitionists of the antebellum years who made the bell famous by making it the symbol of their cause—which is the actual genesis of the bell's status as a tourist attraction.

7 PHILOSOPHICAL HALL
(AMERICAN PHILOSOPHICAL SOCIETY)
104 South 5th Street, between Chestnut and Walnut Streets
1785–89, Samuel Vaughan

LIBRARY HALL (OF THE AMERICAN PHILOSOPHICAL SOCIETY)
105 South 5th Street, between Chestnut and Walnut Streets
1954, Martin, Stewart & Noble

Since 1789 the Federal-style building on the west side of 5th Street has been the headquarters of the nation's oldest learned society, the American Philosophical Society, founded by Benjamin Franklin in 1743. On the east side of the street is the library and offices of the American Philosophical Society, on the site where the Library Company of Philadelphia, the colonies' first subscription library, had its headquarters from 1789 to 1888, when its building was demolished. In the 1950s a new building by Martin, Stewart & Noble re-created the façade of the Library Company's 1789 building, designed by William Thornton, the original architect of the U.S. Capitol in Washington. I daresay it is one of the best things built in Philadelphia in the 1950s.

7 *Philosophical Hall*

8 SECOND BANK OF THE UNITED STATES
420 Chestnut Street, between 4th and 5th Streets
1818–24, William Strickland

Here's Charles Dickens in 1842:

> We reached the city, late that night. Looking out of my chamber-window, before going to bed, I saw, on the opposite side of the way, a handsome building of white marble, which had a mournful ghost-like aspect, dreary to behold. I attributed this to the sombre influence of the night, and on rising in the morning looked out again, expecting to see its steps and portico thronged with groups of people passing in and out. The door was still tight shut, however; the same cold cheerless air prevailed; and the building looked as if the marble statue of Don Guzman could alone have any business to transact within its gloomy walls. I hastened to inquire its name and purpose, and then my surprise vanished. It was the Tomb of many fortunes; the Great Catacomb of investment; the memorable United States Bank.

Handsome and dreary: two words one seldom hears used in conjunction with each other. Outside there are austere octastyle Doric porticoes on either end, copied from pictures of the Parthenon in Stuart and Revett's *Antiquities of Athens,* with minimal decoration (there are triglyphs and metopes in the entablatures) and undecorated pediments. It lacks the funky inventiveness of the Merchants' Exchange, but the Second Bank's

handsome dreariness seems somehow more expressive of the virtues, such as they were, of the young republic. On the sides are arched windows, and inside is a Roman rotunda. This was highly usual for large Greek Revival public buildings because no one was all that concerned about stylistic purity. In any event, this is a really grand building.

WILLIAM STRICKLAND (1788–1854)

William Strickland was born in New Jersey. When the family moved to Philadelphia, his father worked as a carpenter for Benjamin Henry Latrobe, the city's—and the young nation's—most important architect. Then young William was apprenticed to Latrobe and spent two years in the master's office before deciding to strike off on his own—as a painter. But, in 1815 he decided to enter the competition for the design of the new Second Bank of the United States and, thus, one of the most important architectural careers in American history was well and truly launched. Beginning with his design of the Second Bank, Strickland, though he dabbled in a variety of styles, set the first true national architectural style of the young republic. His Greek Revival swept the new nation like wildfire. At first he relied upon James "Athenian" Stuart and Nicholas Revett's pattern book, *Antiquities of Athens* (1762), the first book to make available to architects and builders archaeologically accurate representations of Greek buildings of the fifth century B.C. (including the Parthenon and the Erechtheion). But Strickland soon enough was doing some pretty original stuff, as in his circular portico to the Merchants' Exchange. He designed St. Stephen's Church (Episcopal), built in 1822–23 at 10th and Market, in a picturesque "Gothic" (that bore little relation to the Ecclesiological Gothic of, for example, Notman's St. Mark's of 1847–49). He designed the beautiful U.S. Naval Hospital, built in 1827–33 at Gray's Ferry Road and Bainbridge Street in South Philadelphia, in Greek Revival with an octastyle Ionic portico, based on illustrations in Stuart and Revett. (This was the first home of the U.S. Naval Academy.) But perhaps the building for which he is today best known is not in Philadelphia. The financial panic of 1837 that followed President Jackson's closing down the Second Bank of the United States led to a standstill in new building in Philadelphia. Strickland moved to Nashville where he won the commission to design the new state capitol. The Tennessee State Capitol—the "Parthenon" of which Tennesseans love to boast (though the building is more closely modeled on the Erechtheion)—was built in 1845–59. Though it was completed five years after the architect's death, the project was supervised to the end by Strickland's son, Francis. The elder Strickland is buried in Nashville.

8 *Second Bank of the United States*

The Second Bank was formed by the federal government in 1816, five years after Congress revoked the charter of the First Bank. The new bank puttered along until 1822 when Nicholas Biddle was placed in charge of it. But the same populist forces that had put an end to the First Bank, with its conservative fiscal policy, led as well to the demise of the Second Bank when President Jackson vetoed Congress's renewal of the bank's charter, which expired in 1836. The following year, without the bank's brake on the money supply, runaway inflation led to the nation's first major depression.

THE GREEK REVIVAL

The Greek Revival differed from eighteenth-century classicism in that the former appealed not only or even primarily to the aesthetic sense but to the sense of virtue. We are now in the midst of the Romantic movement: art seeks to recover that which has been lost. In the landscape paintings of the "Wissahickon School" (William Trost Richards, Thomas Moran, et al.) or of New York's Hudson River School (Thomas Cole, Frederic Edwin Church, et al.) there is the attempt to record Arcadian nature. In the historical novels of Sir Walter Scott or of Philadelphia's own Charles Brockden Brown, there is the evocation of an idealized past. Frederic Church painted the Parthenon as though it were part of nature. The operative idea is the recovery of virtue.

And so the Greek Revival was the first architectural style the young republic self-consciously adopted. To be sure, the Greek Revival was a worldwide phenomenon, but nowhere was it clasped to a people's bosom as in America. Beginning with Strickland's Second Bank of the United States, the Greek temple mode and its variations caught on like wildfire across the new nation. Small-town courthouses, banks, urban row houses and southern plantation houses, churches of all denominations—every region of the country and every type of building was affected by the Greek vogue.

Why?

Within the young republic there was a natural identification with ancient Athens and its democracy. There was an atavistic element to the American project, not so much a sense of a new nation exploring uncharted terrain but a sense of *going back* to a less corrupted state. And to top it off, in the 1820s and 1830s, Americans paid keen attention to the Greek war of independence from the Turks. Americans identified with the Greeks, seeing in their struggle a reflection of the American Revolution. Indeed, the Greek war of independence was the sort of international cause célèbre that the Spanish Civil War would be a hundred years later. Lord Byron, the Romantic figure par excellence, died in Greece after going there to fight for the

Greeks, in the manner of Orwell or Malraux fighting beside the Spanish Republicans in the 1930s. For all kinds of reasons, Americans went in for things Greek. Don't forget how many American place names—Troy, New York; Athens, Georgia; Syracuse, New York; Spartanburg, South Carolina; and so on—have ancient Greek origins. This, too, was part of the Greek Revival.

So identified with America did Greek architecture become that when in 1832 Samuel Francis Smith wrote the words of "America" (i.e., "My Country 'Tis of Thee"), he included the lines:

I love thy rocks and rills,
Thy woods and templed hills.

All those "templed hills" are the progeny of William Strickland's design for the Second Bank of the United States.

Strickland was still around in the 1840s to remodel the building into the Customs House, which remained here until Ritter & Shay's tower went up in the 1930s.

Inside the Second Bank is a branch of the **National Portrait Gallery,** the "main branch" of which is in Washington's Old Patent Office Building. Here you will find much of interest, including Charles Willson Peale's portraits of Alexander Hamilton and Robert Morris, Henry Inman's portrait of William Penn, and William Rush's life-size carved-pine figure of George Washington.

9 CARPENTERS' HALL
320 Chestnut Street, between 3rd and 4th Streets
1770–74, Robert Smith

The Scotsman Smith, prominent member of the Carpenters' Company (i.e., guild) for whom this was built, did a variation on a cruciform Palladian villa (via pattern books) in red brick. This was the first Philadelphia appearance of the Greek cross plan, derived from such works of Andrea Palladio's as the Villa Rotonda in Vicenza from the 1560s. (Carpenters' Hall was closer in time to Palladio than we are to Carpenters' Hall.) The style of the handsome main doorway, with its keystoned arch resting upon pilasters, with flanking Doric columns and a triangular pediment, was introduced to

Philadelphia at Captain MacPherson's Mount Pleasant in 1761–62.

The Carpenters' Company, founded in 1724, is the oldest trade organization in the country. It was founded, at a time when the pace of building construction in the city was quickening, "for the purpose of obtaining instruction in the science of architecture and assisting such of their members as should by accident be in need of support." The Company's *Rule Book,* setting forth architectural and constructional standards and practices to be observed in Philadelphia, had a very carefully controlled circulation, and even Thomas Jefferson, as late as 1817 (he'd already been president!) was denied a copy when he requested one. In the year Carpenters' Hall was completed, it was let to the First Continental Congress for their meetings.

10 FIRST BANK OF THE UNITED STATES

120 South 3rd Street, between Chestnut and Walnut Streets
1795–97, Samuel Blodget
1901, James Hamilton Windrim

This is one of the best, most "finished" works of public architecture of the eighteenth century in the United States. Blodget (1757–1814), charged with housing the first national bank of the new republic, was apparently—and happily—inspired by Thomas Cooley's and James Gandon's contemporary works in Dublin. The hexastyle Corinthian portico, the Corinthian pilasters, and the sculptural pediment are worthy of the Beaux-Arts in the boldness of their conception if not in the crispness of their execution, though the latter is also quite high for the date in Philadelphia. The fully marble façade is in stark contrast to a work such as the central section of Pennsylvania Hospital, built around the same time, using red brick with marble trim.

In 1791 the Bank of the United States was established, largely through the efforts of Alexander Hamilton, as the central bank of the federal government. It was never entirely clear whether the Constitution permitted the federal government to operate such an institution, but no matter. It was Hamilton's dream. The bank controlled the money supply of the young republic, and it was largely because of the bank's conservative fiscal policy and the opposition that this aroused among businessmen and farmers who wanted easier credit that the U.S. Congress revoked the bank's charter in 1811. In 1812 the building was purchased by Stephen Girard, who operated it as a private bank (which eventually became Girard Trust Co.).

10 *First Bank of the United States*

11 INDEPENDENCE NATIONAL HISTORICAL PARK

East of Independence Square, bounded by 2nd, 5th, Walnut, and Chestnut Streets

INDEPENDENCE MALL

North of Independence Hall, bounded by 5th, 6th, Chestnut, and Race Streets

About Independence Mall, here's the English architectural critic Ian Nairn in 1965:

> . . . a vast formal axis galloping off to nowhere, focused on a building (Independence Hall) which is too small to stand up to it and which is dominated anyway by a skyscraper behind and off-center. Worse still is the historical zoo that is being constructed at the back of Independence Mall in which the monuments stand in landscaped grounds like gooney-birds, sterile and unrelated, to be looked at as museum specimens. The bums don't use the prairie barrenness of Independence Mall—they stay in the sleazy but live Franklin Square, nearby—and neither does anyone else. It is all unreal paper planning, the creation at enormous cost of an elaborate substitute for urban life. The often-derided Colonial Williamsburg has a far more organic pattern than this. (*The American Landscape,* New York: Random House, 1965, p. 124)

Beginning in 1948, over two hundred buildings in the three blocks east of Independence Square were cleared away by the National Park Service for Independence National Historical Park. Among these were undoubtedly many fine old buildings that just did not happen to have a direct connection with the lives of the Founding Fathers. In 1952 the Commonwealth of Pennsylvania followed suit and scorched three blocks of earth north of Independence Hall. The first block of Independence Mall, from Chestnut to Market, was built in 1952–54. The second block, from Market to Arch, was completed in 1957. The third block, from Arch to Race, was completed in 1963. The whole shebang was deemed finished when in 1967 the underground garage below the Market-Arch block was completed, along with the group of arcaded structures flanking the "public forum" in the same block. Not only did the Commonwealth destroy most of what was in these three blocks, but the city used its power of eminent domain to clear away many buildings, including many nineteenth-century commercial buildings, from adjacent streets, so as to allow redevelopment with several of the most hideous modern structures in the city. These included the ghastly U.S. Mint (1969, Vincent G. Kling & Associates), occupying the entire block bounded by 4th, 5th, Arch, and Race Streets; and the even ghastlier Police Administration Building (1963, Geddes Brecher Qualls Cunningham; note the bureaucratizing of the name of what we used to call police headquarters) on 7th and Race, across the street from Franklin Square (one of Penn's original squares), into which Independence Mall shades at its northern boundary. The Mint and Police buildings are two of the ugliest buildings ever allowed to disfigure the historic core of a great city.

As for the buildings that were felled for this progress, one need only point to one to stand for the rest: on the south side of Chestnut between 3rd and 4th there is today a reconstruction of the Joseph Pemberton house from 1775 and, to the east, an allée leading to Carpenters' Hall. The site of both of these had been occupied by Furness & Hewitt's Guarantee Trust Building, demolished in 1956 with not a peep of protest. It had no connection with the Founding Fathers. By my own reckoning, perhaps six buildings designed by Furness were knocked down to create Independence Mall and Independence Park.

Ian Nairn was right. It is well that Philadelphia should seek to preserve and honor the great buildings associated with our nation's founding, but the manner in which this was carried out, in the name of "renewal," created an open wound in the heart of the city.

There are plans afoot, at this writing, to try to make Independence Mall—the bit stretching north from Independence Hall—better than it is. The plan is by the Philadelphia-based landscape architect Laurie Olin, who is responsible for, among many other things, the magical transformation of New York's Bryant Park. In Olin's plan, new buildings, sensitively designed according to strict guidelines, will reoccupy some of the vast and amorphous open space. The Liberty Bell will be removed from its hideous "pavilion" and moved to a new setting in the remaining open space. At this writing, I do not know how much of this is certain to transpire, but I am under the impression that it is all systems go, and though the proposed solution falls well short of the total makeover that is required, it is hard to think it could be worse than what is currently there.

CHAPTER 4

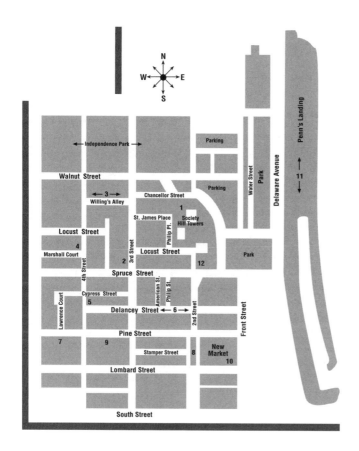

N
W—E
S

Independence Park

Walnut Street

← 3 →
Willing's Alley

Chancellor Street

Parking

Parking

Water Street

Park

Penn's Landing

Delaware Avenue

11

St. James Place

1 Society Hill Towers

Philip Pl.

Locust Street

4

Marshall Court

3rd Street

2

Locust Street

12

Park

Spruce Street

4th Street

Cypress Street

5

American St.

Philip St.

Lawrence Court

Delancey Street ← 6 →

2nd Street

Front Street

Pine Street

7

9

Stamper Street

8

New Market

10

Lombard Street

South Street

SOCIETY HILL

1 *Society Hill Towers*

CHAPTER 4

SOCIETY HILL

Society Hill is named for the Free Society of Traders, a stock company that invested in William Penn's colony and had its offices above Dock Creek (later filled in and called Dock Street). This is to dispel two common misconceptions: that *Society* in *Society Hill* refers to high society, since this was once as it is again an affluent area, or that *Society* refers to the Society of Friends, since many of the area's original residents were indeed Quakers. But neighborhood names are seldom so simple.

For the purposes of this book, Society Hill is defined as the area bounded by the Delaware River on the east, a line (roughly continuous with Chancellor Street) just south of Walnut Street to the north, 5th Street to the west, and Lombard Street to the south. It is that northern boundary that might throw people off. My reason for not including any portion of Independence Park under the Society Hill heading is that I think of Independence Park as a scorched-earth urban-renewal district that stands unto itself as an abstract entity with none of its traditional relations either to the neighborhood to the north (Old City) or to the neighborhood to the south (Society Hill).

Be advised, though, that it is very easy to combine strolls in Society Hill with strolls in Independence Park, the Washington Square area (which is contiguous to the west), and Queen Village (which includes the South Street shopping area and is contiguous to the south).

Today Society Hill is probably the most celebrated part of Philadelphia, whether rightly or wrongly, and everyone's favorite example of successful post–World War II urban renewal.

1 *Society Hill Towers*

1 SOCIETY HILL TOWERS
2nd and Locust Streets
1964, I. M. Pei & Associates

By the 1950s Society Hill, as every Philadelphian will tell you, had become a vast slum. Yet for a variety of reasons the area seemed to have promise. For one thing, it was directly adjacent to the historic core of the city, which was being redeveloped as a tourist precinct. As well, it offered an exciting waterfront location for new middle-class housing. So in 1958 the Philadelphia Redevelopment Authority held a competition among developers and their architects for the renovation of Society Hill, a competition won by the developers Webb & Knapp (headed by William Zeckendorf) and their architect, Ieoh Ming Pei.

The Towers are three severely Miesian poured-in-place concrete jobs that added instant chic to central Philadelphia. There was then and there is now really nothing quite like them anywhere else in the city, which is one of the several things that makes Philadelphia so physically distinct from New York or Chicago. Because these towers aren't replicated on every street as they are in New York or Chicago, they don't offend. So a bit of postwar Miesianism was added to the beguiling stew of Philadelphia architecture.

At least they're good by their own standards (unlike the Penn Center office towers).

The seven hundred or so apartments in the three towers were supplemented by a group of three-story town houses, also designed by Pei. They are across Philip Place from the towers, at 3rd and Locust. The houses face inward across a paved courtyard. Their design features red brick laid in the Flemish-bond pattern characteristic of the eighteenth- and nineteenth-century row houses in the neighborhood, arched doorways, and windows in scale with those of the surrounding older town houses. The idea was to create town houses that were clearly modern as well as good, deferential neighbors to the older houses. Most people would agree that the new houses are largely successful in realizing this goal.

In concert with the other new and rehabilitated row housing throughout Society Hill, they form one of the handsomest residential districts in the United States. Still, there's a lingering sense that it's all a little too, well, *perfect*. That sounds like an odd thing to say, but it's all a little too manicured—and uniform. It is uniform because it was determined, as part of the redevelopment, that everything from before 1840 had to be saved and rehabilitated, which meant of course mostly Georgian row houses. Anything from after 1840 could, and largely did, come down, to be replaced by the modern houses that were, as I noted, so handsomely fitted in with the older houses. It is little remembered today that, prior to this redevelopment, Society Hill was rich in Victorian buildings, almost all of which are gone: all those modern "infill" houses did not go up on land that just happened to be vacant!

The upshot is a kind of Colonial Williamsburg regimentation to the streets. Don't get me wrong: it's all quite marvelous (I like Colonial Williamsburg). But it lacks a certain something—a lived-in quality, perhaps, or a sense of the organic growth of a traditional neighborhood—that one can still find in some of the rehabilitated sections of New York or Boston, or, for that matter, Philadelphia (for example, some of the streets near Rittenhouse Square). This is why I favor Rittenhouse Square over Society Hill, even as the latter showed that *something* handsome and potentially long-lived might have emerged from the drawing tables of modernist planners.

2 POWEL HOUSE

244 South 3rd Street, between Locust and Spruce Streets
1765

The Powel (note spelling) house was restored and opened to the public as a house museum before the Second World War, which is to say well before any of Society Hill's large-scale renewal occurred.

Samuel Powel was the last mayor of colonial Philadelphia and the first mayor of independent Philadelphia. He married Elizabeth Willing, the daughter of Charles Willing and Ann Shippen, and the sister of Thomas Willing, who with his partner Robert Morris helped finance the Revolution. The Powels were good friends of George and Martha Washington, who often dined in this house and who reciprocated by having the Powels to Mount Vernon several times. Mrs. Powel was a famous hostess, and others among her guests included Benjamin Franklin, John Adams, and the Marquis de Lafayette. Adams wrote of an evening at the Powels':

> [A] most sinful feast again! Everything which could delight the eye or allure the taste; curds and creams, jellies, sweetmeats of various sorts, twenty sorts of tarts, fools, trifles, floating islands, whipped sillibub, &c., &c., Parmesan cheese, punch, wine, porter, beer, etc.

(A "fool" is a dessert of pureed fruit mixed with cream or custard and served cold. "Trifle" is sponge cake soaked in rum or brandy and topped with cream. "Sweetmeat" can be any kind of candy but is usually dried fruit. A "floating island" is custard with stiff, beaten egg whites floating on its surface. Whipped "sillibub," more commonly spelled "syllabub," is a dessert made with whipped cream, lemon, wine, and sugar.)

Samuel Powel and his brother-in-law Thomas Willing were among Benjamin Franklin's six pallbearers in 1790. Powel died three years later, in 1793's yellow-fever epidemic, following which Elizabeth sold the house. As the house fell on hard times, the Metropolitan Museum of Art in New York bought and removed the rich paneling from the first-floor dining room, and the Philadelphia Museum of Art bought and removed the paneling and the fireplace from the second-floor ballroom. In 1930 the house was about to be knocked down but was saved by the Philadelphia Society for the Preservation of Landmarks, which had been formed for that purpose by Frances Anne Wister, the granddaughter of Fanny Kemble, daughter of Dr. Owen Jones Wister and Sarah Butler, and sister of the novelist Owen Wister. Under the Society's auspices, the house was opened as a museum in 1933. The paneling that was removed had to be reproduced, but the ballroom ceiling

2 *Powel House*

is original. (The Society still owns and operates the Powel house as well as the nearby Hill-Physick-Keith house and Germantown's Grumblethorpe, the only one of the houses with a connection to the Wister family.)

Powel was a Quaker who became an Anglican, and it has been said that the house exhibits this duality: the exterior is restrained, while the interior is richly and luxuriously appointed. (The paneling, the elaborate plaster-work, and the Santo Domingo mahogany stairway are often noted.) The colonial carpenter extraordinaire and Scotsman Robert Smith worked on the interior.

The Powel house is open to the public Wednesday to Saturday from noon to 5:00 P.M. and on Sunday from 1:00 to 5:00 P.M. Admission is $3, $2 for students and seniors. (215) 627–0364.

3 WILLING'S ALLEY
South of Walnut Street, from 4th to 3rd Streets

At 212 South 4th Street, between Walnut Street and Willing's Alley, is the **Philadelphia Contributionship for Insuring Houses from Loss by Fire,** built in 1835–36. Thomas Walter adapted his Portico Row design from

1831–32 but substituted a tetrastyle Corinthian portico with fluted marble columns for the three-columned Ionic porches of the earlier design. This is the first and only permanent home of the oldest fire insurance company in America, founded by Benjamin Franklin in 1752. (Prior to this building, the Contributionship met in coffeehouses and taverns.) They wanted their new building to look like an elegant residence, and it included an apartment for the company's treasurer. The offices were on the ground floor and the apartment was on the top two floors. In 1866 Collins & Autenreith (the Lit Brothers' architects) expanded the apartment by adding the mansard.

Across 4th Street is Willing's Alley, a passage to 3rd Street. On the north side of Willing's Alley is **St. Joseph's Church,** built in 1838. The original St. Joseph's, built in 1733, was the first Roman Catholic Church in Philadelphia. It was replaced in 1755; the present church is the third on the site. The Marquis de Lafayette and the Comte de Rochambeau worshiped in the original church on this site when they were in Philadelphia. The present church was spared in the horrible anti-Catholic riots of 1844 (unlike St. Augustine's, which was burnt to the ground), possibly because it is rather hidden: the church is in a courtyard that is entered through an archway off Willing's Alley. Catholics in Philadelphia did not wish to be conspicuous. Agnes Repplier described St. Joseph's as "a church as carefully hidden away as a martyr's tomb in the catacombs."

It is a simple "Georgian Gothic" building constructed of brick, notable for the circular mural on its ceiling painted by the excellent Filippo Costaggini

3a *Willing's Alley, Entrance to*
St. Joseph's Church

3b *St. Paul's Church from Willing's Alley*

(1837–1900), who completed Constantino Brumidi's frieze in the rotunda of the U.S. Capitol in Washington. There is also an impressive Crucifixion painting, in the manner of Rubens, over the altar.

In 1689 King William III (regnant 1689–1702) and Queen Mary (regnant 1689–94) outlawed the Catholic Mass in the colonies, but in 1707 Queen Anne (regnant 1702–14) decreed that Catholic Masses could be said in the colonies but only in private houses. Thus when the Jesuit Father Joseph Greaton came to Philadelphia in 1729 he had to create a chapel in his house. Four years later, he tested the public waters when he built the first St. Joseph's Church. Amid the public uproar, the Charter of Privileges of 1701—the basis of Penn's "holy experiment" in religious toleration—was upheld and the church was allowed to operate.

On the north wall of the courtyard is a plaque commemorating William Penn, with the inscription:

> When in 1733 St. Joseph's Roman Catholic Church was founded and Dedicated to the Guardian of the Holy Family it was the only place in the entire English speaking world where public celebration of the Holy sacrifice of the Mass was permitted by law.

St. Joseph's congregation grew from fifty permanent parishioners in 1733 to 378 in 1757, when the land was purchased for St. Mary's, the city's second Roman Catholic church, which opened in 1763.

At the 3rd Street end of Willing's Alley is **St. Paul's Church,** opened in 1761 as the home of the city's third Episcopal congregation (after Christ Church and St. Peter's). The Georgian church was remodeled in 1830 by Strickland in a modified, austere, and handsome Greek Revival style. I am not sure if it was then or later that the brickwork was stuccoed over, which adds to the building's attractiveness. It's no longer an active church but has been the headquarters of the Episcopal Community Services of Pennsylvania since 1904. In its churchyard is buried the once famous actor Edwin Forrest (1806–72), whose fans' feud with the fans of the English actor William Macready precipitated the Astor Place riot in New York in 1849, in which thirty people were killed. The Forrest Theater on Walnut between 11th and 12th Streets was named for Edwin Forrest.

4 ST. MARY'S CHURCH (ROMAN CATHOLIC)
252 South 4th Street, between Locust and Spruce Streets
1763, 1782, 1810–11, 1886

Founded in 1763, St. Mary's was the city's second Roman Catholic church after the original St. Joseph's (built thirty years earlier). It became the city's first Roman Catholic cathedral, serving in that capacity from 1810 to 1838. And it is the oldest extant Catholic church in Philadelphia. In the words of E. Digby Baltzell, St. Mary's was "the most prominent Catholic church in America at the nation's founding." George Washington is known to have attended Mass here twice: in 1774, when he was a delegate to the Continental Congress, and in 1787, when he was a delegate to the Constitutional Convention. The third anniversary of the signing of the Declaration of Independence was commemorated here in 1779; the Te Deum was chanted.

After John Adams attended a Mass at St. Mary's, he wrote to his wife, Abigail:

> [T]he music, consisting of an organ and a choir of singers, went all the afternoon except sermon time, and the assembly chanted most sweetly and exquisitely. Here is everything that can lay hold of the eye, ear, and imagination, everything which can charm and bewitch the simple and ignorant. I wonder how Luther ever broke the spell.

The present flat Gothic façade was added in 1884, when the entrance was placed on 4th Street. Originally, the church was hidden from 4th Street by a row of houses, and one entered through the cemetery on 5th Street. Like St. Joseph's, St. Mary's was designed to be as demure as possible in a city in which anti-Catholic prejudice might flare into mob violence at any time.

Among those buried in St. Mary's cemetery are Thomas FitzSimons, a parishioner and one of two Catholics to sign the Constitution (the other was Daniel Carroll of Maryland). (There is a statue of FitzSimons in front of the Catholic cathedral at Logan Circle.) Also buried here is Michel Bouvier (1791–1874), the excellent furniture maker, the great-great-grandfather of Jacqueline Bouvier Kennedy Onassis and the first of the Bouvier clan to come over from France.

Inside the church are a crucifix sculpted by William Rush and an organ case designed by Thomas Ustick Walter.

5 HILL-PHYSICK-KEITH HOUSE
321 South 4th Street, between Cypress and Delancey Streets
1786

This is a superb freestanding Federal house. There are thirty-two rooms, including a first-floor ballroom. It would appear to be one of only two freestanding Federal town houses extant in the city. (The other is the Reynolds-Morris house at 225 South 8th Street near Washington Square.)

The house was built by Henry Hill, an importer of Madeira and the executor of Benjamin Franklin's will, who died, like Samuel Powel, in the yellow-fever epidemic of 1793. The occupant from 1815 to 1837 was Dr. Philip Syng Physick, one of the many Philadelphians with an honored place in the history of modern medicine. Physick is sometimes called the "father of American surgery," and plied his trade in the surgical amphitheater under the skylight of Pennsylvania Hospital. He is credited with being the first to use catgut ligature in surgery, and the first doctor ever to use a stomach pump.

The façade is lighter and airier than that of the earlier Powel house. The broad, centrally placed, semi-elliptical fanlight—one of the best you'll ever see—above the front door is the façade's most distinctive and dominant feature.

The adjacent early-nineteenth-century garden is a gem. It is laid out in the romantic manner popular in the late eighteenth century, with serpentine paths and antique sculpture reflecting an upper-class taste for whiffs of the remote past. All the plants are ones that might have grown in such a garden in the early nineteenth century.

5 *Hill-Physick-Keith House*

The house is open to the public during the winter from Thursday to Saturday, 11:00 A.M. to 2:00 P.M., and during the summer from Thursday to Sunday, noon to 4:00 P.M. Guided tours are offered on the hour. Admission is $3, $2 for students and seniors.

6 DELANCEY STREET, 4TH TO FRONT STREETS

Extending east along Delancey Street from the Hill-Physick-Keith house is where Philadelphia comes true for many people. It's not just that Delancey itself is delightful. But additional short streets and pedestrian pathways and even a small park are thrown in mid-block. Between 3rd and 4th Streets there's **St. Peter's Way,** which extends from Pine Street on the south to Locust Street on the north, anchored at either end by a fine church (St. Peter's on the south, St. Joseph's on the north). St. Peter's Way bisects Delancey Street at **Three Bears Park,** a small park with a playground and a whimsical sculpture of three friendly bears (papa bear, mama bear, and baby bear). This and similar open spaces in this neighborhood are part of the greenway plan of Edmund Bacon, the urban planner who masterminded the redevelopment of Society Hill in the 1950s. In this plan, pedestrian paths and small parks in the interiors of blocks are separated from vehicular conduits—it is the "superblock" imposed on a neighborhood of Georgian town houses.

On the other side of Three Bears Park from Delancey Street is the one-block Cypress Street. Another short block to the north, to the left around the corner from St. Peter's Way, is the **Girard Row** of town houses at 326–34 Spruce Street. Built in 1831–33, these middle-class houses are notable for their fully marble-revetted ground floors, a contrast with the conventional uniform red-brick façade with stone trim. A block north on Locust Street between 4th Street and St. Peter's Way is **Bingham Court,** a group of row houses designed by I. M. Pei & Associates and built in 1967, five years after Pei's Society Hill town houses, a block east at 3rd and Locust. The Bingham Court houses have unwindowed brick bases with second stories of glass, brick, and steel; they are reminiscent of Philip Johnson's famous Rockefeller guest house in Manhattan, built in 1950.

Across the street from Bingham Court at the northwest corner of Locust and 4th is the **Shippen-Wistar** house, built in 1765 by Dr. William Shippen (1711–1801), who received his medical training in the office of Dr. John Kearsley, the builder of Christ Church. The house passed to Dr. William Shippen Jr. (1736–1808), a prominent physician and one of the first American doctors to use cadavers for anatomical dissection, a practice illegal at the time. In 1762 Shippen Jr. established Philadelphia's—and America's—first maternity hospital. He was one of the five original

6a *Three Bears Park*

6b *Bingham
Court Houses*

6c *Shippen-Wistar House*

lecturers at the medical school, the first in the country, at the College of Philadelphia (the forerunner to the University of Pennsylvania) in 1765. When the University of Pennsylvania was established in 1791, Shippen Jr. became professor of anatomy, surgery, and midwifery. He was a founder of the College of Physicians and Surgeons. Shippen Jr. married into the Lees of Virginia, and many members of that distinguished clan were guests in this house.

(In the cliché-ridden 1959 movie *The Young Philadelphians,* starring Paul Newman, Robert Vaughn, Barbara Rush, and Alexis Smith, the villain is a physician and an Old Philadelphian named Dr. Shippen Stearns. Like Dr. S. Weir Mitchell, he is a world-renowned neurologist. One wonders how much of this was accidental, like the Philadelphian Hockley in the recent *Titanic,* and how much intentional. I am not going to research it: the film isn't good enough.)

The Shippens sold the house to yet another well-known Philadelphia physician, Dr. Caspar Wistar (1761–1818). A guest of Dr. Wistar's in this house was his friend, Alexander von Humboldt, the German naturalist. By the way, the wisteria (or wistaria) vine is named after Dr. Caspar Wistar, an avid botanist and horticulturist.

From 1836 to 1987 the Shippen-Wistar house and the neighboring **Cadwalader house** (240 South 4th Street) were the headquarters of the Mutual Assurance Company, the "Green Tree." This was the second oldest fire insurance company in America after the Philadelphia Contributionship. The green tree became its symbol because they, unlike the Contributionship, would insure houses that had trees in front of them. Today the two houses form the Pennsylvania headquarters of the Episcopal Church. The Cadwalader house, by the way, was built in 1826 and purchased in 1837 by the distinguished Judge John Cadwalader (1805–79).

Mid-block between 2nd and 3rd, Philip Street runs north one block from Delancey to Spruce Street. Philip Street is anchored on its south end by the **Franklin Roberts house** at 230 Delancey, a good example of a modern Society Hill town house built at a scale and with materials to blend in with its historic surroundings. This one was designed by the renowned Mitchell/Giurgola and built in 1969. (Mitchell/Giurgola also designed the house at 110–12 Delancey Street.) At the north end of Philip Street is a fine Georgian town house, the **Abercrombie house** at 268–70 South 2nd Street, built in 1759. Built at four and a half stories on high ground, the decked gable roof must have commanded quite a prospect in the colonial city, kind of like living high up in Society Hill Towers today.

Among it all is not a single masterpiece, but who cares? We have mid-Georgian, Federal, Greek Revival, and modern houses both freestanding and in rows, and churches, all harmoniously related in materials and scale along short blocks with open spaces and surprising vistas. It doesn't get any better than this.

7 OLD PINE STREET CHURCH (PRESBYTERIAN)
412 Pine Street, between 4th and 5th Streets
1768, Robert Smith
1837
1857, John Fraser

In 1837 the pedimented octastyle Corinthian portico was added to the Georgian body that the Scotsman Smith designed for this congregation of his countrymen. This is the only Presbyterian church still standing from pre–Revolutionary Philadelphia. Big deal, you say? Believe it or not, by

7 *Old Pine Street Church*

1739, when George Whitefield came a-preaching Philadelphia way, the Presbyterians, not the Quakers or Anglicans, were the most numerous religious denomination in the city.

The first of the city's Presbyterian churches went up in 1704; it was called the First Presbyterian Church. In 1739 came Whitefield, who fomented the Great Awakening that both aroused the religiously disaffected and also sowed dissension in the ranks of the established Protestant churches. The Greatly Awakened among the Presbyterians decided they had to form their own church; they called it the Second Presbyterian Church. One of the leading Great Awakeners, Gilbert Tennent, was made its pastor. Eventually, as the city and the number of its Presbyterians grew, the First Presbyterian Church had to expand; their new church was called the Third Presbyterian Church. (The Presbyterians have a way with names.) It is more familiarly and charmingly known as the Old Pine Street Church.

Buried in the churchyard are David Rittenhouse and Eugene Ormandy.

8 HEAD HOUSE SQUARE

2nd Street, between Pine and Lombard Streets
Market sheds: 1745
Head house: 1804

This is a superb survivor of eighteenth-century colonial urbanism. Once the central market of the city, it was restored in 1960. The head house was added to the market sheds half a century after they were built and is a fine example of a utilitarian structure in the Federal style. But the market sheds in the middle of the street are the special thing here. It's the way the sheds open up Second Street and enhance its density. In other words, a commercial street like this must be dense or it doesn't succeed. At the same time, the very density that is its requirement can work against it by being oppressive. Open up the street too much, and the appropriate density is lost. Don't open it up, and the density might be too much. It's a delicate balance. But here, with the strip of open sheds down the middle of the street, you pull off the miracle of increasing the openness and the density at the same time. From either side of Second Street you can look across both to the market sheds and through them to the other side of the street. Within the sheds you are open to either side of Second Street. It's as though a new dimension's been added to the street. It's marvelous, and odd that it hasn't, to my knowledge, been replicated in the neo-urbanist planning of recent years.

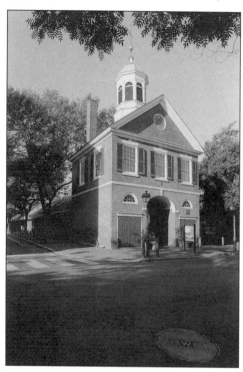

8 *Head House Square*

9 ST. PETER'S CHURCH (EPISCOPAL)
313 Pine Street, between 3rd and 4th Streets
1758–61, Robert Smith, carpenter
Steeple: 1852, William Strickland

This is another work by the peripatetic Scotsman who gave us Carpenters'
Hall, among much else, and who also worked on Christ Church, where he
was a parishioner. Smith was a pattern-book Palladian through and through,
though here he's quite restrained. Still, there's a bravura Palladian apsidal
window. The spire atop Smith's boxy six-story tower was added by Strickland
in the 1850s.

9 *St. Peter's Church*

In 1753, the Christ Church vestry decided they needed to build a second church, both to handle their overflow and for the convenience of parishioners who lived in fashionable Society Hill. St. Peter's was thus a "chapel of ease" of Christ Church. The land for the church was donated by William Penn's son Thomas, an Anglican convert. The first service was held in 1761.

Inside, there is an unusual arrangement in which the altar is at the east end, but the pulpit is at the west end. In any event, it would have been the pulpit, not the altar, that commanded attention in an eighteenth-century Anglican church, where the sermon, not any sacrament, was what mattered. Note the wooden angels flanking the organ case: they were carved by William Rush.

Buried in St. Peter's churchyard are Nicholas Biddle, Benjamin Chew (of Cliveden fame), Charles Willson Peale, and Dr. John Morgan. In 1765, Morgan was the founder of the medical school, the country's first, at the College of Philadelphia (the forerunner of the University of Pennsylvania).

10 NEW MARKET

2nd Street, between Pine and Lombard Streets
1973, Louis Sauer Associates

Across from the market sheds of Head House Square is this example of 1970s urbanism at what has to be reckoned its best, which may be damning with faint praise. Ghirardelli Square in San Francisco was all the rage, and Faneuil Hall Marketplace in Boston was soon to follow, as old cities "rediscovered" their waterfronts with these shopping and restaurant pavilions. How ineffably exciting it must have been to drive in from the suburbs around the time of the Bicentennial to eat at the Rusty Scupper! Alas, it was a fleeting thrill, as the '70s waterfront-pavilion thing, just like the '70s atrium-hotel thing, became a cliché in rather short order.

11 PENN'S LANDING

Delaware River, from Lombard to Market Streets
begun 1967

For years whenever I'd come to Philadelphia I went looking for Penn's Landing. I had credible information it existed. But as I prowled the waterfront in the nether region on the other side of I-95, I was never quite sure if I was in Penn's Landing. Alas, Penn's Landing is an ill-coordinated jumble of ill-

conceived recreational and commercial uses. There's the big concert bowl and a maritime museum (another of those "interactive" museums for people with short attention spans), landing stages for the sailing vessels in which it is indeed a joy to ride about the river, the ghastly World Sculpture Garden (I have concluded that anything with *world* in its title is bound to be worthless or dangerous), an ice-skating rink, a Chart House restaurant (no historic waterfront would be complete without one!), and whatnot. If you never set foot in its forty-some-odd acres, you won't be missing a damn thing. That said: a missed opportunity. Waterfronts are a terrible thing to waste.

The development of Penn's Landing, once a bustling working waterfront, began in 1967.

12 MAN FULL OF TROUBLE

127 Spruce Street, northeast corner of 2nd Street
1759

An inn and a tavern, forthright in its colonial Georgian, the Man Full of Trouble opened in 1759. One of many such places of repast and respite in the rough, dirty, fetid, fledgling burg, this Great Good Place operated for 125 years. Travelers stayed in the second and gambrel-roofed attic stories. The bar and dining room were on the first floor, the kitchen in the basement. It's the only city tavern remaining from colonial Philadelphia and is interesting to compare with a colonial-era country inn/tavern, the Green Tree (1748) in Germantown, and a later city inn/tavern, the St. Charles Hotel (1851) on North 3rd Street.

N
W ← → **E**
S

9   8
1   Benjamin Franklin Bridge

Race Street

Cherry Street

Elfreth's Alley
2

6   3

Arch Street

7   3   3

4th Street   3rd Street   2nd Street

5

Church Street   4

Market Street

13

Front Street

← 10

← 11   ← 12 →   14 →   Chestnut Street   15

16

↓

OLD CITY

1 *Benjamin Franklin Bridge*

CHAPTER 5

OLD CITY

1 BENJAMIN FRANKLIN BRIDGE

At Delaware River, between Race and Vine Streets
1926, Paul Philippe Cret

The great Cret gave us one of America's most beautiful suspension bridges, the equal, really, of any of New York's justly renowned East River spans. It was, when built, the longest suspension bridge in the world. And it can be traversed on foot!

That rapid-fire blinking-light business at night was added for the Bicentennial by Venturi, Rauch & Scott Brown.

2 ELFRETH'S ALLEY

Bounded by Arch, Race, 2nd, and Front Streets
1720s anon.

As Head House Square is to the commercial urbanism of the colonial city, so Elfreth's Alley is to the residential urbanism. Every Philadelphian will tell you that this is the oldest continuously inhabited street in the United States (or something like that). There's a mix of early-eighteenth-century houses, modest two-and-a-half-story structures entered directly from the street, and somewhat grander, late-eighteenth-century Federal houses, three-and-a-half stories with porches. It's a pleasant jumble, that quality being a hallmark of colonial urbanism, as is the close-packed density.

2 *Elfreth's Alley*

3 *Smythe Stores*

3 CAST-IRON FRONTS NEAR FRONT STREET

Probably the grandest cast-iron front in Philadelphia belongs to the old **Smythe Stores,** built in 1855–57 at 101–111 Arch Street, at the northwest corner of Front. Note, however, that the central section was reproduced in fiberglass when the building was converted to chichi apartments in the 1980s. That section had been removed in 1913 for a trolley turnabout. **The Tutlemann Brothers and Faggen Building,** at 56–60 North 2nd Street, between Church and Arch Streets, was built in 1830–36 with a brick façade, replaced by cast-iron in 1900–1901, which is quite a late date for that. It was one of the first old loft buildings to be converted to apartments when Old City became trendy in the 1970s. On the other hand, the old **St. Charles Hotel,** at 60 North 3rd Street at the southwest corner of Arch, has a cast-iron façade nearly as early as the Tutlemann Brothers' is late: 1851. It's also a good example of an antebellum hostelry, bar on ground floor and guest rooms up above—an updating of the Man Full of Trouble of an earlier era.

4 *Girard Warehouses*

4 GIRARD WAREHOUSES

18–30 North Front Street, northwest corner of Church Street
1810

There's plenty of rugged splendor to the old waterfront neighborhood here, as in these warehouse/store/countinghouses not dissimilar to Schermerhorn Row in New York. The first floors are faced in granite, the upper floors in brick. There's a similar row up Front Street at Nos. 36–44.

5 CHRIST CHURCH (EPISCOPAL)

2nd Street, northwest corner of Church Street
1727–44

Philadelphia's most famous colonial church is a fully realized essay in Georgian ecclesiastical architecture. The main church was "designed" by Dr. John Kearsley (1684–1772), an Englishman, a physician, and a local sophisticate who may have known Wren's postfire churches in the City of London. It appears to be under Wren's influence that the church, with its single square tower, first began to take shape in the twenties. Of greater significance, though, are the Palladian elements that indicate the later influence of Gibbs's pattern books. (These elements include the double rows of arched windows along the sides, vertically separated by pilasters; the balustraded parapets;

5 *Christ Church*

and the large Palladian window of the east end.) Gibbs may have entered the picture via the Scotsman Robert Smith (1722–77), the parishioner who designed the 209-foot-high steeple that was added in the fifties. (Smith later designed St. Peter's to handle the Christ Church overflow.) Indeed, this is said to be the first church in the colonies to show the direct influence of Gibbs's St. Martin in the Fields in London, completed only a year before construction began on Christ Church. Clearly, thirty years of pattern-book pickings were bound to lead to the occasional infelicity. But on the whole there's an impressive dimensionality and finish that mark this as one of the major buildings of colonial America. Architectural historian William H. Pierson Jr. called it "the most advanced and completely English church in the colonies."

It was here that in 1789 the first General Convention of the American Episcopal Church, under Bishop Samuel Seabury, was held. The American Episcopal Church is part of the Anglican Communion that has its origin in the Church of England, which formed when Henry VIII broke from the Church of Rome in 1534. The regional and national churches that make up the Anglican Communion are independent of the authority of the Church of England. These various churches are bound together largely by a shared body of basic theological beliefs and liturgical practices.

6 BETSY ROSS HOUSE

239 Arch Street, between Bread and 3rd Streets
1740

Did any of us really need to know that Betsy did not in fact design the American flag? That, indeed, she may never even have sewn one? We are not even sure that this was the seamstress Betsy Ross's house! If it is, then we have the splendidly preserved home and burial place of an ordinary colonial seamstress, which is in itself no bad thing since it's well to see how seam-stresses, as well as the elite, lived in the colonial city. Betsy's dates are 1752–1836, and she's buried (or so we've been told) in the courtyard of this simple and handsome Georgian house.

7 ARCH STREET FRIENDS MEETINGHOUSE

330 Arch Street, between 3rd and 4th Streets
1803–5, 1810–11, Owen Biddle

Long, three-winged, triple-porticoed, central-pedimented: say as much, and you might picture Independence Hall. This is, not surprisingly, infinitely plainer, as it's a meetinghouse of the Society of Friends, William Penn's Quakers.

It is the oldest Friends meetinghouse still in use in Philadelphia, and the largest in the world. Quaker meetinghouses are generally simple as can be—the *reductio* of the Protestant tendency to the desacralization of the worship service, though in contrast to the Protestant sects, there's not even a pulpit. And of course there's nothing like religious iconography—there is a horror of ostentation. A Meeting of Friends involves sitting together in silence, with people speaking as the spirit moves them. There are no formal prayers nor is there a formal liturgical shape to the proceedings. Being anti-clerical, the Quakers are also antiritualistic. They believe that God speaks to each individual through the "still, small inner voice." At a Meeting, there-fore, silent communion may be interrupted by spontaneous testimony or "witness." At Arch Street, the yearly Meetings take place in the west wing, and the monthly Meetings in the central section. The east wing is now a museum with displays, including dioramas, on the life of William Penn.

The Religious Society of Friends was founded in seventeenth-century England by George Fox (1624–91). It was the ultimate anticlerical sect, maintaining that an individual's relationship to God requires no clerical intermediaries but rather the guiding light of the Holy Spirit calling him to a Christlike life. The Society takes its name from John 15:6–16 ("You are my friends if you do what I command you.") Originally, the term *Quaker* was apparently a derogatory name given to Friends for their "trembling" or "quak-ing" before God but was soon enough cheerfully adopted by Friends (in much the way that the derogatory *Methodist* was adopted by Wesley and his followers in the eighteenth century). Persecuted in England, the Quakers, under William Penn, formed their own colony of Pennsylvania in 1682.

The Arch Street meetinghouse was begun in 1803 and completed in 1811. It was in 1819 that New York's Elias Hicks first came to Philadelphia. Speaking at Philadelphia Meetings, the charismatic Hicks preached a vision of radical Quakerism holding to a belief in the absolute authority of the Inner Light and the basic irrelevance of Scripture. Hicks's appeal to large numbers of Philadelphia Friends led to the schism of 1827 in which Quakers became divided between "Orthodox" and "Hicksite" factions. The Ortho-dox faction maintained its home at the Arch Street meetinghouse. To out-siders, all Quakers may seem like one. Among Quakers, though ecumenism

7 *Arch Street
Friends Meetinghouse*

has been on the steady rise in recent years, the distinctions among the sects (more factions were added later) are of paramount if parochial importance. (Bryn Mawr and Haverford Colleges were founded by Orthodox Friends; Swarthmore by Hicksites. I suspect that few if any of the students at these schools today care or even know very much about such distinctions.)

Owen Biddle, who "designed" the Arch Street meetinghouse and was long among its prominent members, was a clock maker and a member of the American Philosophical Society. Apparently he was not a practicing Friend when he fought as an officer in the Revolutionary War. (I do not know if he joined the "fighting Quakers" whose meetinghouse was located at Arch and 5th Streets.) But he shortly returned to the fold in time to build the new meetinghouse, and he remained staunchly Orthodox though many among his famous descendants in Philadelphia became Hicksites or even Episcopalians, the latter as they assumed roles of greater importance in society (as opposed to the Society).

Arch Street is home to the Philadelphia Yearly Meeting of Friends, which covers southern New Jersey, Delaware, and parts of Maryland. (Pennsylvania is no longer the largest Quaker state, by the way, which comes as a great surprise to many people: the title now belongs to Indiana, with Pennsylvania pulling up second. Indiana Quakers are Orthodox followers of Joseph John Gurney, whose teachings produced another schism among Philadelphia Orthodox Quakers. Jessamyn West's 1945 novel *Friendly Persuasion* and William Wyler's 1956 film of that novel, starring Gary Cooper, Dorothy McGuire, and Anthony Perkins, are set among the Gurneyite Quakers of Indiana.)

The grounds of the meetinghouse have been used as a burial place since 1701. Among those buried here are James Logan (of Stenton fame), in an unmarked grave (why is this?), and the Gothic novelist Charles Brockden Brown (1771–1810), author of *Wieland* (1798) and an important figure in the evolution of American literary romanticism (he is considered an influence on Hawthorne and Poe). (In a town not known for its novelists, Brown may be historically the most significant that Philadelphia has ever produced.)

8 ST. GEORGE'S CHURCH (UNITED METHODIST)
235 North 4th Street at New Street, between Race and Vine Streets
1769

St. George's is the oldest Methodist church in continuous use in the United States and was the center of colonial Methodism in America. Before the church was built, Philadelphia Methodists met in private homes. The church is Quaker plain and was the site of the first three conferences of American Methodism (1773, 1774, and 1775) and of the first Methodist Book Concern, the publishing arm of the Methodist Church.

St. George's came near to being torn down in 1921 when the Benjamin Franklin Bridge was built. To spare the church, the bridge was actually moved fourteen feet, though the sidewalk had to be lowered, which explains why St. George's is entered via steps at its second level.

Richard Allen (1760–1831), the founder of the African Methodist Episcopal Church in 1816, was licensed at St. George's in 1784 as the first African American Methodist preacher.

The Methodist Church grew out of the Church of England through the teachings of John Wesley (1703–91), an Anglican priest. From 1735 to 1737, he accompanied James Oglethorpe (1696–1785) to the recently formed Georgia colony, where the works of Moravian missionaries had a profound impact on Wesley. (The Moravians, founded by Jan Hus in Bohemia in the fifteenth century, had a great deal in common with Methodism as it would be developed by Wesley.) On May 24, 1738, at a prayer meeting in London, Wesley had a revelation that it is by complete surrender to God's mercy alone that man might be saved. Equipped with this truth, Wesley set out to preach, especially to those who were disaffected from the established church. He proved enormously persuasive and a great organizer, and almost superhumanly energetic. He did not at first conceive of what he was doing as forming a new sect but rather as offering a new route into the Church of England. But opposition to his methods from the Church hierarchy caused his followers to form their own denomination in 1795, four years after Wesley's death. (Wesley went to his grave considering himself a member of the Church of England.) The Methodists almost immediately began to splinter; indeed, they were worse in this regard than even the Quakers.

Also in 1738, Wesley's friend George Whitefield (1714–70) made the first of his several trips to America, where his fiery preaching touched off the "Great Awakening." Eventually, Whitefield would break with Wesley and form a new branch of Calvinistic Methodists.

Methodism came to Philadelphia, unbeknownst to Wesley, in 1766 via the English preacher Captain Thomas Webb. Upon learning this, Wesley sent the Englishman Francis Asbury (1745–1816), considered the father of American Methodism, to Philadelphia in 1771. During the Revolution, Wesley himself opposed American independence. This might have been death for American Methodism but for Asbury, an outspoken supporter of the Revolutionary cause who, at a time when the prestige of the Church of England was ebbing in America, gained many converts to Methodism. The Methodist Episcopal Church in America was founded in Baltimore on December 24, 1784, with Asbury and the Welshman Thomas Coke (1747–1814) as co-superintendents. (They soon changed their title to bishop, which Wesley, being opposed to bishops, did not like.)

Methodist was at first a derogatory term used by Wesley's opponents in much the way that George Fox's opponents referred to his followers derogatorily as Quakers. Methodist referred to Wesley's and his followers' strict or "methodical" habits. As with Quaker, the epithet was proudly adopted by its followers.

9 ST. AUGUSTINE'S CHURCH (ROMAN CATHOLIC)
4th and New Streets
1847–48, Napoleon LeBrun

The original St. Augustine's was built in 1798 but burned to the ground by an anti-Catholic mob on May 8, 1844. The church was rebuilt in 1847–48 by LeBrun in a Palladian style prefiguring that of the Catholic cathedral, designed in part by LeBrun, at Logan Circle. The tower was completed by the outstanding and underappreciated Catholic architect Edwin Durang (designer of the glorious Church of the Gesù in North Philadelphia) in 1867. Inside are ceiling frescoes by (the outstanding and underappreciated) Filippo Costaggini (1837–1900), who was Constantino Brumidi's assistant and successor. There's also a beautiful white marble altar, its domed baldachin raised on Corinthian columns.

The Order of St. Augustine founded St. Augustine's Academy at this site in 1811. This school evolved into today's Villanova University.

10 THE BOURSE
11 South 5th Street, between Ludlow and Ranstead Streets
1893–95, G. W. and W. D. Hewitt
Renovated in 1982, H2L2

The Bourse was once home to the Philadelphia Stock Exchange, among other financial institutions, and was renovated in the 1980s into a shopping mall and office building. The building is another good one by the redoubtable brothers Hewitt, and it is always a small miracle whenever

9 *St. Augustine's Church*

Philadelphia manages to preserve a Victorian structure. The renovation was sensitive: there's much in the way of decorations and in the grandeur of the atrium to recommend a visit here. The atrium space was originally a trading floor ringed by offices. The mall is filled with those cheesy chain eateries staffed by uncouth adolescents.

11 CHESTNUT STREET, BETWEEN 4TH AND 5TH STREETS

This encompasses Bank Row, appropriately enough, right across the street from Strickland's grand Second Bank of the United States. From west to east: the **Pennsylvania Company for Insurances on Lives and Granting Annuities** (only in Philadelphia do buildings have names that long) at No. 431, designed by the Quaker Addison Hutton and built in 1871–73; the **Farmers' and Mechanics' Bank** at No. 427, designed by John M. Gries and built in 1854–55; and the **Bank of Pennsylvania** at No. 421, also by Gries, built in 1857–59.

Of these the most interesting is the Farmers' and Mechanics' Bank, with its lovely Italianate marble façade, with fifteen arched openings rhythmically disposed in a horizontally tripartite composition with cornices, quoins, heavy modillions, and relief panels. It was sparklingly restored in the 1980s by Bower Lewis Thrower. Hutton's Pennsylvania Company is the last remaining post–Civil War structure on Bank Row, which once boasted not one but two banks designed by Frank Furness.

11   *Farmers' and Mechanics' Bank*

12 CHESTNUT STREET, BETWEEN 3RD AND 4TH STREETS

This is a continuation of Bank Row above. At 323 Chestnut Street is the **Philadelphia National Bank,** built in 1898. The architect was Theophilus Parsons Chandler (1845–1928), who founded Penn's school of architecture in 1900. To the east at 315 Chestnut is the **First National Bank,** built in 1865–67. The architect here was John McArthur Jr., famous for City Hall, which began construction shortly after this bank was completed.

The most important, in architectural terms, of all the Bank Row buildings, however, is gone: Furness & Hewitt's Guarantee Trust Company, on the south side of Chestnut between 3rd and 4th, obliterated in 1956 in the Independence Park scorched-earth campaign.

13 FRANKLIN COURT
312–22 Market Street, between 3rd and 4th Streets
1973–76, Venturi & Rauch with John Milner Associates

Benjamin Franklin's house and print shop were in the courtyard in the interior of this block but were destroyed; instead of what would have been a highly speculative reconstruction, the National Park Service went high concept, engaging Venturi & Rauch to put up "ghost structures"—bare steel frames outlining what the original buildings might have looked like. The museum of Frankliniana is underground. This was, I suppose, the genesis of the Venturi exploding-semiotica plaza, with quotes and such cut into the pavings. It's a semi-goofy idea but it kind of gets to you.

14 MID-NINETEENTH CENTURY LOFT BUILDINGS AROUND CHESTNUT AND 3RD STREETS

At 235–237 Chestnut Street, between 2nd and 3rd Streets, are the **Elliott and Leland buildings,** built in 1854–56. Their architect was Joseph C. Hoxie, who designed the sumptuous Arch Street Presbyterian Church in 1853–54. Like the church, these commercial loft buildings are in the Italianate style, here handsomely rendered in granite. Around the corner to the north at 37–39 South 3rd Street is another building called, confusingly, the **Leland Building.** Designed by Stephen Decatur Button (1803–97), it was built in 1855. Button's use of continuous vertical piers, projecting slightly beyond the plane of the windows and spandrels, and his very sparing use of ornament are said to have greatly impressed the young Louis Sullivan when he lived in Philadelphia while working for Furness & Hewitt in 1873.

15 WELCOME PARK
2nd and Walnut Streets
1982, Venturi, Rauch & Scott Brown

What Venturi and Rauch began at Franklin Court, they adapted for other "semiotic plazas," as I like to call them, in which words and images are

13 *Franklin Court*

etched in stone and combined with textual panels to impart information and evoke a sense of history. Washington's Freedom Plaza on Pennsylvania Avenue is a famous example, as is Welcome Park here. It was created to commemorate the three-hundredth anniversary of William Penn's founding of the Pennsylvania colony (his ship was called the *Welcome*), and, in the manner of Franklin Court, Welcome Park is laid out on the site of Penn's house (demolished in 1867). Penn's original plan for Philadelphia is reproduced in the marble paving, and in the center of the park is a miniature version of Alexander Milne Calder's statue of Penn from City Hall. The textual panels on the surrounding walls feature quotes from and commentaries on Penn and his plans for Philadelphia.

Fronting the square is a cozy bed-and-breakfast that was originally the home (built in 1769) of Dr. Thomas Bond, the founder of Pennsylvania Hospital. My wife and I had the experience of staying the night in the Bond House in a room overlooking the park, which I then realized is best viewed from above, and is especially affecting in the still of night. By the way, Old Original Bookbinder's around the corner is not the original Bookbinder's; at any rate, it is neither as venerable nor as good as Bookbinders' Seafood House on 15th Street, which is the true Philadelphia classic. This joint on 2nd Street is an overpriced tourist trap, about which kind of thing the visitor to this city must be constantly vigilant.

16 SECOND STREET SUBWAY STATION
2nd Street, northeast corner of Market Street
1976–79, Murphy Levy Wurman

This is worth noting both as an example of an interesting station in Philadelphia's maligned subway system and as a work by the firm that included the redoubtable Richard Saul Wurman, author of *Man-Made Philadelphia* and editor of the innovative and invaluable Access guides to the world's great cities (including Philadelphia), among much else of note. He's a New Yorker now, though he was taught at Penn by Louis Kahn and, like so many of the great man's acolytes, established his practice in Philadelphia, the environment of which has since the last century been the beneficiary or victim of the products of Penn's renowned architecture school.

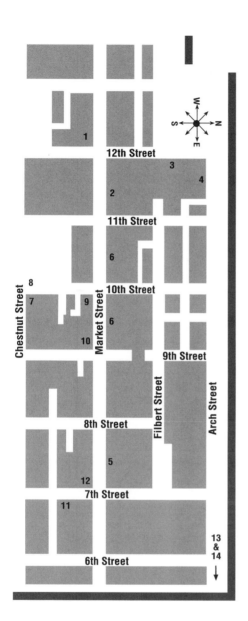

12th Street

11th Street

10th Street

9th Street

8th Street

7th Street

6th Street

Chestnut Street

Market Street

Filbert Street

Arch Street

1
3
4
2
6
8
7
9
6
10
5
12
11
13
&
14

W N S E

CHAPTER 6

MARKET EAST/CONVENTION

1a *PSFS Building*

CHAPTER 6

MARKET EAST/ CONVENTION

1 PSFS BUILDING

12 South 12th Street, southwest corner of Market Street
1930–32, Howe & Lescaze

What a modern classic this has become! There must be twenty buildings in New York, from town houses to apartment buildings to office skyscrapers, that were directly influenced by the PSFS. But as with Raymond Hood's McGraw-Hill Building in New York, where once the PSFS was held up as something special because of its International Style mannerisms, it's now beloved for the very things that mark it off from the International Style- and Bauhaus-inspired buildings that came to dominate the American urban scene after World War II. This may be those later buildings' daddy, but it's a cusp building, and its sleekness and stylization give off a strong whiff of Art Deco.

It is, in a word, *jazzy.* And of how many of the productions of the later crops of modernist buildings can that be said? Forget all that prattle about functional differentiation and expression. There was nothing new in that, and without the use of ornament to accentuate those properties, that kind of thing became banal. No, what people like here is the cool, sleek way the polished black-granite base, with its cantilevered strip windows, curves around 12th Street, with those shiny smooth surfaces and the curved glass. And people like the stylized "PSFS" lettering high above the city.

The received wisdom is that the PSFS "is the finest twentieth-century building in the city." Is this really so? Here are some other twentieth-century Philadelphia buildings: the Bellevue-Stratford, John Wanamaker's, the Museum of Art, 30th Street Station.

It is thirty-six stories containing about 300,000 square feet of office space: puny by New York or Chicago standards. At this writing, there appear to be plans afoot for converting the building into a hotel.

1b   *PSFS Building*

2 READING TERMINAL

Market Street, between 11th and 12th Streets
1891–93, The Wilson Brothers and Francis Hatch Kimball

The Wilsons' Broad Street Station may be no longer, but in spite of the vicissitudes of Center City redevelopment, Reading Terminal is miraculously with us still.

This was the Reading's first and only Center City facility. The only possible suitable site was occupied by the Franklin Market, as it was called, at 12th and Market. The deal that was worked out was that the railroad could have the site—if it incorporated the market into the station.

The façades of the head house were designed by one of New York's best and most underappreciated architects, Francis Kimball. What a wonderful building it is! It's heavily and beautifully worked—the extensive coursework of the second and third stories, through which rise the arcaded loggia with paired banded colonnettes; the balustrades at the second, fourth, and attic stories; and the oculi in the rich terra-cotta frieze. But the glory is in the way the slice is taken from the corner but for the curved arcaded bay (topped by a balustrade) at the fourth story, with the courses a story down gracefully sweeping up to a point. It is ineffably grand, and alone takes the weight out of what might otherwise have been the somewhat ponderous rectangular mass of the main block. Genius.

(By the way, Teitelman and Longstreth refer to Kimball's head house as "an undistinguished station building.")

The train shed survives, too (sort of): it's the last remaining single-span arched train shed in the country, from steam days. (It was the largest train shed in the world—for about a year, when the Wilson Brothers expanded their shed at Broad Street.) It's been incorporated (1993–94) into the Convention Center. It is always amazing when Philadelphia decides to preserve something that's not associated with the Founding Fathers. But here you have it: as exciting a thing as there is in the city, particularly with the associated food market.

2a   *Reading Terminal, Head House*

2b *Reading Terminal Train Shed, 1998*

2c *Reading Terminal Train Shed, 1984*

3 READING TERMINAL MARKET
12th Street, between Filbert and Arch Streets

As exciting in its way as the Terminal itself is this venerable marketplace, alone reason enough to come to Philadelphia. Sticky buns, eggs, fresh hot soft pretzels, tub butter, muffins, coffees, teas, cut flowers, smoked meats, smoked fish, free-range poultry, fresh seafood, ducks, geese, sausages, nuts, spices, herbs, cheeses, famous 4th Street cookies, and Bassett's ice cream are just some of the hundreds of foodstuffs purveyed in this market where Philadelphia, long a town gustatorily to be reckoned with, spreads out its culinary wares in mouth-watering, nose-tingling cornucopial glory.

Be sure to visit Wednesday through Saturday when the Pennsylvania Dutch Amish bring in their produce and baked goods from Lancaster County, as they have done continuously since 1892. The Amish are not on the premises Monday or Tuesday, and the market is closed Sunday.

4 PENNSYLVANIA CONVENTION CENTER
Bounded by Arch, Race, 11th, and 13th Streets
1993–94, Thompson, Ventulett, Stainback & Associates, et al.

The some half million square feet of exhibition space of the convention center that Philadelphia's civic leaders felt—probably correctly—the city desperately needed required the extirpation of about four square blocks of Center City—the biggest bit of scorched earth since the 1950s heyday of Penn Center and Independence Park. Big convention centers are nearly everywhere and always thumping blights on the cityscape, though in recent years there's been some recognition of this condition and an attendant attempt to rectify the problem, as in the recent convention centers in Boston and New York. Here, a panoply of postmodernist mannerisms, like the Arch Street front's ceaseless row of abstracted gables, abstracted colonnades, oriels, complexly mullioned windows, limestone and granite revetments, and so on, are the architects' earnest effort to make this a friendly presence.

The "Grand Hall" has been placed in the old and glorious train shed of Reading Terminal, probably the only way that space could have been saved from the wrecker's ball. Although great care was taken to preserve the spatial integrity of the shed, it's a pale shadow of what it once was. One can enter the old train shed three ways: via the Arch Street bridge reached through the main block's three-story skylighted pedestrian passage, which also leads

to the main exhibition hall; through the main entrance of the head house on Market; or across the pedestrian bridge over 11th Street from the gargantuan new Marriott Hotel.

CHINATOWN

Bounded roughly by Vine Street on the north, Arch Street on the south, 12th Street on the west, and 8th Street on the east is Philadelphia's compact Chinatown. In contrast to New York's Chinatown, which seems at times as though it might devour all of Manhattan, Philadelphia's is hemmed in, nestled among the Convention Center, the Gallery, and the Vine Street Expressway. There is no direction in which it can grow. The area has long been a kind of nether region, a war zone even, with its adjacency to the winos and porno shops, expressway construction, and so on. Amazingly, though, this little Chinatown has hung on here since the Civil War. It began with a laundry at 913 Race in the 1860s, and in the next decade, that was also the location of Philadelphia's first Chinese restaurant. (It is commemorated with a plaque on the building at that address.) There's nothing here to do with the Founding Fathers, so the planners haven't gussied it up, which is just as well. What is here, in addition to the smattering of Chinese institutions and shops, are several restaurants featuring cuisines from various Chinese and other Asian (Vietnamese, Thai, Burmese) regions and provinces. It's not New York or San Francisco, of course, but good eats are to be had, and one real standout is **Ray's Cafe** at 141 North 9th Street between Arch and Race. Ray's is noteworthy not so much for its Chinese dishes as for its excellent coffees, brewed and served in an improbably ritualistic manner and with a fanatical attention to quality that no nouvelle espresso joint could hope to match.

5 LIT BROTHERS

Market Street, between 7th and 8th Streets
1859–1907
Renovated in 1989, Burt Hill Kosar Rittlemann with
John Milner Associates

Now let's see if I can get this right: the Lits opened on the corner of Market and 8th in 1891 when the block was already occupied by several commercial structures dating back as far as 1859. The Lits progressively purchased the entire block between 1895 and 1907 and built new structures at either end of the block, retaining three buildings in the interior. The brothers' architects were Collins & Autenreith. It was sort of like the Gallery of its day. Nos. 719–21 are cast-iron fronted, the other mid-block buildings are revetted in marble or granite with terra-cotta and iron trim. Lit Brothers, long a major Philadelphia department store, remained in business here until 1977. The whole block was then in danger of demolition but has since been saved (it's the only intact block of Victorian commercial structures in a city that set out systematically to destroy its Victorian architectural legacy) and renovated into elegant offices and stores. It looks grand.

5 *Lit Brothers*

6 THE GALLERY

Market Street, between 9th and 11th Streets
1974–77, Bower & Fradley
1982–83, Bower Lewis Thrower and Cope Linder Associates

As with Penn Center, it's a little hard to recall the enthusiasm that greeted the Gallery when it was first developed. I was an untraveled lad growing up in Chicago when the Gallery was built, but I remember looking in my father's *Time* magazine and seeing a feature on the urban revival then going on (I didn't then realize that there's *always* an urban revival going on, if only in the pages of *Time*) in which chic new retail developments were taking shape in Minneapolis, Houston, Boston, and Philadelphia. There were photos of the Gallery, showing happy people shopping and eating ice-cream cones amid greenery and waterfalls and, by golly, Philadelphia *was back*. Reading this inspired my own fledgling urbanity, then nourished by the occasional foray with my aunt to downtown Chicago, and when I was finally of age and went to Philadelphia, I determined that the Gallery was one of the first things I'd look in on.

Boy, was I disappointed. I—and *Time*—had rather overestimated the place.

Attached to the Gallery is the venerable **Strawbridge & Clothier** department store. Justus Strawbridge opened his dry-goods store in 1861 and later teamed with Isaac Clothier in founding what was, for a long time in this city, a strong second to Wanamaker's. These Quakers apparently had no objection to going into the business of selling frilly things. The present building dates from 1896 with numerous additions up to the 1930s. Strawbridge's is probably most famous for its Food Hall.

7 FEDERAL RESERVE BANK

10th and Chestnut Streets
1931–35, Paul Philippe Cret
Garden: 1941, Cret
Seventh story: 1952–53, Harbeson, Hough, Livingston & Larson (Cret's successor firm)

This is another of the numerous gems from the great Cret. It's Greekly austere, with its phalanx of Doric-topped three-quarter box columns. The heavily fenestrated upper portion, containing offices (the banking room is

7 *Federal Reserve Bank*

8 *Victory Building on left,*
Federal Reserve Bank on right

below), is much lighter. The whole composition, while it has been called "stripped classical" or "classic modern," is in fact just plain classical. And Cret, Beaux-Arts man that he was, does not neglect embellishment: note the fine marble reliefs—*Wisdom* and *Commerce*—by Alfred Bottiau (1889–1951) on either side of the main entrance. It is a complete winner.

8 VICTORY BUILDING

1001 Chestnut Street, northwest corner of 10th Street
1873–75, Henry Fernbach

Built as a branch office of the New York Life Insurance Company, this was originally three stories with a mansard. But three more stories were added—beneath the mansard—and a balustrade marks the point where the mansard once began. Faced in granite, this is an exuberantly foreshortened Second Empire pile with loads of character, though it appears to be endangered.

9   *St. Stephen's Church*

9 ST. STEPHEN'S CHURCH (EPISCOPAL)

19 South 10th Street
1822–23, William Strickland
North transept and vestry room: 1878–79, Frank Furness
Parish house: 1888, George C. Mason

This was erected on the site where Benjamin Franklin flew his kite. Strickland goes Gothic, with less than inspiring results. Inside, however, is plenty that is of interest, including the *Angel of Purity* by Augustus Saint-Gaudens, a beautiful marble reredos, a marble baptismal font by Carl Steinhauser, and, over the altar, a huge mosaic of the Last Supper.

10 UNITED STATES POST OFFICE AND COURT HOUSE

9th and Market Streets
1934–40, Harry Sternfeld

The co-architect of the exuberantly Art Deco WCAU Building (*see* chapter nine)—and a former student of Paul Cret's—also gave us this monumental "stripped-classic" structure. The site was once occupied by the University of

10 *United States Post Office and Court House*

Pennsylvania's campus, beginning in 1800. In 1829 the University had Strickland design handsome twin buildings here. But the University moved to what it felt to be the salubrious countryside of West Philadelphia in 1870, leaving this space for Alfred B. Mullett's Second Empire galoot of a post office, erected from 1873 to 1884. The construction of Mullett's post office was supervised by John McArthur Jr., whose City Hall was taking shape on Broad Street. (McArthur was offered Mullett's job as supervising architect for the federal government, and turned it down, mainly so he could see City Hall through to completion.) Festooning Mullett's mansard were sculptures by Daniel Chester French, *Law, Prosperity,* and *Power,* now in Fairmount Park (*see* chapter twelve). Sternfeld's limestone replacement post office is decorated on its 9th Street side with relief panels by Edmond Amateis (1897–1981) featuring muscular postal workers. On Market Street are other muscular figures, *Justice* and *Law,* by Donald De Lue (1897–1988), the sculptor responsible for the *Rocket Thrower* at the 1964 New York World's Fair.

11   ATWATER KENT MUSEUM

15 South 7th Street, between Market and Chestnut Streets
1825, John Haviland

The building was originally the home of the Franklin Institute, back when the Franklin Institute played a vital role in the culture of the city, before it became an "interactive" entertainment environment for people with short attention spans. The early Franklin Institute offered the first architectural courses in America, with teachers such as William Strickland and Thomas Walter. They taught in a building designed by their fellow Greek Revivalist, Haviland. It's an austere design that bears a close resemblance to Paul Cret's nearby Federal Reserve Bank, built over a hundred years later.

When the Franklin Institute moved to its present Parkway location in 1933, this building was in danger of being knocked down. To the rescue came the radio magnate A. Atwater Kent, who bought the building and transformed it into a charming museum of Philadelphiana, opened in 1938, featuring everyday artifacts spanning three hundred years of the city's history. The renovation of the building into the museum was undertaken as a WPA project during the Great Depression.

Open Tuesday to Saturday from 9:30 A.M. to 4:45 P.M. Admission is free.

12 DECLARATION HOUSE
7th and Market Streets
1975

The present house is a complete reconstruction dating from the year before the Bicentennial. The house that originally stood on this site was built in the eighteenth century and was known as the Jacob Graff house. It was where, in rented rooms on the second of three floors, Thomas Jefferson drafted the Declaration of Independence between June 10 and June 28 in 1776. In 1798 Graff sold the house to Simon and Hyman Gratz (brothers of the fabled Rebecca Gratz), who added the fourth floor, which means that the present four-story house is not a reconstruction of the house as it appeared when Jefferson stayed there. The original house was taken down in 1883 when it was replaced by Frank Furness's exuberantly gabled Penn National Bank. Furness gave his bank a series of rather odd quasi-Palladian windows in an apparent attempt to relate his building to the Georgian tradition of eighteenth-century Philadelphia architecture. The bank also had a prominently featured bronze plaque at its entrance telling of the history of the site. Furness's bank was, in its turn, knocked down in the 1930s, so there's one nineteenth-century loss we can't blame on the scorched-earth makeover of the 1950s.

13 FREE QUAKER MEETINGHOUSE
In Independence Mall, Arch and 5th Streets
1783

This was the meetinghouse from 1783 until 1834 of the "fighting Quakers," as they were known, a faction that broke off from the Arch Street Friends Meeting in order to bear arms in the Revolutionary cause. Since they wished to continue to be Quakers, they established their own, short-lived meetinghouse. Betsy Ross worshiped here, and the most prominent of the founders was Samuel Wetherill (1736–1816). Inside is Sully's portrait of Samuel Wetherill Jr. (1764–1829).

14 CHRIST CHURCH BURIAL GROUND
5th and Arch Streets

This is not nearly as exciting as it sounds.

Across 5th Street from Independence Mall is the burial ground affili-ated with Christ Church, which is four or so blocks away in the heart of Old City. The thing here is that you can peer through the gate (you cannot enter) at the grave of Benjamin Franklin. Also buried here are Dr. Benjamin Rush (1745–1813), Dr. Philip Syng Physick (of Hill-Physick-Keith house fame), and Bishop William White of Christ Church.

CHAPTER 7

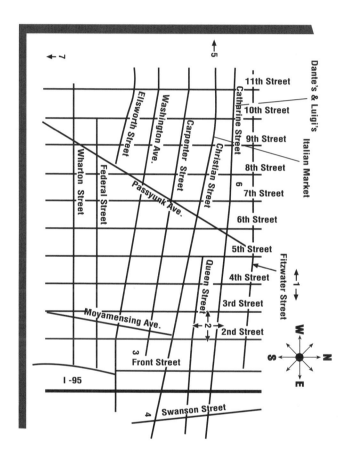

11th Street
10th Street
9th Street
8th Street
7th Street
6th Street
5th Street
4th Street
3rd Street
2nd Street

Dante's & Luigi's Italian Market

Catharine Street
Christian Street
Queen Street

Ellsworth Street
Washington Ave.
Carpenter Street
Wharton Street
Federal Street
Passyunk Ave.
Moyamensing Ave.

Front Street

I-95

Swanson Street

Fitzwater Street

N
W   E
S

SOUTH

1a *South Street Overpass*

CHAPTER 7

SOUTH

This, admittedly, is a bit of a catchall chapter covering everything south of South Street, a vast and varied area. At its northeasternmost section, it extends from Queen Village—which is the oldest part of Philadelphia and, as of the late 1990s, recently fashionable—to the sports stadium complex, at its southernmost tip. In between, the area of most note is the Italian section of South Philadelphia. An area of little physical distinction, this section includes many of the things that in the years since World War II have come to dominate people's perceptions of Philadelphia: the established Italian American community, the numerous Italian pop-music stars (Frankie Avalon, Fabian, Bobby Rydell, Mario Lanza), Sylvester Stallone, the fragrant Italian Market, the Mummers, and so on. It would seem that Philadelphia's two most renowned "sons" are Benjamin Franklin and the troglodytic Rocky Balboa.

1 SOUTH STREET
Front Street to 8th Street

If the Orlons are to be believed, South Street was "the hippest street in town" way back in 1963. (March 1963, to be precise. Besides the Orlons' "South Street," other popular songs of that month included "He's So Fine" by the Chiffons, "I Will Follow Him" by Little Peggy March, "On Broadway" by the Drifters, and "Puff the Magic Dragon" by Peter, Paul & Mary. There have been better months in the history of American popular music.) South Street, a thriving Jewish commercial strip, went downhill, and, just as it looked as though a new expressway might destroy it, the hippies saved it. The hippie phenomenon was always commercial at root—i.e., there would have been no such phenomenon if entrepreneurs, whether drug dealers or

131

2   *South Street*

record companies, did not think they could turn a buck from it. The mercenary component was there nearly from the beginning. As Joseph Epstein wrote in the 1970s, "The most important influence of that assemblage of 1960s youth and its camp followers was not on politics, or philosophy, or art, or social organization, but on retailing." Today's South Street, vaunted for its diversity, is in fact the same tawdry mess of trendy clothing boutiques, record stores, glorified fast-food eateries, and surly attitudes that is the "hippest street" in any of a score of American cities. The kids who were weaned on the "interactive" displays at the Franklin Institute now browse in Zipperhead and Condom Nation, the latter a store Benjamin Franklin himself might have founded.

There are some diamonds in the rough. Book Trader (501 South Street at 5th Street) is a very good secondhand bookstore. Jim's Steaks (400 South Street at 4th Street) is a worthy institution of its kind.

Miss South Street and, frankly, you've missed nothing.

2 QUEEN VILLAGE
Bounded by Lombard Street on the north, Washington Avenue on the south, Front Street on the east, and 5th Street on the west

The busiest stretch of South Street is in Queen Village, a popular neighborhood the name of which dates only from the 1960s. It is the oldest neighborhood in Philadelphia.

The area was first settled by Swedes, the first European group to inhabit what would become Philadelphia. Originally called by the Indian name of Wicaco ("dwelling place"), it was later called Southwark, after the district in South London. (Note the many London names in Philadelphia: Kensington, Southwark, Mayfair, Richmond. Old neighborhood names that are no longer used include Westminster, Adelphi, and Greenwich.)

South Street may have been spared its expressway and is now one of the thriving commercial thoroughfares in the city, but a good bit of Queen Village was sacrificed to the infernal I-95 along the Delaware.

A gastronomic landmark as well as a vestige of the neighborhood's Jewish past is the **Famous Delicatessen** on 4th and Bainbridge, recommended not only (and not mainly) for its standard Jewish deli specialties (pastrami, lox and bagels, etc.) but for its nonpareil chocolate-chip cookies (also available at the Famous 4th Street Cookie Company concession at Reading Terminal Market) and chocolate malted milks (made with Breyer's ice cream, real malt, and light cream, and not, so far as I know, available at Reading Terminal Market). Don't even walk on the same side of the street as this deli if you are on a cholesterol-restricted diet. It's quite the best attraction in the neighborhood.

In the blocks east of the Famous Delicatessen, in the heart of Queen Village, can be found the interesting:

3 WORKMAN PLACE
742–46 South Front Street
1748, 1812

One group of houses at Workman Place was built by George Mifflin (grandfather of the Thomas Mifflin who built Fort Mifflin and was governor of Pennsylvania in the 1790s) in 1748 (the date is boldly incised in the brick side of one of the houses). John Workman, who bought the Mifflin houses and created the courtyard, put up another group of houses in 1812. These are examples of small rental houses built for poor immigrants by property owners on their rear lots. The houses were taken over in this century by the Octavia Hill Association (the president of which at one time was Dr. George Woodward, one of the principal developers of Chestnut Hill).

Another interesting group of eighteenth-century houses, comparable to Elfreth's Alley, is nearby at 109–25 **Kenilworth Street.** All the old houses in this area were built for maritime workers, whether dockhands or seamen or sail makers or, as legend has it, pirates. Since the 1960s the

3a *Workman Place*

3b *Kenilworth
Street*

neighborhood has become popular as a less-expensive and pleasantly funkier (though every bit as venerable) alternative to the nattily redeveloped Society Hill across South Street to the north.

Everyone knows how Dr. Woodward, when he developed Chestnut Hill, was inspired by Ebenezer Howard and Raymond Unwin and their attempts to mix different housing types to avoid suburban monotony. Could it be that Dr. Woodward was inspired as well by the remarkable diversity of housing in Queen Village, almost all of which has clear correlatives in Chestnut Hill? Queen Village features traditional terrace housing, freestanding town houses, courtyard housing, and apartment houses—all the types of housing that such a point was made of incorporating into the fabric of Chestnut Hill beginning in the 1910s, only shortly after the Octavia Hill Association took over the Mifflin houses.

4 GLORIA DEI

916 South Swanson Street, between Columbus Boulevard and Christian Street
1698–1700

The Swedes were in the Delaware Valley before the English, arriving in the 1630s. The city's last remaining building constructed by the early Swedish settlers also happens to be the oldest church still standing in the state of Pennsylvania. Originally a Swedish Lutheran church, though now Episcopal, Gloria Dei was built by English carpenters and masons in the local red brick. With its play of steeply sloping roofs and gables, it is a tad eccentric and picturesque, particularly amid its churchyard with its close-packed gravestones. It seems a miracle that Gloria Dei has survived: not only have there been the usual pressures of urban development and expressway construction and so forth, but the church itself has periodically threatened to topple over from funky construction.

BROAD STREET

The last entry in the chapter "Around City Hall" is for the University of the Arts at Broad and Pine Streets.

Continue south on Broad Street and you will come to fabled South Philadelphia. It is fabled, mainly, for the scads of Italian American teen-idol singers of the 1950s and 1960s who grew up here and for the Mummers—eccentrically outfitted neighborhood clubs that put on the annual New Year's

4ₐ   *Italian Market*

4b   *Italian Market*

Day parade on Broad Street, judged as "that repellent spectacle" by John Lukacs, though much beloved by many different kinds of Philadelphians. Mummer apparently derives from *mumme,* a German word meaning mask, while the spectacle of Mummery had its origin in England, where in the eighteenth century said spectacle immigrated to, of all places, Philadelphia. Today the phenomenon is not at all associated with those of English descent but primarily with the Italian Americans of South Philadelphia. (There is, for those who are truly curious, a **Mummers Museum,** designed by Ueland & Junker and built in 1976 at 2nd Street and Washington Avenue.)

The best of "South Philly" is to be found in its vast **Italian Market,** the northern terminus of which is at Christian and 9th Streets, roughly ten blocks south and five blocks east of the University of the Arts. Operating Monday through Saturday from 9:00 A.M. to 5:00 P.M., the market offers all the meats (including game meats), fish, olive oils, cheeses, sausages, etc., that you would expect. En route, you will unexpectedly encounter:

5 RIDGWAY LIBRARY
901 South Broad Street at Christian Street
1873–78, Addison Hutton

Home to the august Library Company of Philadelphia from the 1870s to the 1960s, this is a wholly surprising Greek Revival behemoth by the Quaker architect Addison Hutton, quite late for such a pure rendition of this style. The library was named after Phoebe Ridgway, the wife of Dr. James Rush, whose million dollars got the thing built. Dr. Rush insisted that it be built in the forlorn quarter of South Broad Street, since he was certain that this was to become the heart of the city. He miscalculated slightly. The Library Company, never particularly pleased with the structure, sold it to the city in 1964 for use as a community center.

At 10th and Catharine Streets near the Italian Market is Dante's and Luigi's, one of the oldest and most popular of the Italian restaurants in the neighborhood. Near Dante's and Luigi's is, unexpectedly, the:

5   *Ridgway Library*

6 SAMUEL S. FLEISHER ART MEMORIAL
709–21 Catharine Street, between 8th and 7th Streets

This is a series of structures, including the former Church of the Evangelists (a Romanesque Revival church designed by Louis Baker of Furness, Evans & Company in 1884–86) and the former St. Martin's College for Indigent Boys (built in 1906, also designed by Baker), taken over by an industrialist and art collector named Samuel Fleisher. It served as the home of his Graphic Sketch Club, founded in 1899 and at one time the only free art school in the country. Fleisher took over the school building in 1916 and the church in 1922. He urged the working people of Philadelphia to regard "the Sanctuary," as he called his deconsecrated church, as their place of meditation and prayer.

The art school has been operated since Fleisher's death in 1944 by the Philadelphia Museum of Art, which has supplemented Fleisher's collections, exhibited in the Sanctuary, with paintings from the museum's own collections. The church already contained a mural by Nicola d'Ascenzo, and in

1929 Fleisher commissioned the remarkable Philadelphia artist Violet Oakley to create her *Life of Moses* reredos. In 1934 Fleisher commissioned an iron gate from Samuel Yellin, and in the 1950s the three stained-glass panels by John LaFarge (1835–1910)—*Apelles, Sabia Muni Sitting Under the Bo Tree,* and *Pan and Nymph*—were acquired. These panels had been in the Edward W. Bok house in Merion.

The renowned modernist architect Louis Kahn once was a student here. (He was also a Central High alumnus.) The elegant and Quakeresque Louis Kahn Lecture Room at the Memorial was designed in 1982 by the artist Siah Armajani.

If Siah Armajani's modernist austerities have put you in the mood for something a bit *zaftig,* then you might enjoy knowing that you are within hailing distance of the center of the cheese-steak universe. The street to the west of the Fleisher Art Memorial is 8th Street. Take a left and head south a few blocks to Passyunk Avenue, which comes in around Washington Avenue. Continue south on Passyunk to 9th Street. At 9th and Passyunk are the two most famous purveyors of cheese steaks in the world: **Pat's** and **Geno's.** What are cheese steaks? They are sandwiches of thinly sliced fried beef piled with greasy fried onions onto a pliant, chewy roll. Where does the cheese come in? It never does, really: the authentic Philadelphia cheese steak is made not with real cheese but with a repellent processed-cheese confection called Cheez Whiz, which is applied to the roll from an aerosol canister. The Cheez Whiz, by the way, is considered de rigueur by cheese-steak aficionados (one hesitates to say connoisseurs). I for my part quite like the things—sans Cheez Whiz. At some of the cheese-steak establishments

6 *Geno's Steaks*

you can get other, truer cheeses on your roll. That I prefer; even as it marks one down to the purists as a yuppie. But I don't think I'm inauthentic: legend has it that the Philly cheese steak was invented by Pat Olivieri, founder of Pat's, in 1930. Well, I hate to burst anyone's bubble, but Cheez Whiz had not yet been invented in 1930, which means that, originally, something like real cheese must have appeared in the sandwich. By the way, the Olivieri family also maintains an outpost in Reading Terminal Market (who doesn't?). Both Pat's and Geno's are open twenty-four hours.

BROAD STREET, EVEN FARTHER SOUTH

Near land's end is Philadelphia's stadium complex. Here you will find the new and relatively pleasant (this is damning with faint praise) CoreStates Center (also know as the "new Spectrum"), where the 76ers (of the National Basketball Association) and the Flyers (of the National Hockey League) play; it was opened in 1996. The "old" Spectrum, which still stands, opened in 1967. The new CoreStates Center was erected on the site of John F. Kennedy Stadium, an outdoor venue for rock concerts.

Outside of the old Spectrum is the bronze statue of Rocky Balboa. A. Thomas Schomberg, a specialist in modern sports heroes, created the statue in 1980. Rocky is Philadelphia's most admired citizen after Benjamin Franklin. Unlike Franklin, however, Rocky never actually lived: he is, of course, Sylvester Stallone's fictional creation from a series of movies set in Philadelphia. The first *Rocky* (1976) was an entertaining movie, but this civic identification with its troglodytic hero is embarrassing. Even worse was that this statue was originally placed on the steps of the Philadelphia Museum of Art (a gift from Stallone himself). It was, blessedly, removed from there. But the Museum of Art has nonetheless deemed it appropriate to include on its steps a pair of bronze footprints indicating where Rocky stood in the movie. It's enough to make you throw up.

Also in the complex is:

7 VETERANS STADIUM
Broad Street and Pattison Avenue

The home of the Phillies of baseball's National League is possibly the single ugliest and most unpleasant major-league baseball stadium in the country (it is also home to the Eagles of the National Football League). The Vet was built in 1971 and was designed by, among others, Hugh Stubbins, who later that decade gave us New York's Citicorp Center. It's also where the annual Army-Navy football game is played.

It is well to note that many people were very excited by the modern stadiums and arenas that were built in a big wave in the late sixties and early seventies. Old, small, antiquated facilities like Philadelphia's venerable Shibe Park (built in 1909, renamed Connie Mack Stadium in 1953, and retired in 1970) had become symbols of urban decline. The new stadiums were spacious, sleek, with superior sight lines and cleaner rest rooms, and dazzled their early visitors. This was as true of the Vet as of Pittsburgh's Three Rivers Stadium or Cincinnati's Riverfront Stadium or St. Louis's Busch Stadium. Not least, these stadiums ushered in the Astroturf era in baseball history, in which the game itself became sleeker and more modern, with a premium placed upon slick fielding and speedy base running. Power was out; speed was in. For a while, it looked as though every old ballpark would be knocked down and replaced by an Astroturf joint.

Our finest baseball writer, Bill James, wrote:

> Stadium architecture . . . is the one largest dynamic of change in baseball; if you put the baseball players of today in the parks of the 1920s, with all of the other differences—the racial composition of the players, the schedule differences, the expansion, the different strike zone—with all of those, in three months they would be playing baseball pretty much the way it was played in the 1920s.

When old Shibe Park was built, it was probably even more dazzling to fans than anything we've witnessed in our time. Bill James also wrote: "[T]he concept of the huge, permanent, sturdy, fireproof, grand, spacious, elegant thing that we now call a ballpark sprang into existence rather suddenly in 1907 or 1908."

Shibe Park, opened in 1909, the first ballpark built of steel and concrete, was probably the very first of these modern ballparks. (By the way, its builder, Benjamin Shibe, that same year further revolutionized the game by his invention of the cork-centered baseball.)

The trend has changed, however. And it's really a microcosm of what's become of modernist architecture in general: it may dazzle at first, but it does not weather well. Only a few years into the Vet, it had become a dreary and tawdry place, with none of the compensating funky charms of old Shibe Park. Thus began the start of the new, and current, trend of designing new ballparks emulating the old (with the necessary allowances for luxury boxes and that crap). So Baltimore has its Camden Yards and Cleveland its Jacobs Field, and we will wait to see how they weather, and whether the fans, who adore the new parks now, will still like them a few years down the road. My guess: the new parks will weather much, much better than their sixties and seventies counterparts; which is not to say the fans, fickle as are all consumers, won't be demanding something new and different.

The Phillies team was founded in 1883, and from 1887 to 1938 played in the Baker Bowl at the northeast corner of Broad Street and Lehigh Avenue in North Philadelphia. Shibe Park opened as the home of the Philadelphia Athletics in 1909 in the block bounded by Lehigh Avenue and Somerset, 20th, and 21st Streets in North Philadelphia. From 1938 both the National League Phillies and the American League Athletics shared the modern, state-of-the-art Shibe Park. The Athletics, founded in 1901, shared the Baker Bowl with the Phillies until Shibe Park was built. The Athletics abandoned Philadelphia in 1954 for Kansas City (they subsequently moved to Oakland, where they are abbreviatedly known as the A's).

Under their legendary manager Cornelius McGillicuddy ("Connie Mack"), the Athletics were generally a successful team that appeared in eight World Series, winning five of them. The Phillies, on the other hand, are notoriously the losingest franchise in the history of baseball, perhaps in all of professional sports, which, when combined with Philadelphians' native self-deprecating quality, results in the curious phenomenon of a city that seems to *hate* its baseball team. The Chicago Cubs can lose year after year, yet Chicagoans embrace their team as though it were a hurt puppy. But nowhere will you hear such jeers directed by "fans" toward their hometown team as you will at Veterans Stadium during a Phillies contest. As E. Digby Baltzell said, "Cheering against the home team is a time-honored tradition in Philadelphia," and it seems to go as much for Penn football games at Franklin Field as for Phillies games at the Vet.

In any event, the Phillies *have* had a few seasons in which they did not stink. There were the "Whiz Kids," with the young stars Richie Ashburn and Robin Roberts, who made it into the World Series in 1950 (only to lose in straight games to the Yankees). In 1964, under manager Gene Mauch and led by the stars Richie Allen and Johnny Callison, the Phillies registered perhaps the most spectacular last-week-of-the-season collapse in history. They were six and a half games in first place with twelve games left in the season and lost the pennant to the St. Louis Cardinals. More impressively, the Phillies were actually one of the consistently mighty teams from 1975 to 1983, including defeating the Kansas City Royals in the World Series in 1980 under manager Dallas Green and with the stars Mike Schmidt, Greg Luzinski, and Steve Carlton. This is the only time in their one hundred and fifteen years that the Phillies have won the World Series. (The annus mirabilis of the new sports center was 1980. The Spectrum's 76ers [basketball] and Flyers [hockey], and the Vet's Eagles [football], as well as the Phillies, made it to their respective sports' championship matches, the only time in the city's history that there has been such sporting prowess across the board in a single year. Only the Phillies, alas, were ultimately victorious, but it was a year to remember.) In 1993, with a motley group including Lenny Dykstra, John Kruk, and Darren "Dutch" Daulton, the Phillies once again made it to the Series, and lost. At this writing, the Phillies are as pathetic as ever.

Check out the philosopher Bruce Kuklick's book *To Every Thing a Season: Shibe Park and Urban Philadelphia, 1909–1976,* published by Princeton University Press in 1991.

Outside of Veterans Stadium is the bronze statue of Connie Mack by the Philadelphia sculptor Harry Rosin (1897–1973). Originally placed in front of Shibe Park in 1957, the statue was moved to its present location in 1972. Rosin worked for Samuel Yellin in his Arch Street studio, then studied under Charles Grafly at the Pennsylvania Academy of the Fine Arts, where Rosin taught for over thirty years.

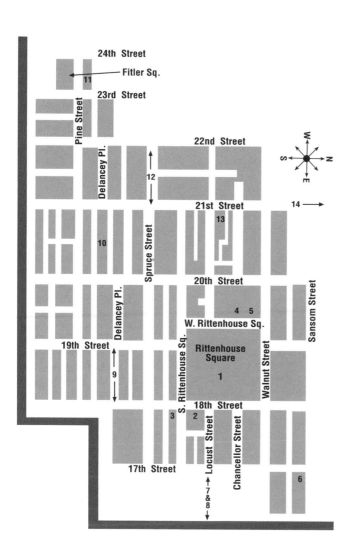

24th Street

Fitler Sq.

11

23rd Street

Pine Street

22nd Street

Delancey Pl.

12

21st Street

13

14 →

Spruce Street

10

20th Street

4   5

W. Rittenhouse Sq.

Delancey Pl.

Sansom Street

19th Street

Rittenhouse
Square

1

Walnut Street

9

S. Rittenhouse Sq.

18th Street

3   2

Locust Street

Chancellor Street

17th Street

6

7
&
8

RITTENHOUSE SQUARE

1   *Rittenhouse Square*

CHAPTER 8

RITTENHOUSE SQUARE

This chapter covers the rather large area west of Broad Street, south of Market Street, north of Lombard Street, and east of the Schuylkill River. It is—as much as New York's Greenwich Village or Boston's North End—the ideal Jane Jacobs neighborhood, as she herself stated in her classic *Death and Life of Great American Cities* in 1961 (*see* page 146). What is most striking to the visitor is the easy urbanity of the mixing together of residences and businesses along narrow streets and alleys. It is not so manicured as Society Hill and breathes more easily for it. In no other major American city are so many and such charming and neighborly residential streets insinuated in so casual a manner right into the heart of "downtown." It is heavenly.

The Rittenhouse Club and Le Bec Fin, Nan Duskin and Newman Galleries—this, not Society Hill, is the most moneyed quarter of central Philadelphia, and it has been so for about a century and a half, hardly letting up. Old City and Manayunk may be chichi, but so, still, is Rittenhouse Square. It is a splendid survivor.

1 RITTENHOUSE SQUARE
Bounded by 18th Street on the east, South Rittenhouse Square (roughly continuous with Latimer Street) on the south, West Rittenhouse Square (just west of 19th Street) on the west, and Walnut Street on the north Remodeled 1913 et seq., Paul Philippe Cret

This is the heart, if not of historic Philadelphia, then of urbane and patrician Philadelphia, and long was it so. The lees of this vintage still gives off a whiff of something special.

In her book *The Death and Life of Great American Cities* (1961), Jane Jacobs wrote about Rittenhouse Square. Looking around her from within the square, she noted an impressive variety of uses to which the surrounding buildings had been put. There were clubs, galleries, old houses and newer apartments, office buildings, schools, shops, a church, a public-library branch, a restaurant, and so on. The buildings themselves varied tremendously in height, age, and style. She noticed that many people used the square, and for a wide variety of purposes, including sitting and talking, sitting and reading, walking dogs, sunning themselves, meeting people, playing with children, and so on. This spot, she felt, was everything a city is supposed to be. It was popular, diverse, interesting, handsome, and safe. There were openness and density at the same time. It was exactly the sort of place modern planners found chaotic and were trying to get rid of through their scorched-earth makeovers of inner cities. Ms. Jacobs showed, however, that places like Rittenhouse Square are only seemingly chaotic; they actually possess an order that is highly complex. "Rittenhouse Square is busy fairly continuously for the same basic reasons that a lively sidewalk is used continuously: because of functional physical diversity among adjacent uses, and hence diversity among users and their schedules."

In 1965, the English architectural critic Ian Nairn saw it differently: "Rittenhouse Square . . . for all its leafiness, has so much pointless and formless variety to the buildings around it (from four to forty stories) that it ceases to read as a square at all. It has become a pedestrian traffic circle: you can never feel happy in it."

Nairn is wrong (for once): I have felt happy in Rittenhouse Square.

And I have felt happy in its nearby streets, especially the stretch of Walnut to the east, with its liveliness, its shops, its architectural diversity, and its perfectly scaled sidewalks. Few commercial streets in the country are so delicious.

The current layout of the square is largely Paul Cret's, and it is lovely.

Of the several sculptures in the square, note the bronze cast of *Lion Crushing a Serpent* by Antoine Louis Barye (1796–1875). Barye was probably the most famous of the nineteenth century's animaliers and was a teacher of Rodin. The original of this work was created in 1832. Through the efforts of Thomas Hockley (*see* page 157 for his Furness-designed house) of the Fairmount Park Art Association (which is responsible for the embellishment of all the city's open spaces), this cast was obtained and installed in the square in 1892.

2 CURTIS INSTITUTE OF MUSIC
1726 Locust Street, southeast corner of 18th Street
1893, Peabody & Stearns

KNAPP HALL
Locust Street, southeast corner of Mozart Place
1908, Horace Trumbauer

1718 Locust Street
1903, Cope & Stewardson

The Curtis Institute was founded in 1924 by Mary Louise Curtis Bok Zimbalist (her first husband was Edward W. Bok, her second was Efrem Zimbalist) as a free musical academy for scholarship students. Among its original faculty were Josef Hofmann, Leopold Stokowski, Efrem Zimbalist, and Leopold Auer. It is one of the most renowned music schools in the world. The Institute counts among its alumni Leonard Bernstein, Gian Carlo Menotti, Ned Rorem, Samuel Barber, Anna Moffo, Vincent Persichetti, and Gary Graffman (who is currently the director of the Institute). Fritz Reiner, the legendary conductor of the Chicago Symphony Orchestra from 1953 to 1962, taught at Curtis from 1931 to 1941. Among the "big five" American orchestras, 30 percent of the positions are occupied by Curtis alumni—a very impressive statistic.

2 *Curtis Institute of Music*

The Institute is housed in a trio of former town houses. The main building is the former George Childs Drexel house at 1726 Locust. (George Childs Drexel was the son of Anthony Joseph Drexel, founder of Drexel Institute and co-owner of the *Public Ledger*. He named his son after George W. Childs, Anthony Drexel's *Public Ledger* partner and best friend.) Knapp Hall, across Mozart Place (which used to be called Bouvier Street), was originally the home of a man named Theodore Cramp, then became an Elizabeth Arden salon, and now serves as the Institute's library. Knapp Hall was named for Mary Louise Curtis Bok Zimbalist's mother, Louisa Knapp (who was the founding editor of *Ladies' Home Journal*). Mary Louise's father was Cyrus H. K. Curtis, founder of Curtis Publishing Company, at one time the most successful publisher of magazines in the United States (*Ladies' Home Journal, The Saturday Evening Post*), with headquarters at Washington Square. It was this magazine fortune that Mary Louise Curtis used to found her Institute. Her husband, *Ladies' Home Journal* editor and huckstering autobiographer Edward William Bok, was the major early benefactor of the Philadelphia Orchestra (even though he knew nothing about music).

3 PHILADELPHIA ART ALLIANCE
251 South 18th Street
1909, Frank Miles Day & Brother

This is a slightly forbidding essay in rustication and banded columns. It was originally a house, not a mausoleum. It's the former Samuel Price Wetherill house and has, since 1926, been the Art Alliance, founded in 1915 by Wetherill's daughter, Christine Wetherill Stevenson, who grew up in this house.

A much better building by the architect Frank Miles Day (1861–1918) was the Art Club on Broad and Chancellor Streets, built in 1888 and demolished in 1975 to make way for a parking lot for the Bellevue-Stratford. Thus, the Art Alliance is probably Day's most noteworthy building standing in central Philadelphia. Philadelphia-born and Penn-educated, Day studied at the Royal Academy School of Architecture in London and later taught at the architectural school at Penn. He established the firm of Frank Miles Day & Brother with H. Kent Day in 1892 and later the firm of Day & Klauder with Charles Zeller Klauder (*see* Drexel Building, chapter one).

3 *Philadelphia Art Alliance*

4 RITTENHOUSE HOTEL
210 West Rittenhouse Square, between Walnut and Locust Streets
Alesker, Reiff & Dundon

The thirty-three-story, white "horizontal ziggurat" is the most earnest effort to date to see how far you can go in designing a hideous building on Rittenhouse Square before you destroy the square. Well, they didn't quite destroy the square, but it is sensible to sit with your back to this behemoth. Better yet, go inside to one of the bars or restaurants—the views are superb, not least because you can't see this building.

One of the better things about the Rittenhouse Hotel is the statue and fountain, *Welcome,* in its driveway: it is by Evangelos Frudakis, one of our best contemporary sculptors carrying on the traditions of neoclassical and Beaux-Arts sculpture.

5 HOLY TRINITY CHURCH (EPISCOPAL)
Walnut Street, northwest corner of West Rittenhouse Square
1856–59, John Notman

On the heels of St. Mark's, Notman goes Romanesque. This is Low Church, distinct from the High Church of St. Mark's. This is a perfect building on the square: the street-wall character of the broad planar façade with its lovely receding-arch central portal, and the big, square, finialed tower that an-

5   *Holy Trinity Church*

chors the corner both help to define the open space of the square.

The pastor here at one time was the Reverend Phillips Brooks (1835–93), also associated with Boston's Trinity Church. Though renowned as a preacher in his own day, he is best remembered for writing the standard Christmas hymn "O Little Town of Bethlehem."

6 FIRST BAPTIST CHURCH
17th and Sansom Streets
1898 or 1899, Edgar V. Seeler

A fine Byzantinesque concoction in brownstone by the one-time École des Beaux-Arts wunderkind Seeler. Note the Byzantine stained-glass panels in the dome. This church is curiously ignored in surveys of Philadelphia architecture.

AMERICAN INSTITUTE OF ARCHITECTS BOOKSTORE
117 South 17th Street at Sansom Street

This bright shop, operated under the auspices of the Philadelphia Chapter of the American Institute of Architects, is Philadelphia's best source for current architectural books (and architecture-related gift items). Philadelphia's leading architects shop here.

Sansom Street, a narrow, dense shopping street, abounds in interesting stores (the How-to-Do-It Book Shop at No. 1608) and restaurants.

JOSEPH FOX BOOK SHOP
1724 Sansom Street, between 17th and 18th Streets

Fox's, a small, cramped, serious bookstore, has been here since 1951: a survivor. The art section is renowned.

7 LOCUST STREET, 16TH TO 17TH STREETS

This is a street of startling and charming variety, with works by several of Philadelphia's notable architects: Nos. 1604, 1620, and 1622 are Notman's from the 1850s, complementing his St. Mark's in the middle of the block; No. 1618 is an 1850s house remodeled by Eyre in 1888. It was at one time the brothers Rosenbach's rare-book store, in which choice specimens from among the books or manuscripts were displayed in the small projecting bay window. Nos. 1631 and 1633 are neo-Georgian jobs by Cope & Stewardson, who designed the men's dormitories at Penn; No. 1629 is a white-limestone Beaux-Arts affair by Trumbauer from 1892, much the sort of thing one finds in the Upper East Side of Manhattan (where Trumbauer also worked). Around the corner at 235 South 17th Street, the gabled and bay-windowed job is Frank Miles Day's.

8 ST. MARK'S CHURCH (EPISCOPAL)

1625 Locust Street, between 16th and 17th Streets
1847–49, John Notman

St. Mark's is a superior work of Ecclesiological Gothic to Upjohn's slightly earlier Trinity Church in New York, even though Notman, unlike Upjohn, was no True Believer (in the Ecclesiological Society's architectural dicta, that is). But the plans were apparently sent for review to the Cambridge Camden Society, and a remarkable purity was achieved. The asymmetrical plan, the tower placed off to the side, and the broached spire were all Ecclesiologically prescribed elements. So was the exposed-truss oak ceiling—something Upjohn wanted to do but was prevented from doing by a conservative vestry at Trinity.

8 *St. Mark's Church*

JOHN NOTMAN (1810–65)

John Notman was, like so many other gifted Philadelphia architects (Robert Smith, John McArthur), a Scot. Born in Edinburgh, he came to the U.S. in 1831, having trained as a carpenter, just like his close contemporary the Englishman Richard Upjohn (1802–78), who came to the U.S. in 1829. Notman is credited with introducing the Italianate style to the U.S., and his house "Riverside"—built in 1837–39 in Burlington, New Jersey, for George Washington Doane, bishop of New Jersey—was admired by Andrew Jackson Downing, the enormously influential theorist of the picturesque in antebellum America. The first Italianate building in Philadelphia was Notman's Athenaeum near Washington Square in 1845 (*see* chapter two). Bishop Doane was the first American to be elected to membership (1841) in the Ecclesiological Society, an English group allied with the Oxford Movement of John Henry Newman and the Cambridge Camden Society of John Mason Neale, which sought to return the full Catholic liturgy, as well as the Gothic architecture of the English Middle Ages, to the Church of England. Notman designed the bishop's Chapel of the Holy Innocents (1845–46) in Burlington, although the bishop turned to Upjohn for the more important St. Mary's (1846–48) in Burlington. Notman's Gothic work is best exemplified by St. Mark's. He was one of only five architects practicing in America who were officially approved by the New York Ecclesiological Society (Upjohn was another). But the Scotsman was equally adept at designing Romanesque churches for "low" Episcopal congregations, as Holy Trinity, built in 1856–59 at Rittenhouse Square, and St. Clement's, built in 1855–59 at 20th and Cherry Streets, attest. And then off he went to do the monumentally Palladian Catholic cathedral on Logan Circle, built in 1846–64.

The Lady Chapel of St. Mark's was designed by Cope & Stewardson and added in 1899–1902.

9 DELANCEY PLACE
18th to 19th Streets

Yes, this is the same Delancey Street we encountered in Society Hill, though somewhere between there and here it did a vanishing act, only miraculously to reappear again as a residential street of beguiling charm. Here the north side of the block is a lovely sequence of semi-elliptical fanlights, low stoops,

shuttered windows, dormers, and stone lintels from the Italianate fifties. No. 1824 is by Eyre from 1895.

10 ROSENBACH MUSEUM AND LIBRARY
2010 Delancey Place, between 20th and 21st Streets

This 1860s town house was the home of rare-book dealer Abraham Simon Wolf Rosenbach (1876–1952) and his antique-dealer brother Philip H. Rosenbach (1863–1953) from 1926 until the early 1950s. A. S. W. Rosenbach was Penn educated (B.S., 1898; Ph.D., 1901) and had taught English at Penn for six years when he decided to go full-time into bookselling. It is believed that the Rosenbach Company was the most lucrative rare-book business in the world.

Since 1954 the brothers' house and collections have been one of the world's most beguiling small museums. Inside are numerous splendid pieces of eighteenth-century English furniture (Hepplewhite, Sheraton, Chippendale, Adam), over a thousand portrait miniatures, 30,000 rare books, and 300,000 rare manuscript pieces. Included in the collection are the following: a *Bay Psalm Book* (1640, the first book printed in what is now the United States, purchased by the Rosenbachs for $151,000 in 1947, then a record price paid for a rare book); the manuscript of *Ulysses;* three-quarters of all of Joseph Conrad's known manuscripts (including *The Secret Agent, Lord Jim,* and *Nostromo*); leaves from the manuscript of Boswell's *Life of Johnson;* Erasmus's 1519 edition of the *New Testament* (with engravings by Holbein); the finest known copy of the first edition of *Don Quixote* (1605); John Tenniel's original illustrations for *Alice's Adventures in Wonderland* and *Through the Looking-Glass;* letters (six hundred of them) and photographs by Lewis Carroll; parts of the manuscripts of *The Pickwick Papers* and *Nicholas Nickleby;* several thousand drawings by Maurice Sendak; and much of Marianne Moore's Greenwich Village flat (reconstructed here in period-room fashion). There are autograph letters and papers from Franklin, John Adams, Jefferson, Washington, Lincoln, and Grant. There are works on paper by Fragonard, Blake, Doré, Daumier, Cruikshank, and others.

There's no idle wandering around in here, but the personable guides will show you what you want to see—come mid-afternoon on a weekday, and you may get a guide all to yourself. In addition to being a public museum, this is an enormously important research library for literary scholars.

Be sure to see Thomas Sully's mesmerizing portrait of the beautiful Rebecca Gratz (1781–1869), of Sephardic Jewish descent (she is buried in the Mikveh Israel Cemetery on Spruce between 8th and 9th Streets), the daughter of the prominent merchant Michael Gratz. Rebecca's best friend was Matilda Hoffman, who died while she was Washington Irving's fiancée. Subsequently, Rebecca and Irving became close friends, and it was Irving who described her to his friend Sir Walter Scott, who used her as the model for the character of Rebecca in his *Ivanhoe* (1819). Sully's rather flowery portrait captures not only Rebecca's great beauty but also a sense of resignation in her gaze: because she would not marry outside of her faith, she was forced to reject the only man (Samuel Ewing) she ever loved enough to marry. Thus, the most celebrated Philadelphia beauty of her day never wed, devoting her life instead to charitable works for orphans and unwed mothers of all faiths.

A. S. W. Rosenbach was instrumental in building such important American libraries as Henry Folger's in Washington, Henry Huntington's in San Marino, California, J. Pierpont Morgan's in New York, and Harvard University's Harry Elkins Widener Library. It is fitting that the last, funded by Philadelphians in honor of their bibliophilic son who perished on the *Titanic,* should also have involved the Philadelphian Mr. Rosenbach, from whom young Harry Widener bought many books. The Rosenbachs spent around $75 million on their book purchases, including eight Gutenberg Bibles and thirty Shakespeare first folios.

9   *Delancey Place, 18th to 19th Streets*

11 FITLER SQUARE
Pine Street, between 23rd and 24th Streets

This charming small park was created in 1896 and was last renovated in 1980. It is named for Edwin Henry Fitler (1825–96), mayor of Philadelphia from 1887 to 1891 and the first mayor to have his office in the present City Hall.

12 SPRUCE STREET, 20TH TO 22ND STREETS

Unlike New York, Philadelphia was never a city dipped in chocolate, but brownstone had its day, as evident in these blocks of Spruce, with their brooding rows of mansarded brownstone houses. Nos. 2111–13 and 2132–34 are Furness's, the fine neo-Georgian house at 2123–25 is Eyre's, and No. 2100 is George Hewitt's.

12   *Spruce Street, 20th to 22nd Streets*

13 *Thomas Hockley House*

13 THOMAS HOCKLEY HOUSE
235 South 21st Street
1875, Frank Furness

Richly variegated with a steep mansard, gables, a gravity-defying jutting bay at the second story, pointed arches with polychrome voussoirs, and, most interesting of all, the unusual recessed corner entrance—like so much of Furness's work, it's just this side of goofy.

By the way, the character played by Billy Zane in the blockbuster movie *Titanic* is a fictitious Philadelphian named Cal Hockley. Writer-director James Cameron was evidently unaware of the Hockley name's association with Rittenhouse Square.

WILLIAM H. ALLEN BOOKSELLER
2031 Walnut Street, between 20th and 21st Streets

Allen's is one of Philadelphia's last general secondhand- and rare-book dealers, as opposed to the ultra-pricey and often pretentious dealers who have lately abounded here, and as distinct from the general secondhand dealers like Book Trader on South Street. This store is crammed and musty and almost unbelievably dusty (people with respiratory ailments be advised), and the assistance may border on the laconic, but it's a marvelous store with an excellent selection of classical history and literature. The store was founded in 1917.

Open, as of this writing, Monday through Friday from 8:00 A.M. to 5:00 P.M., and Saturday from 8:30 A.M. to 1:00 P.M. (215) 563–3398.

14 FIRST UNITARIAN CHURCH
2125 Chestnut Street
1885–86, Furness, Evans & Co.

Furness's father, the Reverend William Henry Furness, was the pastor of this church. And the design, one of the least pleasing of Furness's extant works, gives off a sense of trying too hard. The porch, with that deep-chiseled look and heavy shadow that Furness was able to exploit so well, is the best thing, but the big central gable with the rose window is just plain awkward. For once Furness, whose art required total control, allowed himself to lose control.

The Reverend Furness was one of the remarkable Philadelphia clergymen of his day, a devotee of Ruskin and sharp critic of the Quaker dullness of the streets of Philadelphia—the Reverend Furness, whose son Frank would do more than anyone to liven those Quaker streets. But Frank was not the Reverend Furness's only son to achieve acclaim in his field. Horace Howard Furness (1833–1912), six years Frank's elder (they died in the same year), was one of the leading American Shakespearean scholars of his time—indeed every bit as famous in his field as his brother Frank was in his.

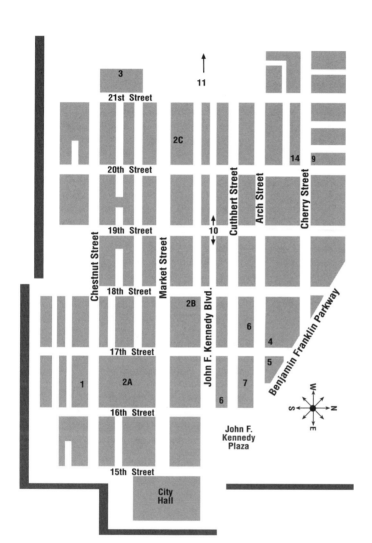

3

21st Street

11

2C

20th Street

14   9

Cuthbert Street

Arch Street

Cherry Street

19th Street

10

Chestnut Street

Market Street

18th Street

2B

John F. Kennedy Blvd.

17th Street

6

4

Benjamin Franklin Parkway

5

1

2A

7

16th Street

6

W

N   S

E

15th Street

John F.
Kennedy
Plaza

City
Hall

MARKET WEST

2a *From left to right; Two Liberty Place, William Penn, One Liberty Place*

CHAPTER 9

MARKET WEST

1 WCAU BUILDING

1620 Chestnut Street, between 16th and 17th Streets
1928, Harry Sternfeld and Gabriel Roth
Renovated in 1983, Kopple Sheward & Day

This is one of the most exuberant Deco salads you'll ever see, and an eye-opener in a city where Deco usually means the relatively subdued efforts of Ritter & Shay. Believe it or not, Sternfeld, who did the exterior, was a student of Paul Cret's. Originally built for a radio station, the studio was in the glass tower, lit up in blue at night when the station was on the air. The building was renovated in the 1980s for the Art Institute of Philadelphia.

2A UNGENTLEMANLY TOWERS: THE MARKET STREET CORRIDOR
LIBERTY PLACE
Market Street, between 16th and 17th Streets

ONE LIBERTY PLACE
1987, Murphy/Jahn

TWO LIBERTY PLACE
1990, Murphy/Jahn

The two zigzag towers by the enfant terrible of Chicago architecture now dominate the Philadelphia skyline. That is the most significant aspect of these buildings, rendering moot any other questions of their architectural quality. They will always be remembered, even when they are no longer the

2b   *Mellon Bank Center*

city's tallest structures, as the ones that were allowed to rise above William Penn. I don't think it matters if the Empire State Building or the Chrysler Building had been put there. Some vital part of the city's soul—one of the last things that made Philadelphia *better* than other American cities—was forever lost in the reckless decision to allow this skyward development.

The earlier tower is sixty stories, the later fifty-eight. The developer was Willard Rouse, the son (or is it nephew?) of the famous developer of the new towns of Columbia, Maryland, and Reston, Virginia, as well as of Boston's Faneuil Hall Marketplace, Baltimore's Harborplace, and New York's South Street Seaport.

As disturbing as these buildings themselves is that certain fashionable Philadelphians mistake Jahn's and Rouse's exhibitionism for chic, and do not realize that Helmut Jahn skyscrapers are nowadays so numerous around the world that they confer no status at all upon a city (if they ever did).

2B MELLON BANK CENTER

1735 Market Street, northeast corner of 18th Street
1990, Kohn Pedersen Fox

On the heels of Liberty Place, the Market Street corridor west of City Hall was further developed with towering behemoths. Here's the entry by Kohn Pedersen Fox, with Murphy/Jahn one of the two firms most associated with the development excesses of the Reagan eighties. Just as Michael Milken gave us junk bonds, these firms gave us junk buildings, though, to be fair, there's undeniably higher quality in KPF's than in Jahn's forays into the speculative wilds. As is illustrated here, Mellon Bank Center is positively stately in comparison to the Liberty Place towers. It is a fifty-four-story obelisk, its crowning pyramid ostentatiously illuminated at night, just in case by sheer height alone it did not eclipse William Penn.

2C COMMERCE SQUARE
Market Street, between 20th and 21st Streets
1987, 1992, Pei Cobb Freed & Partners

The Pei firm has a long association with Philadelphia, as with seemingly every city on the planet, successful as the firm was in garnering urban-renewal jobs. Whenever a bit of "quality" was needed to sell the latest scorched-earth proposal, Pei was at the ready, and, often as not, did something discernibly better than just about anyone else of similar stature would have done under the same circumstances.

So it's no surprise to find the Pei firm in the Market Street mega-office corridor in the eighties. Philadelphia wasn't going to make the same mistake twice: in the fifties and sixties, the working-stiff firms of Kling and Emery Roth got the Penn Center commissions. In the eighties, Market

2c *Commerce Square*

Street was going to get the most chichi Sunday supplement architects. Jahn gave us pure glitz, KPF gave glitz with restraint, and Pei gives restraint with little glitz—sober modernism with careful and slick urbanistic bows. The diamond shapes on top are a false note in this firm's work. The best thing by far is the plaza between the two towers: it's the work of the important Hanna/Olin firm of landscape architects, responsible for, among much else, the magnificent makeover of New York's Bryant Park.

3 COLLEGE OF PHYSICIANS AND SURGEONS

19 South 22nd Street, between Market and Chestnut Streets
1908, Cope & Stewardson

The College of Physicians and Surgeons is neither a school nor a hospital, but rather a not-for-profit organization dedicated to medical history and to the study of current issues in medical practice. Founded in 1787 by Benjamin Rush (1745–1813, a signer of the Declaration of Independence), among others, the college offers exhibits, lectures, and conferences that are open to the public as well as to medical practitioners. The college's library is considered one of the best libraries of medical history in the country.

The college has served in a public health advisory capacity, as during the yellow-fever epidemic of 1793, when the college was consulted on measures to prevent the further spread of the disease. In 1993, the college held a conference called *A Melancholy Scene of Devastation: The Public Response to the 1793 Philadelphia Yellow Fever Epidemic.*

Inside is the **Mütter Museum,** one of the most peculiar museums you will ever see. Fluid-preserved anatomical specimens, anatomical models, medical instruments, mementos of famous physicians, medical illustrations, and so forth are among the objects on display. There are the bladder stones removed from Chief Justice John Marshall by Dr. Philip Syng Physick. There are the connected livers (preserved in a jar) of the Siamese twins Chang and Eng Bunker, along with a plaster cast of their joined torsos. (The twins' autopsy was performed at the college in 1874.) There is Marie Curie's piezo-electrometer, which she herself presented to the college. There are Dr. Benjamin Rush's medicine chest and Florence Nightingale's sewing kit. There's part of President Grover Cleveland's jawbone. There's a piece of John Wilkes Booth's thorax (honest). There are bones in every conceivable state of fracture and pathology. There are outstanding collections of skulls and of eardrums. And if you ever wondered what a syphilitic lesion looked like compared to a tubercular lesion, this is the place to come. But perhaps topping it all is the Chevalier Jackson Collection of Foreign Bodies—i.e., of objects accidentally swallowed by people.

Dr. Thomas Dent Mütter (1811–59) was a professor of surgery at Jefferson Medical College (the end of his tenure there overlapped with the beginning of Dr. Gross's) and an inveterate collector of medical curiosities and memorabilia, most of it for use in his classes. In 1856, upon his retirement from teaching, Dr. Mütter donated his collection, along with an endowment for its perpetuation, to the College of Physicians and Surgeons. The museum was first located in the college's old building at 13th and Locust, built in 1863. The museum moved with the college into its elegant new Cope & Stewardson building in 1908.

4 ROBERT MORRIS HOTEL

1705 Arch Street, northwest corner of 17th Street
1914–15, 1921–22, Ballinger & Perrot

Here are Gothic details in terra-cotta slathered over the steel frame of what was originally an office skyscraper. It was begun a year after the completion of Cass Gilbert's Woolworth Building in New York.

5 BELL ATLANTIC TOWER

Arch Street, northwest corner of 17th Street
1991, The Kling-Lindquist Partnership

This is the clear winner among the newer, higher-than-William-Penn Center City towers. Fifty-three stories sheathed in red granite, with the

5a   *Bell Atlantic Tower, from Swann Memorial Fountain*

5b   *Bell Atlantic Tower*

setback-slab massing we associate with Ritter & Shay's towers of the thirties. Indeed, it's a tribute to Ritter & Shay, and awfully like what that firm would have done had it not observed the antediluvian "gentlemen's agreement" limiting Center City building heights.

6 ARCH STREET PRESBYTERIAN CHURCH
1724 Arch Street, between 17th and 18th Streets
1853–55, Joseph C. Hoxie

Arch Street Presbyterian Church is one of the best churches of its era in the country and one of Philadelphia's most beautiful buildings. This one scores on several counts—its fine tetrastyle Corinthian portico, its wrapping of Corinthian pilasters, and especially its impressively large copper dome. Inside, the coffered dome is spectacular, as is the sanctuary treatment with its aedicular altar, a pedimented Corinthian peristyle. The versatile Hoxie (1814–70) designed the Elliott and Leland loft buildings around 2nd and Chestnut at the same time he was doing this elaborate church.

Arch Street Church would probably be far better known if it weren't practically in the shadow of the Catholic cathedral. But from several vantage points in the environs of the otherwise exceedingly drab Penn Center, it is possible to see not one but two majestic domes. Alas, Arch Street Church appears to have once been (before 1900) more magnificent than it is: gone are its twin towers flanking the portico and the high cupola atop the dome. These elements made it clearer that Hoxie was probably indebted to Christopher Wren's design of London's St. Paul's Cathedral (1675–1710). It is remarkable that Wren's influence in Philadelphia, so pronounced in the mid-eighteenth century (as at Christ Church and at Stenton), should still be strong a century later.

7 INSURANCE COMPANY OF NORTH AMERICA

(I. N. A.)

Arch Street, 16th to 17th Streets
1925, Stewardson & Page
Addition in 1979, Mitchell/Giurgola Associates

The original Stewardson & Page structure, facing east across 16th Street, is a handsome, squat skyscraper with neo-Georgian detailing. It works well in concert with the Suburban Station building, next door to the south, to provide a good street-wall for the open space of Kennedy Plaza. Far more famous—and larger—is the Mitchell/Giurgola annex, attached to the west side of the original, on Arch Street. As with so many Mitchell/Giurgola concoctions, each façade gets its own environmentally correct treatment.

6 *Arch Street Presbyterian Church*

The north wall facing across Arch Street is almost all glass. The south wall has screened windows up top where the sun might get too strong, but farther down, where the wall is in the shadow of nearby buildings, it is fully glazed. The east and west walls have windows deeply recessed behind sunscreen strips. You will recognize the idea from the same firm's United Fund Building on the Benjamin Franklin Parkway. These varying façade treatments are unified by the use of the same smooth aluminum skin on all façades, and by the sleek rounded corners, making for sinuous segues from one façade to another. The principal bow to Stewardson & Page's original building occurs at the fifteenth story of the addition, where the mechanical facilities are expressed by a broad aluminum band that is continuous with the cornice level of the original building.

8 SUBURBAN STATION
16th Street and John F. Kennedy Boulevard
1924–29, Graham, Anderson, Probst & White

The Chicago-based successor firm to D. H. Burnham & Company and the architects of 30th Street Station created this office building/train station combo. It's a fine street-wall building, although once there were little yellow lights on the 16th Street façade that spelled out *Pennsylvania Railroad,* one of those little touches that lends magic to a city; these lights are no longer. This complex was necessitated by the condition that as the new 30th Street Station, with which Suburban Station was built as part of a coordinated plan, usurped the functions of the old Broad Street Station, it left a void in the center of the city for suburban commuters, since 30th Street Station is just a bit too far to the west to serve commuters into the Center City office district. Hence, Suburban Station, about which it has correctly been pointed out that its commuter functions possess none of the larger station's ceremonial splendor. It is stuck in the basement of an office building that seems not to wish to proclaim that it is also a railroad station.

9 ST. CLEMENT'S CHURCH (EPISCOPAL)
20th and Cherry Streets
1855–59, John Notman

This church was actually built to promote a real-estate speculation: build a church, and they will come (and buy houses on the nearby properties).

8   *Suburban Station*

Kind of the same idea that Henry Howard Houston had when he built the Church of St. Martin in the Fields in his new development of Chestnut Hill (*see* chapter fourteen). Anyway, here's Notman in his Romanesque mood, and the church was built over exactly the same years as his Holy Trinity at Rittenhouse Square. The Lady Chapel here is a later addition, and later still are its iron gates by Yellin.

10 JOHN F. KENNEDY BOULEVARD
From Broad Street to the Schuylkill River

It was created as part of the Penn Center makeover of Center City in the fifties, following the dismantling of the Chinese Wall. Planning-guru Edmund Bacon's notion here was to create the kind of dense office corridor that abounds in midtown Manhattan, with a sense of enveloping mass. What emerged, perhaps inevitably, was one of the ugliest streets in the city, a thoroughfare especially dispiriting on weekends when it is largely empty of people. It's the one street I avoid like the plague in my Center City perambulations. Its nadir is the plaza bounded by the Boulevard, and 15th,

Arch, and 16th Streets. The buildings on the west side are fine (Suburban Station and the old I. N. A. Building), and diagonally across the boulevard is glorious City Hall. But all the other surrounding buildings of high Penn Center vintage are banal; and as an open space that mediates between the Benjamin Franklin Parkway and City Hall, it is truly unfortunate. The round tourist information structure has no business there, and the *Love* sculpture by Robert Indiana is enough to make anyone gag.

As John Lukacs has written, "When Philadelphia tries to go modern, she merely follows New York; and when she follows New York, the results are usually, and expectably, indifferent."

11 30TH STREET STATION

30th Street and John F. Kennedy Boulevard
1927–34, Graham, Anderson, Probst & White
Restored in 1991, Dan Peter Kopple & Associates

One of the last of the great train stations, this has been beautifully restored without being turned into a shopping mall. Back in 1974 Edward Teitelman and Richard W. Longstreth had this to say: "Despite its potential to impress, the building's exterior lacks a distressing portion of the needed vitality.

11a *30th Street Station*

11b   *30th Street Station, Main Concourse*

Grouped with the Post Office (1930) across Market Street, it helps create a strangely barren, large-scaled entrance to West Philadelphia." Hmmm.

Here's Sally A. Kitt Chappell, the leading authority on the architects Graham, Anderson, Probst & White:

> Today the Corinthian columns, eleven feet in diameter and seventy-one feet high, form an impressive colonnade and, together with the subordinate wings at the sides, give Philadelphia a sense of dramatic closure on the west. On the north and south the façades are lower, but the tall windows separated by pilasters, capped with an attic story similar to the porticoes, bring harmony to all four sides and mark a key point in the route along the Schuylkill Expressway. In every direction the building fits into the fabric of the city, playing an integral part in the idea of order in urban Philadelphia, as well as expressing its own particular, individual function as a railroad station. (*Architecture and Planning of Graham, Anderson, Probst & White, 1912–1936,* Chicago: University of Chicago Press, 1992, p. 200)

There is agreement, however, about the interior. Teitelman and Longstreth:

> The interior is . . . of a breed becoming rare, and if the experience is not the same exhilaration once rendered by the old Penn Station in New York, there is still the feeling of Having Arrived.

Chappell:

> The lofty columns, gleaming marbles, and glowing lights of the interior transform the functional space into a ceremonial space, a setting worthy of human feelings, where railroad engineering rises to the humanistic art of architecture. (op. cit., p. 202)

11c   *30th Street Station, Main Concourse*

The main concourse is 290 feet long, 135 feet wide, and 95 feet to the flat coffered ceiling. (The concourse of New York's Grand Central Terminal comes in at 460 feet long, 160 feet wide, and 150 feet to the crest of the vaulted ceiling.) The floor is Tennessee marble, the most comfortable stone mankind has ever discovered for treading upon. Karl Bitter's relief *The Spirit of Transportation* in the north waiting area was originally installed, in 1895, in the waiting room of the old Broad Street Station and was moved here in 1933. The gigantic statue, the *Pennsylvania Railroad World War II Memorial,* on the 29th Street side of the concourse is by Walker Hancock and dates from 1952.

I think the view of the Corinthian portico of the articulated mass of the concourse, with the recessed projecting wings to north and south, as one approaches from Center City along the bridges over the Schuylkill is one of Philadelphia's most stirring sights.

Filbert Street

9

Market Street

Ludlow Street

Chestnut Street

Sansom Street

Walnut Street

Locust Walk

Smith Walk

Spruce Street

Hamilton Walk

South Street

Convention Ave.

Lancaster Ave.

←10

38th Street

37th Street

36th Street

34th Street

33rd Street

32nd Street

31st Street

1

2

3

4

5

6

7

8

N
W   E
S

CHAPTER 10

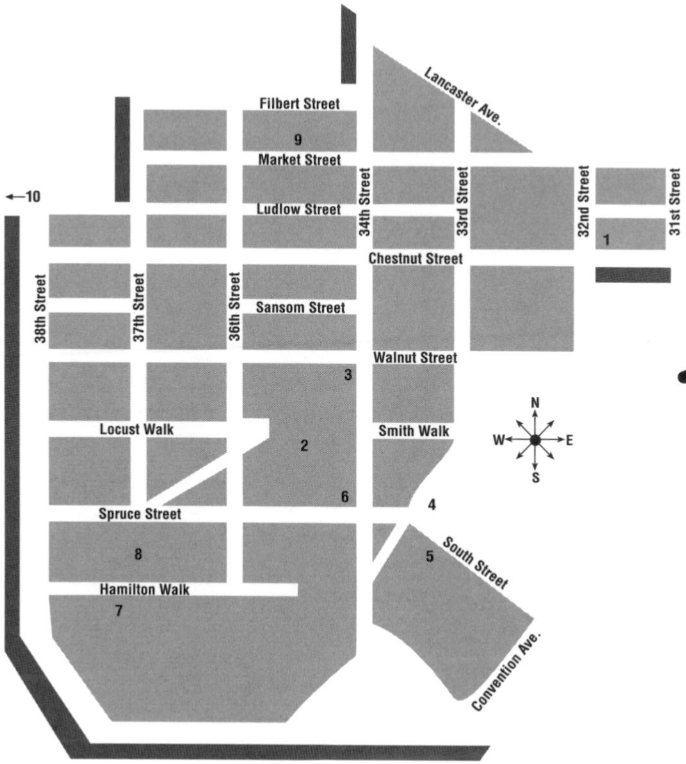

UNIVERSITY CITY

1a *Drexel University, Main Building*

CHAPTER 10

UNIVERSITY CITY

1 DREXEL UNIVERSITY, MAIN BUILDING
32nd and Chestnut Streets
1889–91, The Wilson Brothers

The main building of Drexel is an imposing Renaissance block similar in its articulation of masses and in some of its details to Schwarzmann's Memorial Hall, completed thirteen years before the Drexel building was begun. It's lavishly decorated in terra-cotta, and the articulated central section features an enormous arched entrance (in contrast to the triple-arched portico of Memorial Hall) that leads to the central court, which is this building's glory. It is a soaring, four-story-high, sixty-five-foot-square, galleried and arcaded, light-filled space elaborately ornamented in red tile, white brick, and pink marble with wrought-iron balustrades.

This was the first building of the brand-new Drexel Institute of Art, Science and Industry, which began offering classes in 1891. The school was founded by the famous investment banker and partner of J. Pierpont Morgan, Anthony J. Drexel (1826–93). When he died, only a year after Drexel Institute opened, the firm of Drexel, Morgan & Co. split into the two firms of J. P. Morgan & Co., New York, and Drexel & Co., Philadelphia, though the two firms retained a close relationship. Drexel & Co. metamorphosed into Drexel Burnham Lambert, which famously went belly-up in the overheated 1980s.

Drexel Institute was founded to train young men and women of modest means in business and engineering. The tuition was kept low, the school was liberal in granting scholarships, and night classes and work-study programs were instituted. Above all, the school did not discriminate on the basis of race, creed, ethnicity, or sex. Originally, the institute was a non-degree-granting school, though in 1914 it began to award the bachelor of

1b *Drexel University,*
Anthony Drexel Monument

science degree, in 1927 the master of science degree, and in 1965 the doctor of philosophy degree. In 1936 the school's name was changed to Drexel Institute of Technology and in 1970 to Drexel University. In 1919 Drexel Institute began one of the nation's first so-called cooperative education programs, in which students alternate periods of full-time employment with periods of full-time study; the co-op approach is still going strong at Drexel. In 1988 Drexel became the nation's first university to require that all students possess a microcomputer. There are now about 11,000 students enrolled at Drexel.

The architects of Drexel Institute, handpicked by Anthony J. Drexel, were the brothers Wilson. Joseph Wilson (1838–1902) was born in Phoenixville in Chester County and worked for the Pennsylvania Railroad, for whom he designed various structures and facilities. In 1876 he began a firm with his brother John, who had also worked for the Pennsylvania Railroad. They got their start working on the Centennial Exposition and in the 1880s became one of Philadelphia's most successful firms. They designed the train shed of Reading Terminal (1891–93) for the Reading Railroad and the old Broad Street Station for the Pennsylvania Railroad.

UNIVERSITY OF PENNSYLVANIA

The University of Pennsylvania, today one of the eight Ivy League universities (along with Harvard, Yale, Dartmouth, Cornell, Columbia, Brown, and Princeton), had its origin in a "Publick Academy of Philadelphia" proposed in 1749 by Benjamin Franklin (who else?). Franklin opened his academy in 1751 in a building on 4th and Arch. The academy became the College of Philadelphia in 1755, with the Reverend William Smith as provost. Seized as a Tory bastion by the State of Pennsylvania in 1779, the College became the University of the State of Pennsylvania, thus laying claim to being both the first state-sponsored institution of higher learning in the country and the first "university" (as opposed to "college") in the country. After the Revolution, in 1791, the university reverted to private status, and the name was changed to University of Pennsylvania. In 1802, after the federal government moved from Philadelphia to Washington, the university moved into the former presidential residence at 9th and Chestnut. In 1829 this building was replaced by two handsome new buildings designed by William Strickland. The West Philadelphia campus was developed beginning in 1872 under Provost Charles Janeway Stillé (provost 1868–80). By then the university was going wholeheartedly over to the German model of higher education, with an emphasis upon Ph.D. studies (the University awarded its first Ph.D. degree in 1889) and original research, particularly in the sciences (with other disciplines being transformed along quasi-scientific lines). This process of Germanification reached a crescendo of sorts under the strong leadership of Provost William Pepper (provost 1881–94). (There is an excellent statue of Pepper to the west of Irvine Auditorium on Spruce Street. The statue is by Karl Bitter and dates from 1896.) Another way that Penn was more similar to Central European than to English universities was that it was basically a commuter university, drawing most of its students from the immediate area. (This is no longer the case.) Under Pepper's leadership in 1890 the university graduated 301 students; one hundred years later, Penn graduated 5,634 students. Among Penn's American firsts are the first medical school (established 1765), the first university teaching hospital, the first collegiate school of business, and the first journalism program. The current enrollment is about 10,000 students. The first all-electronic computer, ENIAC, was created at Penn in 1946. Today Penn is most renowned for its Wharton School of Business Management (founded 1881), and for its School of Nursing, though the law and medical schools are also ranked among the top ten in the country.

The university occupies a 262-acre campus in West Philadelphia and is the city's largest private employer.

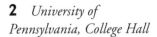

2 *University of Pennsylvania, College Hall*

2 COLLEGE HALL

Locust Walk, between 34th and 35th Streets
1871–72, Thomas W. Richards

It's been mutilated over the years with the amputation of gables and towers, but the outlines are still apparent of an attempt at a grand exercise in High Victorian Gothic, with its contrasting materials, finials, pointed arches, sloping roofs, gabled dormers, etc. This was Penn's first building on its new West Philadelphia campus.

3 FURNESS BUILDING (THE ANNE AND JEROME FISHER

FINE ARTS BUILDING)
34th and Walnut Streets
1888–90, Frank Furness
Renovated in 1991, Venturi Scott Brown & Associates

Begun twelve years after the Pennsylvania Academy of the Fine Arts was completed on North Broad, this was originally Penn's library. It's more "duck" than the PAFA, less "decorated shed." The form is studiously asymmetrical (an articulation of volumes as tortured as at Kahn's Richards Medical Research Building), the profile variegated (multi-gabled and crenellated), the facings—of red-brick, terra-cotta, and fieldstone—earthy and romantic. The battered base works with the steeply sloping roofs to create a sense of the building as a natural rock formation. It's been said, rightly, that the north rounded end looks like a church apse and that the south end looks like a train shed. I detect a whiff here of Mont-Saint-Michel, as at Irvine Auditorium (designed by architects very different from Furness and thirty-nine years later). The four-story, skylighted reading room, with brick and terra-cotta walls and exposed iron beams (influence of Viollet-le-Duc), is one of the great spaces of Philadelphia. Indeed, inside and out, this is one of the city's most amazing buildings.

3 *University of Pennsylvania, Furness Building*

4 FRANKLIN FIELD

33rd and South Streets
1902–4, 1913, 1922, Frank Miles Day & Brother

The gymnasium came first, in 1902–4, and the stadium was added in 1913 and enlarged in '22. "Collegiate Gothic," crenellated, a red brick mass with limestone trim. E. Digby Baltzell, our finest commentator on the virtues of sportsmanship, called it "the finest stadium in America." He may have been right.

The Eagles played in Franklin Field until Veterans Stadium opened in 1971. When the team moved from here into the modern facility in South Philadelphia it was considered progress. Today, progress, for lovers of the city, is a suspect word. But Franklin Field is still home to the famous Penn Relays track meet held every April as well as to Penn football. Is it really necessary that this venerable stadium's playing field be carpeted in artificial turf?

5 UNIVERSITY MUSEUM

South Street, between 33rd and 34th Streets
1893–1926, Wilson Eyre, Frank Miles Day & Brother, Cope &
    Stewardson
1969–71, Mitchell/Giurgola Associates

The University Museum of Archaeology and Anthropology (if that's what it's still called, as they have a disconcerting habit of slightly altering its name every few years, which is why most people just call it the University Museum) is widely acknowledged to have the nation's third finest general collection of ancient art and archaeological artifacts, after New York's Metropolitan Museum and Boston's Museum of Fine Arts. In general, the Philadelphia Museum of Art concentrates on art since A.D. 1000, while the University Museum covers everything before then. So while Philadelphia lacks the kind of encyclopedic museum enjoyed by New York and Boston, by putting together the Museum of Art and the University Museum you have something that is indeed encyclopedic.

While the Pennsylvania Academy of the Fine Arts was inspired by the Royal Academy in London, and the Philadelphia Museum of Art by the South Kensington (now Victoria and Albert) Museum, the University Museum was inspired by the British Museum. The University Museum was

5 *University of Pennsylvania, University Museum*

established in 1887 under Penn's legendary Provost William Pepper, who was an amateur archaeologist. Under Pepper, the university sponsored digs in the Near East, and began amassing the museum's outstanding collections. The support for the University Museum—not only from Pepper's university but also and especially from among well-to-do Philadelphians, many of them with no connection to the university—was startlingly enthusiastic. The digs even became society events.

The museum's first home was in College Hall beginning in 1889. The museum moved the following year into the newly completed library designed by Furness. The present museum building was conceived in 1893 but was not ready for occupancy until 1899.

Eyre's design seems based on twelfth-century Northern Italian Romanesque prototypes, such as San Ambrogio in Milan. With its Japanese-style gate (*not* a Romanesque element!), fine wrought-iron work, landscaped courtyard (with a reflecting pool), tile roof, mosaic panels, rough brick with marble accents, and ivy-covered walls, the original museum building is not only one of the most picturesque but also one of the loveliest sights in Philadelphia. The sculptures on the gateposts—representing Native American, African, Oceanic, and Asian cultures—are works of the redoubtable Alexander Stirling Calder. Inside, the rotunda is composed of self-supporting Mercer tiles, using the vaulting techniques introduced into the United States by the Catalan engineer Rafael Guastavino in 1881.

6 IRVINE AUDITORIUM

34th and Spruce Streets
1929, Horace Trumbauer and Julian Abele

The exterior form of Penn's auditorium is based on the thirteenth-century church of the monastery of Mont-Saint-Michel. The variegated profile, the abundant iconography, and the soaring space of the auditorium make this one of the most characterful, eccentric, and exciting buildings on the Penn campus, and a remarkable work within Trumbauer's oeuvre.

Julian Francis Abele (1881–1950), Trumbauer's assistant who probably played the major role in designing Irvine Auditorium, is a remarkable figure in the history of American architecture. He was the first African American to be graduated from Penn's architecture school and the first African American to attend the École des Beaux-Arts. He may have been the first African American to be a professional architect and was certainly the first to attain distinction as one. Abele joined the Trumbauer firm in 1906. I suspect that in the understandable zeal to promote Abele's accomplishments, his role in the Trumbauer firm has probably been slightly overstated in recent years. The current tendency is to suggest that anything credited to Trumbauer and built after 1906 really ought to be credited to Abele. I cannot say, not being an expert on the inner workings of the Trumbauer firm, if this is so. My gut feeling is that there is enough continuity between Trumbauer's pre- and post-1906 work that even if he did delegate a great deal to Abele, the designs are still clearly Trumbauer designs.

Anyway, of the works by the Trumbauer firm that are noted in this

7   *University of Pennslyvania,*
Richards Medical Research Building

book, the following are pre-Abele: the house at 1629 Locust Street from 1892 (*see* chapter eight); the second Land Title Building, 1902, designed by Trumbauer with Daniel H. Burnham, on Broad and Chestnut (*see* chapter one); and the St. James apartment house from 1900–1904, on Walnut between 12th and 13th (*see* chapter two). The following "Trumbauer" works came after Abele became chief designer: the Union League addition, 1909–11, on 15th Street (*see* chapter one); the Widener Building, 1914, on Chestnut and Juniper (*see* chapter one); the Philadelphia Museum of Art, 1916–28 (*see* chapter eleven); the Free Library, 1917–27 (*see* chapter eleven); the Public Ledger Building, 1924, on 6th and Chestnut (*see* chapter two); and, of course, Irvine Auditorium, begun later than any of them. As of this writing, the university plans to mutilate this wonderful building by carving up the auditorium's space to accommodate a new lobby, a restaurant, a rehearsal studio, and whatnot, all as part of the larger Perelman Quadrangle project designed by Venturi & Scott Brown.

7 RICHARDS MEDICAL RESEARCH BUILDING
37th Street and Hamilton Walk
1957–61, Louis I. Kahn

There is not a building in the world about which it is more boring to read. Almost everything one reads about this building rambles on about its HVAC (heating, ventilating, and air conditioning) systems as a determinant of its form. Everyone says this is so great, but none of these commentators seems willing to let us in on just *why* it's so wonderful that HVAC systems should determine a building's form. Richards presents the famous visual differentiation of "servant spaces" (ventilating systems, elevators, heating plant, and so on) and "served spaces" (the laboratories that are the structure's raison d'être). This apparently *just happens* to give the building its often-noted whiff of the medieval towers of San Gimignano, which whiff is actually quite fragrant in this context. But I wonder if Kahn couldn't have designed the visual profile of his building in any of a number of ways without compromising his HVAC fetish. And does this not mean that he took decisions that were essentially informed by aesthetic rather than purely functional considerations? And does this then not mean that the whole bloated HVAC analysis of the building may be interesting to HVAC engineers but has nothing whatsoever to do with the building's aesthetic presence? As the analysis stands, it seems that Kahn should get no more credit for this building's design than its engineer, August E. Komendant.

Scientists working in the building complain of a lack of privacy and flexibility, qualities that, incidentally, tend to abound in Beaux-Arts buildings.

LOUIS ISIDORE KAHN (1902–74)

Louis Kahn was born in 1902 in Estonia but moved with his parents to Philadelphia when he was three years old. He attended the remarkable Central High School in Philadelphia and also Samuel S. Fleisher's Graphic Sketch Club (where the Louis Kahn Lecture Room, designed by Siah Armajani, opened in 1982). He studied under Paul Philippe Cret at the University of Pennsylvania's School of Architecture (1920–24) and also worked in Cret's office. From 1941 to 1948, Kahn worked with George Howe and Oskar Stonorov, then he taught at Yale from 1948 to 1957 before settling down at Penn from 1957 until his death in 1974. One of the ironies of Kahn's career is that though this architect grew up in Philadelphia, had his practice in Philadelphia, and taught in Philadelphia, making that city a mecca for aspiring modernist architects, his best buildings are all elsewhere. If the Richards Medical Research Building on the Penn campus was one of his first major works, it was also probably among the least felicitous of his major works, some examples of which do indeed rank among the finest achievements of modernist architecture. The great works begin right after the Richards, with the Salk Institute in La Jolla, California, built in 1959–65, which clearly embodies some of the Beaux-Arts precepts Kahn learned from Cret, as do the Kimbell Art Museum in Fort Worth, Texas, built in 1966–72 and generally considered one of the masterpieces of post–World War II architecture (Kahn himself considered it his finest moment), and the Yale Center for British Art in New Haven, built in 1969–74. Among the Philadelphia architects who worshiped at Kahn's feet we may count Romaldo Giurgola, Robert Venturi, and Richard Saul Wurman. If Louis Sullivan's dictum was "form ever follows function," and Mies van der Rohe's was "less is more," then Kahn's was "what does this building want to be?" It is perhaps the most presumptuous of all the modernists' flip dicta.

8 MEN'S DORMITORIES
Spruce Street, between 36th and 38th Streets
1895–1902, Cope & Stewardson
Renovated in 1983–87, Davis Brody & Associates

What a wonderful, visually delightful group of buildings these make! The style has been termed "Jacobethan" (Jacobean + Elizabethan), with what that implies about the loose combination of medieval and classical forms, though here the piquant combinations of Gothic gargoyles with Palladian windows not only have no actual historical precedent but are both more winsome and more finely hewed than anything in postmodernism, which the dormitories' stylistic eccentricities may seem to foreshadow. The keynotes are delight and surprise in both form and detail. There's the main quadrangle and several ancillary open spaces approached through elaborate archways. The big main gate on Spruce and 39th is a four-towered affair with Brighton domes. Its big, bulging curved bay over the archway recalls the same sort of thing in the courtyard of City Hall.

Walter Cope (1860–1902) was born in Philadelphia to a distinguished old Quaker family (he was the great-grandson of Thomas Pym Cope) and also died there. He was educated at Germantown Friends School and came up through the office of the Quaker architect Addison Hutton (designer of the Library Company's Ridgway Library on South Broad Street). Cope then went to work in the office of Theophilus Chandler (who founded Penn's

8 *University of Pennsylvania, Men's Dormitories*

School of Architecture). There Cope met and entered into a partnership with the École des Beaux-Arts–trained John Stewardson. Cope's output—including the campus plans of Penn, Bryn Mawr College, and Washington University, and Alexander Cassatt's estate in Rosemont—was prodigious for an architect who was only forty-two when he died. When John Stewardson died, his place in the firm was taken by his brother Emlyn Stewardson (1863–1936), who was trained at Penn and, in addition to his collaborations with Cope (who was not a Penn man), designed two of Proper Philadelphia's most august private clubs: the Philadelphia Club and the Rittenhouse Club. Thus, between their buildings for Penn and their clubhouses, Cope & Stewardson designed many of the buildings in which Proper Philadelphia carried on its days.

9 INSTITUTE FOR SCIENTIFIC INFORMATION
35th and Market Streets
1978–79, Venturi Rauch & Scott Brown

This is essentially a simple, rectangular, four-story, inexpensively constructed "shed" that Venturi Rauch & Scott Brown decorated in a bright and playful manner with a geometric composition of colored tiles. Or: Market Street is almost all right.

9 *University of Pennsylvania, Institute for Scientific Information*

10   *The Woodlands*

10 THE WOODLANDS
Woodland Avenue and 40th Street
1742, 1788–89

The present house stands on the grounds of the former estate of the re-doubtable Andrew Hamilton, the great colonial lawyer and one of the build-ers of Independence Hall. Hamilton's son built the present house, and it was enlarged in the 1780s by William Hamilton, Andrew's grandson. It is a tremendously important house in the evolution of the Federal style, or late-Georgian style, inspired by the British architect Robert Adam.

On the exterior, the house is in the mid-Georgian Palladian tradition, with its pedimented tetrastyle Doric portico. The tall, slender columns, the semi-elliptical fanlights set within the blind arches of Palladian windows, the delicate, modillioned cornice, and the curved volumes visible from the sides are all hallmarks of Adam design. So was the original stuccoing, since removed. Inside, the entry hall is a laterally disposed rectangular space with semicircular lateral ends. Adjacent to the entry hall on the main axis is a relatively small circular hall, which gives, via stairwells, on a pair of flanking oval rooms. This extensive use of curves, both in the form of rooms and in details such as fanlights and moldings, is characteristic of the Adamesque approach, which is often called "Federal" in the United States.

Woodlands is probably Philadelphia's finest extant example of the Adam influence. To see something by Adam himself, it is not necessary to leave town: the drawing room from Adam's Lansdowne House, London, from the 1760s, is in the Philadelphia Museum of Art and is well worth a visit, particularly in conjunction with an appraisal of Woodlands.

1

3

18th Street

Callowhill Street

19th Street

Logan
Circle
2

Vine Street

4

6

20th Street

5

7

Hamilton Street

Pennsylvania Ave.

21st Street

Spring Garden Street

Benjamin Franklin Parkway

Race Street

8

22nd Street

Pennsylvania Ave.

10

N

E

W

S

9

11

PARKWAY

1 *United Fund Building*

CHAPTER 11

PARKWAY

1 UNITED FUND BUILDING

Benjamin Franklin Parkway, between 17th and 18th Streets
1969, Mitchell/Giurgola Associates

This sharply angular modernist building with its varying façade treatments is said by a pair of critics to be "a highly inventive mannerist study in the formal concept of the curtain wall" (Edward Teitelman and Richard W. Longstreth, *Architecture in Philadelphia: A Guide,* 1974). That's a bit too abstract for me.

There are certain similarities between this building and Louis Kahn's Phillips Exeter Academy library (1967–72) in Exeter, New Hampshire. Kahn was the greatest influence on the works of his University of Pennsylvania colleague Romaldo Giurgola.

2 SWANN MEMORIAL FOUNTAIN

Logan Circle, Benjamin Franklin Parkway and 19th Street
1921–24, Alexander Stirling Calder and Wilson Eyre

Logan Circle is one of Penn's five *squares* and was originally called the northwest square. In fact, it originally was square but was turned into a circle with the construction of the Parkway. Once a potter's field and the site of public hangings, it was named for James Logan (of Stenton fame) in 1825, two years after the last hanging took place there, twenty-one years before the cathedral began to take shape on the (then) square's south side, and ninety-nine years before A. S. Calder's fountain was constructed in the center of the (by then) circle.

William Cary Swann, for whom the fountain is named, was a physician

2 *Swann Memorial Fountain*

and the founder of the Philadelphia Fountain Society, which worked to get drinking fountains (for people) and troughs (for horses) built throughout the city. A fountain in his honor was first proposed in 1878, but an adequate site would not be found until Cret and Gréber expanded Logan Circle and suggested it as the site of a major monument in their Parkway scheme in 1918. Eyre was in charge of the overall conception of the fountain, while Calder designed the sculptures. It was Eyre's idea to keep the figures low, so that the visual axis between City Hall and Fairmount Park would not be interrupted, except by the jets of water from the fountain.

The theme is the waterways of Philadelphia. The three figures in the center represent the Delaware, Schuylkill, and Wissahickon Rivers. The Wissahickon is represented by a reclining female figure, her hand holding a water-spouting swan (a pun on Mr. Swann's name). The Delaware, the central figure, is a male Indian, holding a water-spouting fish. The Schuylkill is represented by an older female figure, also holding a swan. The rim of the basin is ringed by water-spouting frogs and turtles. The forms are simplified and slightly abstracted, without the abundant naturalistic detail of the elder Calder's works at City Hall. But the modeling is bold and the composition dynamic, and this is a good fountain. (In the swanky Four Seasons Hotel across the Parkway to the west is a fancy restaurant called The Fountain and a more casual restaurant called the Swann Lounge and Cafe.)

ALEXANDER STIRLING CALDER (1870–1945)

Alexander Stirling Calder was the second of the three famous sculpting Calders. Philadelphia-born, he studied under Eakins and Anshutz at the Pennsylvania Academy of the Fine Arts before going to Paris, where he entered the École des Beaux-Arts in the atelier of Jean-Alexandre-Joseph Falguière, one of Les Florentins, the sculptors who looked to the lively modeling and spontaneity of Florentine Renaissance sculpture in contrast to the prevailing neoclassical mode and had an enormous influence on American sculptors. (A. S. Calder would have been in the atelier Falguière only a couple of years after New York's Frederick MacMonnies, whose works would much more clearly exhibit Falguière's influence.) Upon his return, Calder became a teacher at the Pennsylvania Academy of the Fine Arts and received his first major commission in 1893 when he was chosen to create a statue of Dr. Samuel David Gross for the Army Medical Museum in Washington, D.C. (This is the same Dr. Gross portrayed by Eakins in his famous painting *The Gross Clinic* in 1875, hanging at Jefferson Medical College.) In 1910 Calder moved to New York, where he taught at the National Academy of Design and at the Art Students League and became Karl Bitter's assistant, assuming Bitter's commissions following his death (including the entire sculptural program for the Panama-Pacific Exposition in San Francisco in 1915). His best-known New York work is his statue of President Washington on the west pier of Stanford White's arch (which also contains work by MacMonnies) at Washington Square. Calder died in New York in 1945.

The Shakespeare Memorial on the north side of Logan Circle is also by Calder and dates from 1928.

3 CATHEDRAL OF SAINTS PETER AND PAUL
18th and Race Streets
1846–64, Napoleon LeBrun and John Notman

Teitelman and Longstreth call this "LeBrun's attempt at academic grandeur," a sardonic assessment and a clear indication that these learned (and *academic*) men, writing in 1974, actually consider the United Fund Building to be the superior work of architecture to the Catholic cathedral.

It is one in the succession of America's magnificent Roman Catholic cathedrals built in the antebellum years, as the nation's cities filled with Irish Catholic immigrants. Latrobe's cathedral in Baltimore came first, followed by Philadelphia's, then Renwick's in New York, the first of the bunch to be designed in the Gothic style. Here at Logan Circle, the style is Italian Renaissance classical, executed at an astounding level of refinement. The original plan for the cathedral was devised by a pair of priests, the Reverend Mariano Maller and the Reverend John Tornatore, then reworked by LeBrun. The interior, with its spectacular barrel vault, is largely theirs. The exterior, however, is largely Notman's, working with the Reverend John T. Mahoney, from 1850. They conceived the marvelous dome and the Corinthian portico, similar to such sixteenth-century works of Andrea Palladio's as San Giorgio Maggiore or the Redentore, both in Venice. Also note that the façade uses brownstone, which Notman had only just introduced to Philadelphia in his Athenaeum at Washington Square.

Bear in mind the enormous courage, indeed the bravado, involved in beginning this cathedral, as imposing and sumptuous and conspicuous an edifice as Philadelphia at the time could claim, only two years after the horrible anti-Catholic riots of 1844.

The Diocese of Philadelphia was created by Pope Pius VIII on April 8, 1808.

SAINT JOHN NEPOMUCENE NEUMANN (1811–60)

Probably the most prominent Catholic personage to be associated with this cathedral was John Nepomucene Neumann, a Bohemian emigrant (his father was Bavarian, if you're wondering about the name) who was ordained in New York's *old* St. Patrick's Cathedral in what is now Manhattan's Little Italy. Father Neumann, though he asked not to be given a high administrative position, was named Bishop of Philadelphia in 1852, and, through his multitudinous good works—among other things, he basically created the American Catholic school system—was canonized in 1977. In the words of David Hugh Farmer, in his *Oxford Dictionary of Saints* (1978), "Diminutive in stature, lacking 'presence' and majesty, he spent much time and energy encouraging layfolk to lives of hidden sanctity. Ultimately, this work achieved the recognition which was its due." Father Neumann came to Philadelphia as bishop in 1852 and died in 1860; he was, therefore, the man nominally in charge of a portion of LeBrun's and Notman's continuing work on the cathedral—a responsibility for which the bishop apparently had little taste.

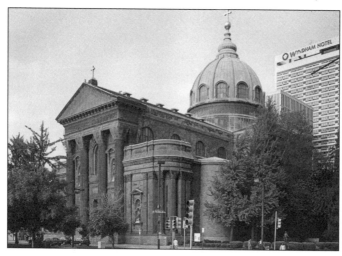

3 *Cathedral of Saints Peter and Paul*

4 ACADEMY OF NATURAL SCIENCES
19th Street, southwest corner of Race Street
1876

Dinosaurs, if you're into that sort of thing.

It's the oldest natural history museum in the country, founded in a coffeehouse in 1812 by John Speakman. It moved to its present site in 1876.

The Academy was the first museum in the world to display a mounted dinosaur skeleton, so the whole *Jurassic Park* business started here. There are mummies and dioramas and "interactive" exhibits. There are stuffed animals set against re-creations of their natural habitats. I think—I could be wrong—that Charles Willson Peale was the first to do this in his Columbianum in 1794.

5 BENJAMIN FRANKLIN PARKWAY
1907, et seq., Paul Philippe Cret, Jacques Gréber, Horace Trumbauer, and C. Clark Zantzinger

Eli Kirke Price, a Proper Philadelphian and a lawyer with a hankering for something more, dreamed the dream; Jacques Gréber and Paul Philippe

Cret realized it. The dream was for a beautiful landscaped parkway, a kind of Champs-Elysées, to link City Hall with Fairmount Park—a way of insinuating the great park right into the heart of Center City: *rus in urbe.*

In 1682 Thomas Holme laid out William Penn's new city as a rectilinear gridiron of streets, punctuated only by the five squares with one in the smack center and the others surrounding it at regular intervals. The plan was so simple, so plain, so abstract that it makes Manhattan's gridiron of 1811 seem drunken in comparison. Here's Dickens from 1842:

> It is a handsome city but distractingly regular. After walking about it for an hour or two, I felt that I would have given the world for a crooked street. The collar of my coat appeared to stiffen, and the brim of my hat to expand beneath its quakery influence. My hair shrunk into a sleek short crop, my hands folded themselves upon my breast of their own calm accord, and thoughts of taking lodgings in Mark Lane over against the Market Place, and of making a large fortune by speculations in corn, came over me involuntarily.

5   *Benjamin Franklin Parkway*

It would appear that the first proposal for the Parkway came from Fred Thorne, an architect in the Wilson Brothers's office, in 1891. But the impact of the World's Columbian Exposition in Chicago in 1893, with its "White City" giving rise to the "City Beautiful" movement, led to ever more grandiose visions of a Parkway connecting City Hall and Fairmount Park. Still, the Parkway gestated slowly. We tend to forget that this was a gargantuan urban-renewal project, involving sundry displacements of people and businesses and the demolition of numerous buildings. The more or less final plan, spearheaded by Cret, was in place by 1907.

It was planned that the Parkway would be the setting for new buildings for Philadelphia's major cultural institutions. The Free Library was housed in City Hall, the Franklin Institute was in the building at 7th and Chestnut that would later become the Atwater Kent Museum, and the Philadelphia Museum of Art was in Memorial Hall in Fairmount Park. Not only was it time to build new quarters for these institutions, but they'd grown sufficiently that monumental new edifices could be justified. In addition, other buildings went up: the County Courthouse (1938–41); Irwin T. Catherine's Board of Education building (1929), on the southwest corner of the Parkway and 21st Street; Charles Zeller Klauder's Boy Scouts headquarters (1929), on the southeast corner of the Parkway and 22nd Street; and Cret and Gréber's Rodin Museum (1927–29). Other buildings that were planned but never built were a new Episcopal Cathedral and a new home (happily not built) for the Pennsylvania Academy of the Fine Arts. It was hoped that in addition to these institutional buildings there would be some private residential development as well to help offset the costs of building the Parkway. While the mansions that were originally envisioned never materialized, several gargantuan and mostly hideous apartment houses did eventually go up.

The Parkway was never—and never will be—completed according to Cret and Gréber's vision. Almost all of the buildings along the Parkway dating from after its first wave of development are of uninspired design and poorly sited. The result is that the space of the Parkway sort of oozes every which way; there is no appropriate sense of enclosure. Of course, there are many fine things here, particularly at the northern and southern ends. But the Parkway was, alas, another botched opportunity.

There are sculptures all up and down the Parkway, most of them uninspiring, but the Civil War Soldiers Memorial, on the north side of the Parkway to the west of 20th Street, is worth a look. The sculptor was Hermon Atkins MacNeil and the date is 1921.

6   *Free Library*

6 FREE LIBRARY
Vine Street, between 19th and 20th Streets
1917–27, Horace Trumbauer

Modeled after Ange-Jacques Gabriel's twin palaces (the Ministère de la Marine and the Hôtel Crillon) from the 1760s and 1770s at the Place de la Concorde in Paris. Trumbauer and the man who was his chief designer at this time, Julian Francis Abele, were both Francophiles and products of the training at the École des Beaux-Arts, which was appropriate, given that the Parkway had been laid out by the Frenchmen Cret and Gréber along Beaux-Arts lines.

As has been pointed out many times by others, the unfortunate thing about the Free Library and its sister across 19th Street, the **County Courthouse** (1938–41, Morton Keast, based on a design from 1931 by John T. Windrim), is that 19th Street is even less the Rue Royale than the Parkway is the Champs-Elysées, and there is of course no Église de Ste. Marie-Madeleine to close the vista. Even so, Trumbauer's is a superb building, one of the great public libraries in America.

Before this building was constructed, the Free Library, which was founded in 1894, was housed in City Hall.

7 FRANKLIN INSTITUTE

20th Street and Benjamin Franklin Parkway
1932–34, John T. Windrim

The Franklin Institute, Philadelphia's museum of science and industry, is visited annually by 1.2 million people—twice the number that visit the Museum of Art. The Franklin Institute, both in its awed worship of the scientific and the technological and in its successful marketing of itself and its exhibitions, would have had Benjamin Franklin, in whose honor the institute was founded, beaming with pride.

The Institute dates from 1824 and was originally housed in the building that is now the Atwater Kent Museum at 15 South 7th Street. There are two main components: the Science Museum and the Fels Planetarium. (The Mandell Futures Center, which sounds more like a financial exchange than a "museum," is housed in a modern addition that, blessedly, does not front the Parkway. This addition was built in 1990 and designed by Geddes Brecher Qualls Cunningham, the same firm that designed the Police Administration Building on Race and 7th Streets in 1963.) Many of the exhibits are automated or interactive: they are carefully designed for the generations weaned on television and other forms of electronic entertainment. They do not require and do not reward protracted attention. Museologically, the Franklin Institute is considered populist and progressive.

The building itself is competent, with its well-proportioned Corinthian porticos facing the Parkway and 20th Street, but it is rather dull and fairly

7 *Franklin Institute*

cries for some sculptural embellishment. Inside, note the massive marble sculpture of a seated Franklin, by the good American sculptor James Earle Fraser (once Saint-Gaudens's assistant, and designer of the buffalo nickel).

8 RODIN MUSEUM

22nd Street and Benjamin Franklin Parkway
1927–29, Paul Philippe Cret and Jacques Gréber

The largest collection of sculptures by Auguste Rodin (1840–1917) to be found outside of France is housed in this elegant and beautiful structure created by the designers of the Parkway itself. It is Cret's only building on the Parkway. The approach has three distinct parts: the entry gate on the Parkway, which is modeled on the one from the château Rodin had reconstructed near his studio in Meudon; a formal garden, laid out by Gréber, containing a reflecting pool; and the museum building itself, a modest, austere, and temple-like structure. This building includes a pair of Doric columns *in antis* (corresponding to the tetrastyle, pedimented Doric portico of the gate structure); empty, pedimented niches in the flanking bays (answering the sculpture-filled arched openings of the gate); and a crowning balustrade (echoing that of the gate). It is an excellent example of that tendency in Cret's work that has been called "stripped classical." The recessed entry doors are adorned with the first bronze cast—commissioned by the motion-picture exhibitor Jules Mastbaum, whose collection forms the museum (and who died before the building was completed)—of Rodin's great, unfinished *The Gates of Hell.*

   The Gates of Hell was commissioned from Rodin by the French government in 1880 for a museum that was never built. Rodin puttered around with the work until his death in 1917, at which time the work was still unfinished. It is an extraordinarily complex work, with more than two hundred distinct images (that's about the same number to be found on the exterior of City Hall), and it became a kind of storehouse of Rodin's ideas. Note, for example, the figure of *The Thinker* at the top. *The Thinker* originated with this work and was originally conceived as a portrait of Dante contemplating his Inferno. (There is a cast of the full-size *The Thinker* facing the Parkway in front of the museum's gate.) Look at the way the figures flow all over the portal, how they jump out from it and dissolve back into it—you can sense the movement of the artist's hands modeling the clay. And you can certainly sense how much Rodin took off from the later work of Michelangelo.

8 *Rodin Museum*

9 WASHINGTON MONUMENT

Eakins Oval, Benjamin Franklin Parkway and 24th Street
1897, Rudolf Siemering

Yikes!

This was originally placed in Fairmount Park in 1897 but moved here in 1928 at the completion (more or less) of the Museum of Art. It's been beautifully restored in recent years.

This is some piece of work. The adjective that most immediately springs to mind is *Wagnerian,* which is not how we're accustomed to seeing George Washington honored. Compare, for example, the austere, elegant obelisk on the Mall in Washington. While there are different Washington Monuments in many cities, no two are less alike than Washington's and Philadelphia's.

Flanking the Washington Monument on Eakins Oval are twin fountains designed by the museum's architects, Horace Trumbauer, C. Clark Zantzinger, and Charles L. Borie Jr. One is dedicated to John Ericsson (1803–89), the engineer who designed the *Monitor.* The other is dedicated to Eli Kirk Price, about whom more anon. Suffice it for now to quote its inscription:

> In memory of Eli Kirk Price (1860–1933) whose wisdom and dedication were responsible for the development of the Parkway and the Museum.

9 *Washington Monument*

10 PARKWAY HOUSE

22nd Street and Pennsylvania Avenue
1952–53, Gabriel Roth and Elizabeth Fleisher

This gargantuan apartment complex was codesigned by the co-architect of the exuberant Art Deco WCAU Building of about twenty-five years earlier on Chestnut and 16th. Of Parkway House, the Foundation for Architecture's *Philadelphia Architecture* says, "It is an exceptionally fine design, with elements from both the Art Deco and International styles." John Lukacs, on the other hand, notes that in the early fifties the Museum of Art was "allowed to be overshadowed by two of the most monstrous apartment buildings ever to disfigure the skyline and the physiognomy of Philadelphia—or perhaps of any great city" (*Philadelphia: Patricians & Philistine, 1900–1950*, 1981, p. 319n). Still, with its views out over the Museum of Art and the Schuylkill, it is hard not to think that this is a pleasant place to live.

11 PHILADELPHIA MUSEUM OF ART

Benjamin Franklin Parkway and 26th Street
1916–28, Horace Trumbauer, C. Clark Zantzinger, and Charles L. Borie Jr.

The two most important names with which to reckon in the history of the museum are Eli Kirk Price and Sidney Fiske Kimball.

Price (1860–1933) was descended from an old Philadelphia Quaker family, though he himself was an Episcopalian as well as a civic improver and a commissioner of Fairmount Park. It was he who led the movement to create the Benjamin Franklin Parkway. Price felt that the Parkway, taking its origin at the monumental City Hall, required an appropriately monumental climax—a Parthenon on the Acropolis that was then a hill occupied by the reservoir of the Fairmount Waterworks.

THE EXTERIOR
The climax came in the form of the stupendous, the Brobdingnagian structure, the design of which was the product of divers hands. Though divvying up the credit has proved difficult, we do know that the basic form of the three temples facing in toward a common court is Trumbauer's. The central "temple" is Corinthian, the flanking "temples" Ionic. The museum, viewed from afar, as from trains pulling into or out of nearby 30th Street Station, is

11ₐ *Philadelphia Museum of Art*

majestic. Up close, it's a bit intimidating. Visitors to Philadelphia frequently walk the length of the Parkway from Center City to the museum, only to discover that they will need to expend that much energy again just to get in the front door of the place. That stair and courtyard are outrageously vast, however good they appear in the long view. That said, the building is a real piece of work.

It is, for a start, appropriately monumental in just the way Eli Kirk Price had hoped. It is fully up to the task of being the Parkway pendant to City Hall. Odd, when you think about it, very odd, indeed, that Philadelphia, the most modest of the nation's major cities, should have erected this pair, this Gargantua and Pantagruel, but there they are. And then, the view from the entry court, raised on the hill, back toward Center City is truly breathtaking. It is, after all, worth the climb.

No matter how overbearing the museum threatens to become, it is always humanized by the fineness of its details. With this museum, we are at the absolute pinnacle of Beaux-Arts craftsmanship in Philadelphia and in the United States. The building is superbly finished in golden Minnesota dolomite with blue tile roofs. Note the brilliant glazed terra-cotta sculptures of thirteen mythological figures in the pediment of the north "temple" (the one to the right as you face the museum); these sculptures, installed in 1933, are by Carl Paul Jennewein (1890–1978), who contributed to several of the notable works of architecture of the period, ranging, in New York, from the Woolworth Building of 1913 (he painted the lunette murals in the lobby) to Rockefeller Center's British Empire Building twenty years later (the *Industries of the British Commonwealth* reliefs). In between, he worked on the Philadelphia Museum of Art. Unfortunately, no complementary groups exist in the pediments of the other two "temples." Jennewein also designed the bronze doors of the elevators inside the building.

There *is* an entrance to the museum at ground level, so it is not, in fact, necessary to ascend the steps, though by not doing so you will not experience the architectural sequence quite properly. Also, the view from the museum's steps back toward Center City is one of the most celebrated views in Philadelphia. It is indeed impressive, though, alas, today one can see all too plainly how the skyline of the city has been unconscionably disfigured by the recent skyscrapers of the Market corridor.

The slightly loopy Lord Dunsany said he thought the Philadelphia Museum was the most beautiful building in the world.

There was already the Pennsylvania Museum and School of Industrial Arts in Memorial Hall. The Pennsylvania Museum was founded on the occasion of the Centennial Exposition and was modeled after London's South Kensington (now Victoria and Albert) Museum, which similarly had its origin in a world's fair (the Crystal Palace Exhibition, 1851) as an institution dedicated to the applied and decorative arts, not the fine arts. The old Pennsylvania Museum had been trudging along for half a century or so when Price got his Parkway built. And when Price conceived of a monumental edifice atop the hill, he had in mind the grand civic gesture of the thing, with little thought of its potential role as a great repository of fine art. To the latter end, Price called in an unlikely man to take charge of the new museum: Fiske Kimball (he never used his first name).

FISKE KIMBALL (1888–1955)

Kimball was born outside of Boston and trained at Harvard as an architectural historian. He was an authority on the architecture of Thomas Jefferson and was teaching at New York University when he was called to Philadelphia. He arrived in town in 1925. The new museum opened three years later. (Some works were exhibited in Memorial Hall, incidentally, until the 1950s.)

Kimball was not the sort one would expect to appeal to a Proper Philadelphian like Price, but then perhaps the Parkway and the new museum were themselves not the sorts of gestures one would expect from a Proper Philadelphian. Still, Kimball lacked refinement and forbearance; he was heavy, loud, vulgar, and brutish, though filled with drive and energy, qualities that seemed to commend him to those who were eager to get the new museum off to a flying start. And, as it turned out, he was the man for the times. As Nathaniel Burt put it, "Other museum directors were ruefully amazed that Fiske could get more out of patrons by insulting them than they could by years of discreet flattery" (we will leave the awkward syntax of that sentence alone). It was an age (we are still in it) in which would-be patrons of the arts wished to have their taste dictated to them, even by—especially by—bullies. And Fiske Kimball was a bully. He was the museum's director for thirty years, until 1955.

It is hard now to recall that when Kimball took over the museum, its collections, such as they were, were still exhibited in Memorial Hall. What's more, the collections were still largely confined to the applied and decorative arts. (The major exception to that was the Wilstach collection, comprising scads of Salon pictures.) But in Philadelphia—the "private city"— were three of the greatest private collections of paintings in the world: those of Peter Arrell Brown Widener (1834–1915), John Graver Johnson (1841–1917), and Albert Coombs Barnes (1872–1951). Kimball's grand plan was to secure the three collections for the new museum on the hill. If the museum could get all three collections, it would be an immediate rival to New York's Metropolitan.

THREE COLLECTORS

All three collectors were Philadelphians by upbringing and all attended the remarkable Central High School, the public high school for gifted boys of modest means. All three were, therefore, self-made men. They did not have the social pedigrees that had always meant so much in Philadelphia.

JOHN G. JOHNSON (1841–1917)

Johnson became the outstanding corporate lawyer of his generation in America. Though he was advisor to robber barons like Morgan and Frick (great collectors both!), he had a reputation for being scrupulously honest; he won in court not by being more devious but by being more brilliant than his opponents. He married a high-born Philadelphia woman, a Powel (she was descended from Samuel Powel, the first mayor of Philadelphia after the Revolution, and the occupant of the famous Powel house on South 3rd Street in Society Hill).

When Kimball took over the museum, Johnson had been dead for eight years, and his will was extraordinarily complicated. He left his collection to the City of Philadelphia with the apparent proviso that the collection be exhibited to the public in his house on South Broad Street (as well as in the house next door, which Johnson had purchased to contain the overflow of his collection). In fact, after several years of trying to figure out what to do, the city opened the Johnson house as a museum, albeit one where the conditions were unacceptable for the proper care and display of the art. This was the situation as it existed when Kimball came on the scene. The Johnson collection finally ended up in the Museum of Art, kept in its own wing, separate from the museum's other holdings. This required a certain amount of legal legerdemain, as did the later decision of the courts in 1989 to allow the museum finally to integrate the Johnson collection with the rest of the museum's holdings. But since Johnson's house on South Broad Street has been torn down, no one is asking too many questions.

Alas, it was the only of the three collections Kimball was able to wangle. He was unsuccessful in the cases of the Widener and Barnes collections.

11b *Philadelphia Museum of Art*

PETER A. B. WIDENER (1834–1915)

Peter A. B. Widener was a butcher (yes, a butcher) who made his initial fortune by selling mutton to the Union Army in the Civil War. He made his real money when he invested his mutton profits in urban traction. (Another Central High alum, Charles Tyson Yerkes, the model of Dreiser's *Financier,* was also an urban-traction magnate, first in Philadelphia, then in Chicago.) Johnson was Widener's lawyer. The Philadelphia society architect Horace Trumbauer, one of the designers of the new museum, was commissioned by Widener to design his palatial house, Lynnewood Hall, in the newly developed (in part by Widener) upper-class suburb of Elkins Park (known today among architecture people not as the site of Lynnewood Hall but of a slightly goofy-looking synagogue designed by Frank Lloyd Wright). (One of Widener's sons, George, and grandson, Harry Elkins Widener, the latter a bibliophile, perished on the *Titanic* in 1912. Harry's parents built the Widener Library, designed by Trumbauer, at Harvard, in their son's memory. Trumbauer also designed the Widener Building in Center City.) But Peter A. B. Widener's son Joseph, to whom the great collection passed, chose not to make a gift of it to the Philadelphia Museum, but left it to the new National Gallery of Art in Washington. There are perhaps many reasons why Joseph Widener did this, but a major reason had to do with his resentment at being snubbed by Philadelphia society—an old story, though such acceptance by society mattered not at all to men of stronger character, such as Johnson. (Johnson, though not highborn, was pretty readily accepted by Philadelphia society, in part because of his wife, but mostly because he was society's lawyer. Still, he cared little if at all for society and kept to himself, his family, his collection, his work, and a small circle of like-minded friends, including the elder Widener.)

ALBERT C. BARNES (1872–1951)

Albert C. Barnes was the son of a butcher who once worked with Peter A. B. Widener. (How unlikely is *that*?) After Central High, Barnes was graduated from Penn's medical school, and, following a period of desultory study and travel in Europe, invented the patent salve Argyrol, which yielded Barnes an immense fortune. One of Barnes's Central High chums was the fine American painter William Glackens, who advised Barnes on his early purchases of paintings. But Barnes, as fierce an autodidact as there ever was, soon became not merely an expert but a highly innovative thinker and writer on art and aesthetics. Barnes befriended John Dewey, who once basically said that he had never known a smarter man than Barnes. Dewey's *Art as Experience* (1934) was dedicated to Dr. Barnes.

Barnes himself wrote several important books on art, demonstrating an encyclopedic command of Western painting. But the collection, though quite broad, is most renowned for its unparalleled stores of modern French paintings by, among others, Monet, Renoir, Cézanne, Pissarro, Van Gogh, and, especially, Matisse. The house that Barnes built, designed by Paul Philippe Cret in suburban Merion in 1925 to contain the collection is itself a work of art, enhanced by a mural Matisse painted expressly for the house (an indication of his genuine respect for Barnes). Barnes established his collection as a teaching tool. His notions of aesthetics were strongly informed by the American philosophy of Dewey, William James, and Santayana, and Barnes's goal was to apply the philosophical and psychological insights of these thinkers to a formal course of education centered around the study of great paintings. To this end he established the Barnes Foundation, a private educational institution and not a public museum.

The upshot was that Barnes was largely uninterested in giving his collection to Kimball's museum. Barnes was even reluctant to lend paintings, since that would deprive the Foundation of their use.

For reasons that are too complex to go into here, Barnes became notoriously irascible as the years went by. There was no way that Barnes and Kimball were ever going to make a go of it. Barnes, though he was undoubtedly Kimball's intellectual superior, was if anything even more volatile and at times even more vulgar than was Kimball.

Legal legerdemain: a specialty, it seems, in Philadelphia, for, as in the case of the Johnson collection, the Barnes Foundation was forced by the courts to open itself to the public following Barnes's death. From the start this was legally very dubious. Today the foundation has devolved, in accordance with Barnes's will, to Lincoln University, which has seen fit to flout entirely Dr. Barnes's wishes. It now not only operates the foundation as a full-fledged museum, but it has also begun lending and touring its paintings and allowing them to be reproduced, as Dr. Barnes squirms from beyond.

THE INTERIOR

Inside the museum, the Great Hall, with its Ionic order, is dominated by Augustus Saint-Gaudens's *Diana,* which had stood atop Stanford White's Madison Square Garden (demolished 1925) in New York. (The *Diana* in the American Wing of the Metropolitan in New York is a smaller copy; the original is the one here.) It is probably the least interesting thing that great

11c   *Philadelphia Museum of Art*

sculptor ever designed. The mobile entitled *Ghost* is by Alexander Calder, the son of Alexander Stirling Calder and grandson of Alexander Milne Calder. Alexander Milne Calder's statue of William Penn atop City Hall faces up the Parkway toward Alexander Stirling Calder's Swann Memorial Fountain at Logan Circle, and past that to the Museum of Art with its mobile by the third Alexander Calder. With the Peales, the Calders, and the Wyeths (not to mention the Hesseliuses and the Lambdins), Philadelphia has been home not only to outstanding artists but to whole families of outstanding artists.

On the walls enclosing the Great Hall are the thirteen spectacular tapestries from the Palazzo Barberini in Rome. (The palazzo, the home of Cardinal Francesco Barberini, was designed by Carlo Maderna, Gianlorenzo Bernini, and Francesco Borromini and is one of the greatest works of seventeenth-century architecture in Rome.) The tapestries, depicting events in the life of the emperor Constantine, were woven to designs by Peter Paul Rubens (1577–1640) and Pietro da Cortona (1596–1669). (The museum also has Rubens's *Prometheus Bound*.)

A WALK THROUGH TIME

Fiske Kimball conceived of the second floor as a "walk through time," in which paintings and sculptures would be displayed with decorative arts and even whole architectural interiors of their periods. The result is that the PMA has what is probably the most lavish collection of "period rooms" to be found in any American museum. The sheer range of these installations is impressive, as is the extent to which whole rooms, and sometimes entire structures, made transoceanic journeys from Europe and Asia to become ensconced in Philadelphia. A remarkable example is the thirteenth-century cloister from the abbey of Saint-Genis-des-Fontaines, within which is placed a fountain from the twelfth-century monastery of Saint-Michel-de-Cuxa. One major donor of medieval antiquities and consultant in medieval installations was the fine American sculptor George Grey Barnard, part of whose collection also went to New York's Metropolitan Museum and formed the basis of the Cloisters in the Rockefellers' Fort Tryon Park in Upper Manhattan. In Philadelphia, Barnard consulted on the installation of the portal from the twelfth-century abbey church of Saint-Laurent and donated many items. Among them were a capital from the cloister of the twelfth-century monastery of Saint-Rémi, a recumbent knight figure from a thirteenth-century Norman tomb sculpture, an amazing Flemish fifteenth-century painted oak Crucifixion group, and an even more amazing Flemish sixteenth-century carved and painted wood altarpiece showing scenes of Christ's Passion (the altarpiece was reunited after centuries with the choir

screen from the chapel, at the château of Pagny, for which the altarpiece was originally made!).

A modern "period room" of great architectural interest is the drawing room from Robert Adam's Lansdowne House, London, from the 1760s. The dining room from this same house can be seen in New York's Metropolitan Museum of Art. For an example of a great Philadelphia house designed in the Adam style, be sure to visit the Woodlands (*see* chapter ten).

THE JOHNSON COLLECTION

Whatever you do, don't miss Jan Van Eyck's *Saint Francis Receiving the Stigmata* (1438–40)—it's the kind of painting people travel from across the world to see. It was part of the John G. Johnson collection.

Other masterpieces from the Johnson Collection include several other quattrocento works, among them the magical *Saint Nicholas of Tolentino Saving a Ship* by the great Sienese Giovanni di Paolo, dated 1457; Rogier van der Weyden's magnificent *The Crucifixion, with the Virgin and Saint John the Evangelist Mourning*, from the 1460s (considered by some the museum's greatest painting); and the elegantly elongated *Enthroned Virgin and Child, with Angels*, from the 1490s, by the Flemish Gerard David. But the Johnson Collection includes some superior modern paintings, as well: see Camille Pissarro's *The Effect of Fog*, 1888—it's one of his best.

More popular among the masses of today's museumgoers, alas, are the works from the Louise and Walter Arensberg Collection, including what may be the museum's best-known holding: Marcel Duchamp's *Nude Descending a Staircase*. It can, in my opinion, safely be missed. On the other hand, the Arensbergs supplied a superlative collection of sculptures by Constantin Brancusi—the best such collection, it is alleged, outside of Paris. It makes for an interesting tour in conjunction with the Rodin Museum down the Parkway.

THOMAS EAKINS (1844–1916)

The PMA's roots in the old Pennsylvania Museum and School of Industrial Arts, that would-be South Kensington Museum, are evident in the marvelous collections of decorative arts and furniture, including choice and thrilling examples of old Philadelphia furniture and silver and much in the way of Shaker crafts. Fine Philadelphia artists, from Charles Willson Peale to Thomas Eakins to Horace Pippin, the African American painter championed by Dr. Barnes, are amply represented here. Eakins's *William Rush Carving His Allegorical*

Figure of the Schuylkill River (1877) is not only a fine painting, it is one artist's tribute to one of his illustrious predecessors as a teacher at the renowned Pennsylvania Academy of the Fine Arts. Rush's sculptures (he did two on the same theme) that he is shown working on in the Eakins painting are, by the way, kept in the museum, in the first floor of the "south temple," where the Eakins painting is also to be found. Copies of Rush's sculptures have been placed at their original location at the Fairmount Waterworks behind the museum, so that the originals could be properly maintained in the museum's indoor, climate-controlled environment. This is standard practice in the curatorial care of public sculptures throughout Europe, though it has met with some resistance in the U.S. (as in New York's Metropolitan's unsuccessful attempt to bring indoors Saint-Gaudens's great Admiral Farragut Monument, and to place a copy in its original location in Madison Square).

HOWARD ROBERTS (1843–1900)
The sculptural equivalent of Eakins's *Gross Clinic* might be Augustus Saint-Gaudens's Admiral Farragut Monument in New York's Madison Square. Or it might be Howard Roberts's *La Première Pose* (1873–76) in the Philadelphia Museum of Art. Few people today think of Howard Roberts, and those who do might dismiss him, as so many excellent nineteenth-century artists are dismissed, as "academic." That would be wrong. Though Roberts—like Eakins, Alexander Stirling Calder, Horace Trumbauer, Julian Francis Abele, Edgar Seeler, and Paul Cret—was trained at the École des Beaux-Arts, his works, like those of the best of the Beaux-Arts-trained artists, incorporate the lessons of the academics but go beyond them, too, to a striking and vitalizing modernity. The special quality that *La Première Pose* possesses is sometimes referred to by historians by some phrase like "lively surface modeling." But, it is more a way of locating the ideal in the real, the real—or the natural—in the ideal. It is a way of making art that is more lifelike than life itself. What Roberts has done is to take the young woman posing nude before the life class, and to express the drama of her situation, to transform it into a genre scene—it is indicated as well in the title of the work. Eakins shows us an unposed Dr. Gross at work in his surgical clinic; Roberts shows us a model at work—posing—in the studio. And just as Eakins's Dr. Gross gives off certain qualities of intelligence, composure, and so on, so, too, does Roberts's young woman give off certain qualities—demureness, beauty, self-consciousness. And in her entwined limbs and contorted torso—Beaux-Arts sculptors loved to show off their virtuoso skills of modeling—there is a spark of sensuousness that is, indeed, more lifelike than life itself.

Roberts was a native Philadelphian who studied under the redoubtable Joseph Alexis Bailly at the Pennsylvania Academy of the Fine Arts before going off to the École des Beaux-Arts in 1866, the same year as his friend Eakins. Roberts and Eakins studied in the same sculptural atelier, that of Alexandre Dumont. Probably the most widely seen of Roberts's works is his statue of Robert Fulton, from 1883, in the rotunda of the Capitol in Washington.

CHAPTER 12

Woodford

Strawberry Mansion

Mount Pleasant Rd.

State Rd.

N. Concourse Street

S. Concourse Street

Parkside Ave.

Memorial Hall

Belmont Ave.

Schuylkill River

Kelly Drive

33rd St.

Sedgely Dr.

Pennsylvania Street

Girard Ave.

West River Dr.

Kelly Drive

Fairmount Ave.

Philadelphia Museum of Art

1. Law, Prosperity, and Power
2. Catholic Total Abstinence Union Fountain
3. Smith Memorial Arch
4. Major General George Gordon Meade
5. Cedar Grove
6. Sweetbriar
7. Letitia Street House
8. Ulysses S. Grant Monument
9. Playing Angels
10. Cowboy
11. Ellen Phillips Samuel Memorial
12. James A. Garfield Monument
13. The Pilgrim
14. Lemon Hill
15. Boat House Row
16. Abraham Lincoln
17. William M. Reilly Memorial
18. Joan of Arc

NORTH BY NORTHWEST

1 *Fidelity Mutual Life Building*

CHAPTER 12

NORTH BY NORTHWEST

This chapter covers the area north and northwest from the Benjamin Franklin Parkway. It takes in the southernmost part of North Philadelphia, just to the north of the Philadelphia Museum of Art (Fairmount Avenue, Pennsylvania Avenue, Girard Avenue); vast and amorphous Fairmount Park; and, on the west side of the Wissahickon Valley and the east side of the Schuylkill River, the community of Manayunk. Greater distances are covered here than in any other chapter of the book.

1 FIDELITY MUTUAL LIFE BUILDING

Pennsylvania and Fairmount Avenues
1925–26, Zantzinger, Borie & Medary
Renovated in 1983, Environmental Design Corp. and David N. Beck

A pair of bravura Beaux-Arts Deco entrances are recessed behind enormous arches that are flanked by what read like pilasters but are actually extensions of the cornice line of the main block of the building; these lines dissolve around the voussoirs into quasi-Michelangesque figure sculptures by Lee Lawrie (1887–1963), who produced scads of naturalistic carvings all over the building. It's one of the best examples you'll ever see of monumental streamlined Beaux-Arts. Githens & Keally's Brooklyn Public Library in New York is in the same vein.

2 EASTERN STATE PENITENTIARY

21st Street and Fairmount Avenue
1823–36, John Haviland

It was called Cherry Hill Penitentiary when Tocqueville and Beaumont came to see it. Haviland's medieval fortress must have looked terrifying to its prospective inmates, though today we prize its picturesque profile (then head to Jack's Firehouse for repast). Within the crenelated stone walls with their lancet slits, there are seven "spokes" radiating from a central surveillance core. The whole thing is based on the notion, advocated by the Quakers and called the "Pennsylvania system," of solitary confinement: the prisoner, in his eight-by-ten-foot cell supplied with a Bible as his only reading matter, would use his solitude and quiet to search his soul and become a better person. But it turned out that prisoners, rather than searching their souls, shut down and went bonkers. Today solitary confinement is considered the most punitive of penological practices. By century's end the "Pennsylvania system" had succumbed not to its harsh criticisms but to overcrowding and the need to make more efficient use of prison space. Eastern State was put out of commission in 1970. Occasional tours are offered.

John Haviland (1792–1852) ranks with Strickland and Walter among Philadelphia's masters of the Greek Revival. Others of his works in that vein include St. George's Greek Orthodox Cathedral (originally St. Andrew's Episcopal Church, where Haviland was a parishioner), built in 1822 at 8th and Spruce; the Pennsylvania Institution for the Deaf and Dumb (now the University of the Arts), built in 1824–26 at Broad and Pine; and the old Franklin Institute (now the Atwater Kent Museum), built in 1825 on 7th between Chestnut and Market. His Eastern State Penitentiary apparently had a tremendous influence on prison design around the world, serving at least in part as a model for prisons in London (Pentonville), Paris, Berlin, Madrid, Milan, Copenhagen, Dublin, and even Beijing—an early instance of an American building influencing architects abroad.

2   *Eastern State Penitentiary*

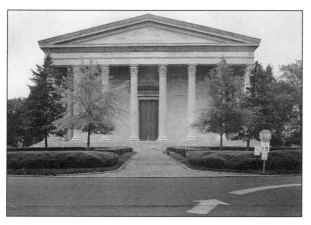

3   Founders' Hall, Girard College

3 FOUNDERS' HALL, GIRARD COLLEGE

Girard and Corinthian Avenues
1833–47, Thomas Ustick Walter

Dickens in 1842:

> Near the city is a most splendid unfinished marble structure for the Girard
> College, founded by a deceased gentleman of that name and of enormous
> wealth, which, if completed according to the original design, will be per-
> haps the richest edifice of modern times.

Well, it was finished according to the original design, five years after Dickens's
American Notes was published. Note that Dickens said "perhaps the richest
edifice of modern times." *Not* the richest edifice of modern times *in America.*
That was an exaggeration, but a telling one. One of America's seminal Greek
Revival buildings is a pedimented Corinthian peristyle built of Chester
County marble. Walter was only twenty-nine when he designed it under
the heavy influence of Nicholas Biddle, one of the college's trustees, who
had visited Greece in 1806 and was probably one of the few Americans of
his time with a firsthand knowledge of Greek architecture. The main lines
of the building were apparently dictated by Biddle; Walter was far too good
an architect to create something so bizarrely unfunctional.

It is hard not to think that besides the Greek temples themselves another possible inspiration here was the Église de Ste. Marie-Madeleine, built
in Paris from 1806 to 1842, thus one of the major buildings in the world at
the time that Founders' Hall was designed and constructed. Ste. Marie-
Madeleine has a main façade of eight Corinthian columns and a crowning

triangular pediment. (Founders' Hall, of course, does not contain the Parisian church's high Roman dome.) The connection between these two structures is also suggested by the circumstance that Stephen Girard, the founder of Girard College, was, of course, a Frenchman. And Nicholas Biddle was a Francophile as well as a Grecophile. I think Founders' Hall would be ideally sited bestride 19th Street east of the Benjamin Franklin Parkway, framed by Trumbauer's Free Library and Windrim's and Keast's County Courthouse, thus completing Philadelphia's Place de la Concorde.

NICHOLAS BIDDLE (1786–1844)

Nicholas Biddle is a fascinating figure and probably the most interesting and accomplished of the many well-known Philadelphians to bear that surname. In the words of E. Digby Baltzell, Biddle "was a scholar, litterateur, statesman, lawyer, architect, agricultural specialist, and farmer, as well as a charming and witty leader in society." Sidney Fisher speculated that had Biddle been born a Bostonian rather than a Philadelphian, he might have achieved lasting fame as a man of letters. In Philadelphia, however, his lasting fame—or infamy—was achieved as a banker. Biddle was only eighteen when, as Secretary of Legation under James Monroe in France, he helped to negotiate the Louisiana Purchase. A Jeffersonian and an anti-Federalist, like his mentor Monroe, Biddle was an early supporter of Andrew Jackson. This is what makes Biddle's subsequent career at the Bank of the United States so ironic, for it was under Biddle that the bank became the object of populist resentment, leading to President Jackson's refusal to renew the bank's charter in 1836. With the ensuing national financial collapse, Biddle became public enemy number one, held responsible for the nation's first major depression. At this time, Biddle bowed out of public life and retired to his country house, Andalusia, an eighteenth-century house in Bucks County that Biddle had Walter remodel in 1834–36. Biddle lived out the last eleven years of his life at Andalusia.

---

4 FAIRMOUNT PARK

Fairmount Park contains some 3,000 to 4,000 acres running north from Center City up both banks of the Schuylkill, thence up Wissahickon Creek for several miles, through Chestnut Hill to the city line at Northwestern Avenue and, in fact, beyond into Montgomery County. It is said to be the largest city park in the United States. Oddly, no two sources one consults seem to agree on the park's total acreage nor even on its precise limits. It is a huge amorphous verdancy.

The idea of the park seems to have emerged in the 1850s, around the time New York started to build its Central Park. Philadelphia already had the landscaped grounds of the Waterworks, which were an immensely popular promenade, and Laurel Hill Cemetery, which, like so many other cemeteries, was developed before the big park-building boom and served as much as a public pleasure ground as it did a place for burial of the dead. The city acquired the 45-acre Lemon Hill estate adjacent to the Waterworks in 1844. But the park was not officially created by an act of the state legislature until 1867, when the Fairmount Park Commission was formed. If any one person is to receive the most credit for the eventual shape the park took, it would probably be the Munich-born engineer Hermann J. Schwarzmann, who we know today as the architect of Memorial Hall. Schwarzmann, who worked as an engineer for the Park Commission, got the job to design the principal buildings for the Centennial Exposition of 1876, the last remaining of which is Memorial Hall. For the fairgrounds, Schwarzmann laid out the roads in the park west of the Schuylkill. But in 1872, the year before he was hired to design the fair's buildings, his plan for the east park had been accepted by the Commission over a plan by Frederick Law Olmsted and Calvert Vaux, who had recently designed New York's Central Park and Prospect Park.

The Benjamin Franklin Parkway, completed in the 1930s, insinuated the park into the heart of Center City. But beginning in 1953, at a time

4a   *Fairmount Park*

4b   *Boathouse Row*

when so much, for good and ill, was being changed in the physical fabric of the city, Fairmount Park received a devastating blow from which it will never recover: the Schuylkill Expressway was cut along the west bank of the river. When you drive along the expressway, the views are splendid. But since when was a city park meant to be viewed from a car, especially at expressway speed? It was a violation of the physical integrity of the city that was not matched until the 1980s, when Willard Rouse imperiously rejected the "gentlemen's agreement" regarding building heights.

The Schuylkill River, expressway or no, is a fine rowing river. In the second half of the nineteenth century various rowing clubs formed the famous Boathouse Row (consising of the Victorian buildings now outlined at night in electric lights), creating one of Philadelphians' favorite images of their city. By the way, among the several boathouses is the **Undine Barge Club** at 13 Boathouse Row. Built in 1882, it was designed by Frank Furness. The local glamour of Boathouse Row is indicated by the name of the bar in the fashionable Rittenhouse Hotel: the Boathouse Row Bar. (The same hotel also has a Cassatt Lounge.)

EIGHTEENTH-CENTURY HOUSES IN FAIRMOUNT PARK

Within the park are nine eighteenth-century houses, all but one of which are open to the public. Five are east of the Schuylkill. From south to north, they are as follows:

LEMON HILL
Lemon Hill Drive, just north of Boathouse Row
1799

Henry Pratt built Lemon Hill on 140 acres that he bought from the 300-acre estate of the financially troubled Robert Morris. (Morris had grown lemon trees on his grounds, hence the estate's name.) The exterior walls are stucco with granite trim. The oval rooms, one of which is boldly articulated on the garden façade of the house, are a Federal element, as are the rich fanlight and sidelights of the front entrance. But the large Palladian window stuck over the front entrance is a holdover from an earlier Georgian style.

The house and forty-five acres of the grounds were purchased by the city in 1844 in order to ensure an undeveloped buffer area around the Waterworks. Thus, Lemon Hill's grounds became the very first part of the vast Fairmount Park.

The house is now maintained by the Colonial Dames. Its last residential occupant was Fiske Kimball, when he was director of the Philadelphia Museum of Art.

MOUNT PLEASANT
(See pages 236–237.)

WOODFORD
Strawberry Drive, near the foot of Strawberry Mansion Bridge
1756, 1772

Woodford was the home of David Franks, George III's customs controller in Philadelphia. Franks's daughter Rebecca was among the belles fêted at the *Meschianza.* She then married General Sir Henry Johnson and lived out her days in Bath (the city in England, not the neighborhood in Philadelphia). Because of his Loyalism, Franks's house was confiscated after the Revolution. He added the second story in 1772, including the big Palladian window.

STRAWBERRY MANSION
Strawberry Drive, just north of Woodford
1797, with some 19th-century additions

Strawberry is the largest if not the fanciest house in the park. The central section is the original house from 1797, while the wings date from 1825.

4c   *Fairmount Park,
Lemon Hill*

The name is from the mid-nineteenth century. It was one of the few non-Loyalist houses in the vicinity: as the home of Charles Thomson (1729–1824), long-tenured secretary to the Continental Congress, and a man described as the "Sam Adams of Philadelphia," the house was ordered burned by General Sir William Howe.

Four are west of the Schuylkill, from south to north, and are as follows:

SOLITUDE
On the grounds of the Philadelphia Zoo (see pages 239–240).

LETITIA STREET HOUSE
Lansdowne Drive, near West Girard Avenue
1713–15

This was originally a row house on the no longer existent Letitia Street, which was between Front and Second Streets in Old City. It was moved to the park in 1883 and is said to be the oldest surviving brick house in America. It is not, unfortunately, open for tours.

It once was open for tours. Poor Letitia Street House: for the longest time people believed that this house had been bought by William Penn who gave it to his daughter. It was an attraction of the city even before it was moved to the park, where it operated as a museum until . . . it was determined that the house had nothing whatever to do with the Penn family. Quietly, in 1965, the house ceased to admit tourists. Today it is the local headquarters of Wildlife Preservation Trust International.

Anyway, it's larger and handsomer than the Betsy Ross house.

SWEETBRIAR
Lansdowne Drive, halfway between the Zoo and Cedar Grove
1797

Sweetbriar was built by Samuel Breck (1771–1862). Here, Breck hosted the Marquis de Lafayette (who seems to have been hosted in every house in Philadelphia) and Charles-Maurice de Talleyrand-Périgord—the French in Philadelphia. The house has windows overlooking the Waterworks, which were completed in 1815. Breck lived here until 1838, so he enjoyed that splendid view for twenty-three years.

CEDAR GROVE
Lansdowne Drive, near Black Road, just east of Memorial Hall
1748, 1752

This gambrel-roofed fieldstone farmhouse originally stood in the Northern Liberties. It was dismantled, moved, and re-erected in the park in 1927. Five generations of Morrises lived in the house.

4d   *Fairmount Park, Sweetbriar*

4e   *Fairmount Park, Cedar Grove*

SCULPTURES IN FAIRMOUNT PARK

The Fairmount Park Art Association, founded in 1872, has long been re-nowned for its sponsorship of sculpture—whether good, bad, or ugly. Here's a brief rundown, the good and the great duly noted.

East of the Schuylkill, south to north:

JOAN OF ARC
Kelly Drive at 25th Street
1890, Emmanuel Frémiet

This gilded bronze equestrian Saint Joan is one of three castings of the work Frémiet created for the Place des Pyramides in Paris. Frémiet was a leading French academic sculptor and an influential instructor at the École des Beaux-Arts.

WILLIAM M. REILLY MEMORIAL
Directly behind the Museum of Art

These Revolutionary War heroes in bronze are here courtesy of the trust established in 1890 by General William M. Reilly of the Pennsylvania National Guard. Reilly wanted the statues placed near Independence Hall. One wonders if the general, in 1890, had any idea that the statues might not look like statues from around 1890, that, in other words, when the statues actually got erected it would be during a period of uncertainty and awkwardness in American public sculpture.

- *General Richard Montgomery*, 1946, J. Wallace Kelly. This was the first of the Reilly statues to go up. Kelly (1894–1976) was responsible for some of the Art Deco ornamentation of Ralph Bencker's N. W. Ayer Building (1929) at Washington Square, for the limestone statue of *Unskilled Labor* (1933–36) on the east terrace of the Philadelphia Museum of Art, and for contributions to the Ellen Phillips Samuel Memorial (*see* page 228).

- *General Casimir Pulaski,* 1947, Sidney Waugh. The sculptor Waugh (1904–63) was himself a highly decorated veteran of World War II.

- *General Friedrich von Steuben,* 1947, Warren Wheelock. The sculptor Wheelock (1880–1960) was a veteran of the Spanish-American War.

- *Marquis de Lafayette,* 1947, Raoul Josset. The sculptor Josset (1899–1957) was known for his contributions to the Century of Progress Exposition in Chicago in 1933.

- *John Paul Jones,* 1957, Walker Hancock. Hancock (1901–99) did the colossal *Pennsylvania Railroad World War II Memorial* (1952) in the concourse of 30th Street Station. He was the chairman of the sculpture department at the Pennsylvania Academy of the Fine Arts. Hancock created the bust of President Bush that is in the Capitol in Washington.

- *General Nathanael Greene,* 1960, Lewis Iselin Jr. Iselin (1913–) created what for 1960 would be considered a real *retardataire*.

ABRAHAM LINCOLN
Kelly Drive at Sedgely Drive
1871, Randolph Rogers

This is an affecting bronze seated Lincoln by one of the important American Neoclassical sculptors. A friend of Hawthorne, Rogers (1825–92) apparently was a model for Kenyon in *The Marble Faun* (1860). When Rogers's seated figure of William Henry Seward was unveiled in New York's Madison Square in 1876, some people charged that the sculptor had used the same body as in his seated Lincoln here in Fairmount Park but placed a different head on the figure. This allegation was repeated as fact for years—even today you will hear New York tour guides retail this story. It is false, and it is a sad thing that it is all most people know of Randolph Rogers.

THE PILGRIM
Kelly Drive at Lemon Hill Drive
1904, Augustus Saint-Gaudens

The bronze pilgrim is a rare costume piece by America's greatest sculptor. If it seems late in his career for this sort of thing, that's because this is a slightly modified version of his much earlier *The Puritan* from 1883 to 1886 in Springfield, Massachusetts. *The Pilgrim* moved to its present site in 1920 from the south plaza of City Hall. Why?

ELLEN PHILLIPS SAMUEL MEMORIAL
Kelly Drive, south of the Girard Avenue Bridge

This is a colossal work composed of three terraces featuring numerous pieces of sculpture commissioned by Phillips, a local philanthropist with an interest in promoting the art of sculpture by sponsoring international exhibitions. Many of the pieces from those exhibitions migrated to this hodgepodge, which is a textbook survey of American mainstream sculpture in its awkward transitional phase from Beaux-Arts to modernist. Who knows if these artists were any good. Sometimes the "spirit of the times" crushes genuine talents at the same time it elevates mediocrities.

SOUTH TERRACE
Everything here is limestone.

• *The Birth of a Nation,* 1942, Henry Kreis. The German Kreis (1899–1963) was an assistant to Paul Manship and Carl Paul Jennewein.

• *The Puritan and the Quaker,* 1942, Harry Rosin. Rosin (1897–1973) was a native Philadelphian who worked for the great Samuel Yellin in his Arch Street studio and then studied under Charles Grafly at the Pennsylvania Academy of the Fine Arts, where Rosin taught for over thirty years. He is known for his statue of Connie Mack from 1957 that stood in front of the old Shibe Park and was moved to its present location in front of Veterans Stadium in 1972.

• *The Revolutionary Soldier and the Statesman,* 1943, Erwin Frey. Frey (1892–1967) was an assistant to Augustus Saint-Gaudens and to Herbert Adams.

• *Settling of the Seaboard,* 1942, Wheeler Williams.

CENTRAL TERRACE
These sculptures are bronze or limestone as noted.

• *Spanning the Continent,* 1937, Robert Laurent, bronze. The French-born Laurent (1890–1970) taught at New York's Art Students League and was among the earliest abstract sculptors. This was the first work installed in the Samuel Memorial.

• *The Miner,* 1938, John B. Flannagan, limestone. Flannagan (1895–1942) is often mentioned along with Laurent and William Zorach. Flannagan was an early exponent of the direct carving of biomorphic forms from rough stone.

• *The Ploughman,* 1938, J. Wallace Kelly, limestone. Kelly (1894–1976) did a lot of work in Philadelphia. See the entry in this chapter for his statue of General Richard Montgomery under William M. Reilly Memorial.

• *The Spirit of the Enterprise,* 1950–60, Jacques Lipchitz, bronze. Fourteen feet long and ten feet high.

• *The Slave,* 1940, Helene Sardeau, limestone. Sardeau (1899–1968) was married to the painter George Biddle, of the distinguished Philadelphia clan, and the man who gave his friend Franklin Delano Roosevelt the idea for the WPA art program, which Biddle then administered.

4f *Fairmount Park, Ellen Phillips Samuel Memorial: The Ploughman*

• *The Immigrant*, 1940, Heinz Warneke, limestone. Warneke (1895–1983), though versatile, was known as an animalier, as in his granite *Cow Elephant and Calf* (1962) near the main entrance to the Philadelphia Zoo.

• *Welcoming to Freedom*, 1939, Maurice Sterne, bronze. Maurice Sterne (1878–1957) attended the National Academy of Design in New York in the 1890s, where he studied under Thomas Eakins. A painter as well as a sculptor, he was, in 1933, the first American artist in any medium to be given a one-man show at the Museum of Modern Art. (Who remembers this?)

NORTH TERRACE
Everything here is granite, except as noted.

• *The Laborer*, 1958, Ahron Ben-Shmuel. Ben-Shmuel (1903–) did the granite *Boxers* (1937) on the east terrace of the Philadelphia Museum of Art.

• *The Poet*, 1954, José de Creeft. This is the sculptor who created the *Alice in Wonderland* group in New York's Central Park in 1959.

• *The Preacher*, 1952, Waldemar Raemisch. Raemisch (1888–1955) did the bronzes *The Great Mother* and *The Great Doctor* at Carroll, Grisdale & Van Alen's Youth Study Center (1953), a once admired modernist building at the southwest corner of 20th Street and Pennsylvania Avenue.

• *The Scientist*, 1955, Khoren der Harootian.

• *Eye and Hand*, 1959, J. Wallace Kelly. See the entry in this chapter on Kelly's statue of General Richard Montgomery under William M. Reilly Memorial (*see* pages 226–27).

JAMES A. GARFIELD MONUMENT
Kelly Drive, south of the Girard Avenue Bridge, near the Samuel Memorial
1895, Augustus Saint-Gaudens

The bronze bust of the Ohioan who was America's twentieth president (elected 1880, assassinated 1881) sits on a granite pedestal designed by Saint-Gaudens with his friend Stanford White. The twenty-foot-high monument

4g   *Fairmount Park,*
James A. Garfield Monument

is a good example of its type, the portrait bust in an elaborate architectural setting.

With this, *The Pilgrim,* and *Diana,* Philadelphia is not without its works by Saint-Gaudens, America's greatest sculptor. But unlike Boston or New York, Philadelphia contains none of the sculptor's masterpieces, and it is a shame.

COWBOY
Kelly Drive, north of the Girard Avenue Bridge
1908, Frederic Remington

Remington (1861–1909) lived in the West from 1880 to 1886, when he returned to New York and became a famous western illustrator. This sculpture, which is not at all bad, is his only large bronze and was created a year before his death.

ULYSSES S. GRANT MONUMENT
Kelly Drive at Fountain Green Drive
1897, Daniel Chester French and Edward Clark Potter

We may infer that Potter (1857–1923), an animalier of distinction and creator of the lions in front of the New York Public Library, did the general's horse, while French (1850–1931), one of the great American sculptors of all time, did the human figure. (Potter had been French's student.) This is a superb equestrian monument in bronze.

Next door to the Grant Monument are:

PLAYING ANGELS
Kelly Drive at Fountain Green Drive
1950, Carl Milles

Milles (1875–1955), purveyor of Cranbrook chic, created five angels for Stockholm in his native country in 1950, and casts of three of them were installed here in 1972. The bronze angels gambol over the park on high concrete columns, and some sense of proportion and movement that is characteristic of Milles's works makes *Playing Angels* a surprising success in its Philadelphia setting.

West of the Schuylkill, south to north:

SMITH MEMORIAL ARCH
North Concourse Drive near Memorial Hall
1897–1912

This sculptural extravaganza was commissioned by the local industrialist Richard Smith as a memorial to the Pennsylvanian heroes of the Civil War. The overall design was by James Hamilton Windrim.

Two slightly concave triumphal arches flank North Concourse Drive, where the entrance to the grounds of the Centennial Exposition was located, with high Doric columns. One column is topped by a statue of Major General John Fulton Reynolds by Charles Grafly (1862–1929) and the other by a statue of Major General George Gordon Meade by Daniel Chester French (1850–1931). (You might want to compare these with John Rogers's statue of Reynolds at City Hall and with Alexander Milne Calder's statue of Meade elsewhere in Fairmount Park.)

On the outer piers of the arches are equestrian figures of Major General Winfield Scott Hancock by the great John Quincy Adams Ward (1830–1910) and of Major General George Brinton McClellan by Edward Clark Potter (1857–1923).

The busts along the bases of the arches include the following: *Admiral*

David Dixon Porter by Charles Grafly; *Major General John Hartranft* by Alexander Stirling Calder (1870–1945); *Admiral John A. B. Dahlgreen* by George Edwin Bissell (1839–1920); *James Hamilton Windrim* (yes, the architect) by Samuel Murray (1870–1941, Murray also did the bronze statue of Joseph Leidy from 1907, in front of the Academy of Natural Sciences on 19th Street and the Benjamin Franklin Parkway); *Major General S. W. Crawford* by Bessie Potter Vonnoh (1872–1955); *Governor Andrew Gregg Curtin* by Moses Jacob Ezekiel (1844–1917); *General James A. Beaver* by Katherine M. Cohen (1859–1924); *John B. Gest* by Charles Grafly; and *Two Eagles* and *Globes* by John Massey Rhind (1860–1936). Rhind did the statue of *John Wanamaker, Citizen* outside of City Hall.

It is as though the entire National Sculpture Society got in on the act. It is a magnificent work and is easy to combine with a visit to Memorial Hall.

4h
*Fairmount
Park, Smith
Memorial Arch*

MAJOR GENERAL GEORGE GORDON MEADE
Lansdowne Drive, north of Memorial Hall
1887, Alexander Milne Calder

A. M. Calder (1846–1923) was hard at work on City Hall when he did his equestrian bronze of the Gettysburg hero who later served as a commissioner of Fairmount Park. It is one of the few things by him that we can point to, aside from City Hall.

CATHOLIC TOTAL ABSTINENCE UNION FOUNTAIN
North Concourse Drive and States Street
1876, Herman Kirn

More than a paean to teetotaling, this is a marble monument to American Catholicism, with its trio of statues of prominent Revolutionary-era Catholics: Archbishop John Carroll, Senator Charles Carroll, and Commodore John Barry. With them is Father Theobald Mathew, a temperance advocate, and in the middle is Moses. Now, what I wonder is this: Were the Carrolls and Commodore Barry all teetotalers? Sculptor Kirn studied in Germany under Carl Steinhauser, who did the baptismal font in Strickland's St. Stephen's Church (*see* chapter six).

LAW, PROSPERITY, AND POWER
South George's Hill Drive, north of the Mann Music Center
1880, Daniel Chester French

This is the marble group that originally stood atop Alfred B. Mullett's Second Empire–style Post Office on 9th and Chestnut (built 1873–84, demolished 1937). The group was placed in the park the following year. French also did the excellent equestrian monument to U. S. Grant (*see* pages 231–32).

5 FAIRMOUNT WATERWORKS
East side of Schuylkill River, near 25th Street, just north of the Museum of Art, in Fairmount Park
1812–15, Frederick Graff

Dickens in 1842:

> Philadelphia is most bountifully provided with fresh water, which is showered and jerked about, and turned on, and poured off, everywhere. The

Waterworks, which are on a height near the city, are no less ornamental than useful, being tastefully laid out as a public garden, and kept in the best and neatest order. The river is dammed at this point, and forced by its own power into certain high tanks or reservoirs, whence the whole city, to the top stories of the houses, is supplied at a very trifling expense.

It's been said that the Greek Revival Waterworks look like one of the ideal templed landscapes in a painting by Claude Lorrain. Built as a group of Greek temples with paved walkways and landscaped grounds, the Waterworks were designed to be visited, with galleries overlooking the modern miracle of the steam-powered machinery that pumped the water. The works served in their intended capacity for about a hundred years, then were converted to an aquarium, remaining thus until 1962. The Waterworks and their vicinity now belong to joggers, fishermen, and sunbathers.

Frederick Graff (1774–1847), Philadelphia born, was a draftsman for Latrobe when he designed the city's first waterworks (1799–1801, demolished 1828) at Centre (Penn) Square. In 1805, Graff became superintendent of the Philadelphia Waterworks, a position he held for the next forty-two years. He became the nation's unquestioned authority on urban water supply. His successor in charge of the Waterworks was his son, Frederic (1817–90)—the elder Graff apparently deciding to Frenchify the son's Christian name—who served through the 1860s.

Atop the north and south entrance houses of the Waterworks are sculptures by William Rush (1756–1833). *The Schuylkill Chained* and *The Schuylkill Freed* are actually fiberglass casts made in 1980 (and installed here in 1989) of the wooden originals from 1825 that were originally here but in 1937 were placed in the Philadelphia Museum of Art for safekeeping. It is *The Schuylkill Freed* that Rush is shown working on in Eakins's great painting *William Rush Carving His Allegorical Figure of the Schuylkill River* from 1877, which is in the Philadelphia Museum of Art along with Rush's original sculpture.

5 *Fairmount Waterworks*

6 *Fairmount Park, Mount Pleasant*

6 MOUNT PLEASANT

*Mount Pleasant Drive, east of the Schuylkill River, in Fairmount Park
1761–62*

Of the many historic houses preserved in and around Philadelphia, Mount
Pleasant may be architecturally the most distinguished. The style is similar
to that of Cliveden (they were built in the same decade), though slightly
more elaborated, particularly with the Palladian window (prominent over
the pedimented doorway) and the crowning balustrade. The walls are local
rubble stone coated with stucco, scored to imitate dressed stone. The quoins
and stringcourses are of brick. Also in contrast to Cliveden is the arched
doorway with its prominent keystone. Otherwise, the slightly projecting
central section with its two pediments, the hipped roof, the shallow porch,
and the nine-over-nine double-hung windows with splayed lintels are iden-
tical to those at Cliveden. The basic style of house represented by both
Cliveden and Mount Pleasant derived from James Gibbs's *A Book of Architecture,* published in London in 1728.

Mount Pleasant was built by Captain John MacPherson, a swashbuck-
ling privateer who ultimately found he could not afford the upkeep of the
lavish house he built for himself. He then sold it in 1779 to the ill-fated
Benedict Arnold (1741–1801). General Arnold acquitted himself brilliantly
in the Saratoga campaign in 1777 but got mad when he was passed over for
promotion. To get even with his superiors, he conspired with Britain's Ma-

jor John André to betray the American post at West Point, New York, to the British. The plot was discovered, Major André was captured and hanged, and Arnold fled to England. This all happened in 1780. Arnold, who had bought Mount Pleasant for himself and his new bride, Peggy Shippen, had to forfeit the house.

Inside are portraits by Benjamin West and by Charles Willson Peale, among other works of art and fine Philadelphia furniture.

The house is open Tuesday to Saturday from 10:00 A.M. to 4:00 P.M. (215) 763–8100, extension 333.

7 LAUREL HILL CEMETERY
3822 Ridge Avenue, from Huntingdon Street to Allegheny Avenue
1836, John Notman

Designed in the English romantic garden manner before there was a Fairmount Park or any other sizable park to speak of in Philadelphia, Laurel Hill Cemetery was a public pleasure ground as well as a cemetery. This phenomenon of the cemetery as pleasure ground was hardly peculiar to Philadelphia. Boston's Mount Auburn Cemetery and Brooklyn's Greenwood Cemetery were similarly employed. In fact, the American urban park movement really took off because of the public demand for parks that was evident from the manner in which these early cemeteries were being used.

The need for large cemeteries resulted from the growing city and the filling up of the small burial grounds attached to many churches in the urban core. The large tracts that were set aside and developed into cemeteries were Americans' first experience of the joys of large landscaped spaces with picturesque vistas, and they became promenades, picnic grounds, and even tourist attractions. Laurel Hill proved so popular that eventually admission had to be charged merely as a means of managing the overflow crowds.

The design was inspired by London's Kensal Green Cemetery, opened in 1833. At Laurel Hill, paths radiate from a central circle—not unlike Eastern State Penitentiary. Here, though, there are lovely trees and shrubs and vistas, not to mention mausoleums designed by Notman, Strickland, and Walter. Today the cemetery covers about a hundred acres.

Notman could of course do creditably well in virtually any style, and, as he proved with St. Mark's, he could do Gothic with the best of them. One might expect Gothic to be the defining style of a cemetery such as this, but it is not. Notman sets the tone of the place with his Palladian gatehouse

(unfortunately much altered over the years) with its Doric order, as at Kensal Green.

8 MEMORIAL HALL

North Concourse, west of Schuylkill River, in Fairmount Park
1874–76, Hermann Schwarzmann

Schwarzmann (1846–91), a Munich-born engineer, had never designed a building when he was hired to design five for the Centennial Exposition. The only one that remains is Memorial Hall, and it is splendid. It is, indeed, one of the more sophisticated monumental buildings of its decade in the United States. Memorial Hall was conceived as an exhibition building, with a vast central space covered by an iron-and-glass dome. Recently, we have seen reenacted the original manner of lighting the dome at night, which must have been a spectacular vision for Philadelphians and visitors to the fair in 1876.

Memorial Hall was the original home of the Pennsylvania Museum and School of Industrial Arts, the forerunner of the Philadelphia Museum of Art. Thus, Schwarzmann's building was the first of the monumental museum edifices to be built in the United States. It continued to exhibit portions of the Philadelphia Museum's collections until as recently as the 1950s. Perhaps oddly, Schwarzmann, in spite of the success of his exposi-

8 *Fairmount Park, Memorial Hall*

tion buildings in Philadelphia, enjoyed at best a modest success, mostly in New York, for the remainder of his career. (If you are interested in Schwarzmann, and happen to be in New York, you may want to look at his old Mercantile Exchange, built in 1882 on Broadway between Bleecker and Houston Streets.)

In front of Memorial Hall are two bronze sculptures of *Pegasus* by Vincenz Plinz. Dating from 1863, they were placed here in 1876. They were originally installed atop the Imperial Opera House in Vienna but removed because they were felt to be out of scale with the building. The sculptures were then purchased by Philadelphian Robert H. Gratz and placed here, where their scale seems fine.

Memorial Hall is open Monday to Friday from 9:00 A.M. to 4:00 P.M. (215) 685–0113.

9 PHILADELPHIA ZOO
34th Street and Girard Avenue
Opened, 1874

The Philadelphia Zoo is the oldest of the nation's public zoological parks. It is located within the confines of Fairmount Park, and its gatehouses were designed by Furness & Hewitt. More recently, the George D. Widener Memorial Tree House, opened in 1985, has received much praise. Designed by Venturi, Rauch & Scott Brown, many consider it that firm's most successful and engaging work. Actually, it's an extensive remodeling of George Hewitt's old Antelope House (1876). The idea behind the remodeled building is to allow children to view the world as various species do. Among the six separate such settings, for example, is one in which children—and adults—view the world as bees do. This effect is achieved through the artificial re-creation, at exaggerated scale, of the other species' natural habitats.

On the grounds of the zoo is:

SOLITUDE
1785

The most charmingly named of all of Philadelphia's houses was originally the residence of John Penn (1760–1834), one of William Penn's two grandsons of that name. This one was the bachelor son of Thomas Penn. The house passed to John Penn's nephew, Granville Penn, and was the last house

8 *Fairmount Park, Memorial Hall*

owned by any member of the Penn family in Pennsylvania. Today it serves as zoo offices.

10 MANAYUNK

East Bank of the Schuylkill, north of Lincoln Drive

"Manayunk" is an Indian name supposedly meaning "drinking place." Today, Manayunk is a place Philadelphians—particularly, I think, suburbanites—flock to for a drink, a meal, and the sundry accoutrements of a young and fashionable "lifestyle."

Nestled upon dramatic hilly terrain between the Schuylkill and the Wissahickon Valley is this former industrial center of the late nineteenth century. As throughout this century most of its industry has moved out, the area has also been progressively rehabilitated, beginning with the creation in the 1970s of a towpath and boardwalk along the old canal, just inland from the river. So successful have these efforts been that the neighborhood, to the amazement of longtime Philadelphians, now stands at the peak of chichi life in the city, an unexpected but not unwelcome circumstance.

Parallel to the canal is Main Street, once a thriving center of commerce for the prosperous industrial community, and now a thriving strip of trendy clothing stores, galleries, cafés and restaurants, antique stores, and such, tending toward the pricey and housed in a beguiling mix of old and rehabilitated quarters from the Manayunk heyday (or is *this* the Manayunk heyday?).

The area that is now Manayunk was first settled in 1693 and incorporated as a town in 1840 at a time when the area had begun to boom as a milling center. Manayunk was consolidated into the city of Philadelphia in 1854. One of the precipitants of the current Manayunk boom came in

1985 when former Philadelphia mayor William Green opened the United States Bar and Grill on Main Street. At around the same time, other trendy restaurants began to open on Main, preceding the marketing of old Manayunk houses to young professionals.

VENTURI & SCOTT BROWN

The old brick building, a former mill, on the corner of Main and Rector is the office of Venturi & Scott Brown, one of Philadelphia's—and the world's—most renowned architectural firms, their name indissolubly linked with the rise of Manayunk chic in recent years.

Venturi was born in Philadelphia in 1925, the son of a produce wholesaler. (Did the elder Venturi conduct business in the old Merchants' Exchange when it was the produce market?) He attended Princeton, worked for Eero Saarinen, and spent 1954–56 in Italy as a *Prix de Rome* recipient, an experience that may have been crucial to his rejection of orthodox modernist architecture. When he returned to Philadelphia, he worked for Louis Kahn and in 1964 formed a partnership with John Rauch, a Penn man who would be Venturi's partner for twenty-four years. Venturi taught at Penn, where he met his wife, the South African Denise Scott Brown (born 1931), who joined Venturi & Rauch in 1967. In 1966 Venturi's book *Complexity and Contradiction in Architecture,* which candidly questioned many of the principles and attitudes of orthodox modernism, was published, and had an immediate and profound impact on young architects. The "postmodernism" of the 1970s and 1980s can be traced back to the influence of *Complexity and Contradiction* as well as to Venturi's second book, *Learning from Las Vegas,* published in 1972. If Louis Sullivan's dictum was "form ever follows function," and Mies van der Rohe's was "less is more," then Venturi's was "Main Street is almost all right." (It is therefore apposite that Venturi & Scott Brown should have their office on a street that is actually called *Main Street.*) Venturi brought a sort of 1960s-Pop sensibility to Jane Jacobs's critique of urban planning orthodoxies.

The high point for Venturi and Scott Brown came when their design for the Sainsbury Wing of London's National Gallery was selected with the imprimatur of the Prince of Wales and built in 1990. (The original competition for this new wing for the museum was held in 1984 and yielded the design by Ahrends Burton & Koralek that Prince Charles famously called "a monstrous carbuncle on the face of a much-loved and elegant friend." Venturi, Rauch & Scott Brown won a later competition.) The critics Edward Jones and Christopher Woodward called Venturi's Sainsbury Wing a "classical billboard," meaning to damn it, though one suspects Venturi rather enjoys such descriptions.

But even these critics agree that the interiors, housing some of the world's greatest Northern and Italian Renaissance paintings, are elegant.

The interiors of the Sainsbury Wing are in my opinion the Venturi firm's finest work. The firm's finest Philadelphia work is unquestionably the George D. Widener Memorial Tree House, built in 1985 at the Philadelphia Zoo. But the most influential of Venturi's local works is **Guild House,** built in 1960–63 on 7th and Spring Garden Streets. (Venturi was, I believe, on his own at this time, while Rauch was employed by the firm of Cope & Lippincott, which associated with Venturi on this project. This is, I think, how Venturi and Rauch hooked up with each other.)

Guild House was built by the Quakers as a home for the elderly. Venturi did a kind of Pop interpretation both of a hackwork modern apartment house or institutional building and of classic Philadelphia Georgian residential and institutional building designs. Its central section is flanked by receding wings *à la* Independence Hall or Pennsylvania Hospital. He gave the main projecting block a horizontally tripartite façade, with the top floor expressed as a kind of broad semi-elliptical fanlight, perhaps referring to their frequent occurrence in Philadelphia Federal–style houses. The main body of the building features four floors each with a double balcony, the uppermost three with deliberately cheesy-looking perforated metal railings. The whole is of red brick except for the base of the central section, in which the brick is painted white. The entrance is recessed behind a single, centrally placed granite pier, and above the entrance, in big, blocky, "superscaled" Pop letters, is the building's name.

Other important works by Venturi's firms in Philadelphia include:

• The renovation of the Furness Library (1888–90) at 34th and Walnut on the University of Pennsylvania campus in 1991 (*see* chapter ten).

• The renovation of the gorgeous Adelbert Fischer house (1909) by Milton Medary at 6904 Wissahickon Avenue in Germantown.

• The Vanna Venturi (Robert's mother) house at 8330 Millman in Chestnut Hill in 1962 (*see* chapter fourteen).

• Franklin Court, 1973–76, at 312–22 Market Street in Old City (*see* chapter five).

• The Institute for Scientific Information, 1978–79, at 3501 Market Street in University City (*see* chapter ten).

• The Clinical Research Building of the University of Pennsylvania, 1991, at 36th Street and Hamilton Walk.

• The Christopher Columbus obelisk at Penn's Landing.

• The night lighting of the Benjamin Franklin Bridge (*see* chapter five).

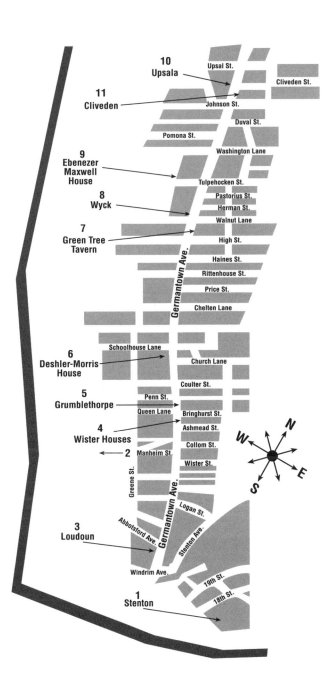

10
Upsala

Upsal St.

Cliveden St.

11
Cliveden

Johnson St.

Duval St.

Pomona St.

Washington Lane

9
**Ebenezer
Maxwell
House**

Tulpehocken St.

8
Wyck

Pastorius St.

Herman St.

Walnut Lane

7
**Green Tree
Tavern**

High St.

Germantown Ave.

Haines St.

Rittenhouse St.

Price St.

Chelten Lane

Schoolhouse Lane

6
**Deshler-Morris
House**

Church Lane

Coulter St.

5
Grumblethorpe

Penn St.

Queen Lane

Bringhurst St.

4
Wister Houses

Ashmead St.

Collom St.

2

Manheim St.

Wister St.

Greene St.

Germantown Ave.

Logan St.

3
Loudoun

Abbotsford Ave.

Stenton Ave.

Windrim Ave.

19th St.

1
Stenton

18th St.

N W E S

GERMANTOWN

CHAPTER 13

GERMANTOWN

Germantown was founded in 1683 by German Quakers led by their own William Penn–like figure, the redoubtable Francis Daniel Pastorius (1651–1720), a lawyer, an educator, and a humanitarian. Pastorius purchased the original 15,000 acres of Germantown from William Penn. The eighteenth-century designation "German" was pretty loose, and Germantown's original settlers were Quakers and Mennonites from the Palatinate (thus, for example, Crefeld Street and Krisheim). There was plenty of German immigration into Germantown through the eighteenth century, but all ethnic bets were off in 1793 when yellow fever sent Philadelphians scurrying thither and yon (including President and Mrs. Washington), and Germantown grew considerably more diverse, a process intensified by the coming of the railroad in the 1830s. Germantown Avenue (originally called High Street) was not paved until 1801, meaning it was still a dirt country road when all the great Georgian houses were built along it. Germantown was annexed by Philadelphia in 1854.

The Battle of Germantown took place October 4, 1777, and though it was a semi-disaster for General Washington, the cleverness of his (albeit ill-fated) battle plan was apparently the final determinant in the French decision to aid the Continental army and, thus, indirectly the cause of the Marquis de Lafayette's heroic attendance at so many dinner parties in and around Philadelphia in the 1780s.

We begin our look at Germantown at its southern extremity.

1 STENTON
Courtland and 18th Streets, just east of where the Reading Railroad tracks cross Germantown Avenue
1728, et seq.

The early Georgian of Stenton is chaster than the middle Georgian of Cliveden and, if lacking the latter's pizzazz, is nonetheless as appealing in its simplicity and stateliness. The materials, the fenestration, and the dormers are pretty similar here to those at Cliveden; absent are the later house's profligacy of pediments and gables, its splayed lintels, and the columns of its porch.

James Logan (1674–1751), Stenton's builder, was, like Benjamin Chew of Cliveden, a Quaker and a local Pooh-Bah. Logan was William Penn's personal representative in the colony following Penn's return to England in 1701. He basically ran the show for half a century. Logan is remembered today in the name of Logan Circle, and for his magnificent library, which formed the nucleus of the Library Company of Philadelphia. His house here originally stood amid some 500 acres, the grounds being whittled down to the present Stenton Park. Logan, something of a colonial polymath, probably designed the house himself. It served as General Washington's headquarters during the Battle of the Brandywine (September 1777), then as General Sir William Howe's headquarters during the Battle of Germantown (October 1777)—I believe it is the only house in Philadelphia to have served both armies in this capacity. Six generations of Logans lived here, and the house is now worthily maintained as a museum by the Colonial Dames. Stenton is open Tuesday to Saturday only from 1:00 to 3:00 P.M. (215) 329-7312.

2 GERMANTOWN CRICKET CLUB

5140 Morris Street at Manheim Street, just east of Wissahickon Avenue
1890–91, McKim, Mead & White

There's surprisingly little McKim, Mead & White in Philadelphia, so it may be worth the detour to the southernmost limit of what we call Germantown to see this elegant and influential neo-Georgian affair credited to Charles Follen McKim, who, with his partner Stanford White, led the late-nineteenth-century revival of colonial style.

GERMANTOWN AVENUE

It's an instructive drive or trolley ride up Germantown Avenue from its intersection with Broad Street. Through Germantown there are the depressing signs of a ravaged neighborhood, with ill-kempt buildings, marginal stores, rubble-strewn lots, unreconstructed burnt-out houses, and such. Gradually, the historic houses appear, beginning with:

3 LOUDOUN

4650 Germantown Avenue at Abbotsford Road
1796–1801, 1829, 1850

This Federal-style house, named after Loudoun County, Virginia, was built in the late 1790s. The Corinthian portico of the south façade was added in 1850.

4 WISTER HOUSES

5203–5 Germantown Avenue, between Ashmead and Bringhurst

These two houses were the home of Dr. Owen Jones Wister and his wife, Sarah Butler, who was the daughter of the great English actress Fanny Kemble, whom E. Digby Baltzell called "the most fascinating and creative woman who ever lived in Philadelphia." (Thomas Sully's portraits of Fanny Kemble can be seen at the Pennsylvania Academy of the Fine Arts.) Here in 1860, Dr. and Mrs. Wister's son, also called Owen, was born: he wrote *The Virginian* (1902), the prototypical Western, and despaired for the future of the Anglo-Saxon race.

SARAH BUTLER WISTER AND HENRY JAMES

Henry James (1843–1916) met Sarah Butler Wister, the wife of Dr. Owen Jones Wister, and her mother Fanny Kemble in Rome in 1869. James was twenty-six and still two years shy of the serialization of *Watch and Ward,* his first novel, in the *Atlantic Monthly.* James wrote of "the terrific Kemble herself, whose splendid handsomeness of eye, nostril and mouth were the best things in the room"—this at the "at home" in Rome to which he had been invited by Mrs. Wister, who was staying there with her husband and young son Owen. (Henry James is perhaps the only writer who ever lived who could get away with describing someone's "splendid handsomeness of nostril.")

Sarah, who was "strikingly handsome and possessed of a magnificent head of hair," in the words of Leon Edel, and eight years James's senior, took an immediate liking to him, as he did to her. He accompanied her on tours of Rome and was "distinctly charmed" by this attractive, intelligent, literary, and strong-willed woman from Philadelphia. Indeed, Mrs. Wister and James went about alone together so often in Rome that had they been only slightly less discreet they would have "set tongues wagging."

James and Mrs. Wister met again in Rome in 1872–73. She had, he wrote, "a very literary mind, if not a powerful one." One finds that James always equivocated in this manner when discussing Mrs. Wister. He would praise her, then point out a fault. Leon Edel, James's prodigious biographer, interprets this as James's strategy for keeping an appropriate emotional distance from the older married woman to whom he was clearly attracted. "[H]er beautiful hair is the thing most to be praised about her. It's on the whole the handsomest I've ever seen." James reported that as the Wisters prepared to return home from Italy, Sarah was "most brokenhearted to exchange Rome for Germantown."

James's relationship with Mrs. Wister found its way into his story "Madame de Mauves" of 1874, and even more explicitly into his story "The Solution" from 1893, in which the character of Mrs. Rushbrook, the older woman who marries the young protagonist, is clearly modeled after Mrs. Wister. James describes Mrs. Rushbrook thus:

> She was extravagant, careless, even slightly capricious. If the "Bohemian" had been invented in those days she might possibly have been one—a very small, fresh, dainty one. . . . She had a lovely head, and her chestnut hair was of a shade I have never seen since. . . . She was natural and clever and kind, and though she was five years older than I she always struck me as an embodiment of youth— of the golden morning of life. We made such happy discoveries together when I first knew her: we liked the same things, we disliked the same people, we had the same favorite statues in the Vatican, the same secret preferences in regard to views on the Campagna. We loved Italy in the same way and in the same degree. . . . She painted, she studied Italian, she collected and noted the songs of the people, and she had the wit to pick up certain bibelots and curiosities—lucky woman—before other people had thought of them.

There is also some of Sarah Wister in Christina Light in Roderick Hudson, a novel of which Mrs. Wister wrote an anonymous review in the North American Review in 1875: "All it lacks is to have been told with more human feeling," she wrote.

In 1875 James visited the Wisters in their home on Germantown Avenue. Seven years later when he met up with the Wisters in France, he noted that Sarah was "a tragic nature, so much worn, physically, that I am sorry for her." Apparently his ardor had cooled.

James visited the Wisters in Philadelphia again in 1905, when he was in town to deliver his lecture, "The Lesson of Balzac," to Agnes Repplier's

Contemporary Club. He had always suffered terribly from stage fright, and that he was able to give his speech to five or six hundred people at the Bellevue-Stratford Hotel (only recently opened on Broad Street) without his feeling debilitatingly nervous he regarded as an enormous success. He, apparently, was the only one who considered his lackluster lecture a success: Miss Repplier was, with her charming introduction of James, far the hit of the evening.

On this, his final visit to Philadelphia, James was put up at the Rittenhouse Club. He liked Philadelphia. He wrote that if Boston was "a state of mind," then Philadelphia was a "state of consanguinity." He admired the city's society for having a sense of and for maintaining its own identity—for "discriminating in its own favor." Philadelphia, "of all goodly villages, the very goodliest, probably in the world; the very largest, and flattest, and smoothest, the most rounded and complete."

The following residences are to the north across Bringhurst.

5 GRUMBLETHORPE

5267 Germantown Avenue, opposite Queen Lane
1744

Grumblethorpe was built by the wine merchant John Wister, German emigrant and progenitor of the distinguished Old Philadelphia clan. (The desk at which Owen Wister wrote *The Virginian* is displayed at Grumblethorpe.)

Constructed of the local schist, Grumblethorpe puts on no airs. A big shingled pent-eave is the dominant note on the house's façade, along with a second-floor balcony over the front door. Note how in addition to the front door there is a door to its left that opens directly into the parlor.

6 DESHLER-MORRIS HOUSE

5442 Germantown Avenue, between Coulter Street and School House Lane
1750–72

The Deshler-Morris House was built by a nephew of John Wister. The house was leased by President Washington during the yellow-fever epidemic

in the fall of 1793, and here he held meetings with Thomas Jefferson, Alexander Hamilton, and other members of his cabinet. George and Martha liked it so much that they returned the following spring, under better circumstances.

Facing across the avenue toward Germantown's Market Square, the house is one of the handsomest in Philadelphia. It has a neat symmetrical façade with a lovely Tuscan-columned and pedimented doorway, and nine shuttered, twelve-over-twelve, small-paned, double-hung windows, and a striking pair of arch-windowed, pedimented dormers. It is coated in stucco, scored to imitate cut stone. The center hall plan was unusual in Germantown at the time, when most houses' first-floor rooms each opened to the outside (as at Grumblethorpe).

After the Battle of Germantown, the house was occupied by General Sir William Howe (who certainly seems to have made the rounds of the neighborhood's houses). By the time George Washington stayed there, the house was owned by Isaac Franks, the brother of the Loyalist David Franks who owned Woodford in what is now Fairmount Park.

7 GREEN TREE TAVERN

6023 Germantown Avenue at High Street
1748

It is interesting to compare the Green Tree Tavern with a city tavern from the same period—the Man Full of Trouble, built in 1760 on Spruce and

6 *Deshler-Morris House*

7 *Green Tree Tavern*

First in Society Hill. It is well to recall that local taverns were once much more than just watering holes. They were community centers, assembly halls, courthouses, post offices, stagecoach stations, and inns. Before telephones and such, it was necessary that there be neighborhood clearinghouses for information, and that's where the tavern came in. The Green Tree was built by Daniel Pastorius, the grandson of the founder of Germantown. By the way, Thomas Jefferson once lodged at the Green Tree Tavern.

It is now a parish office of the First United Methodist Church of Germantown.

Across the street is:

8 WYCK

6026 Germantown Avenue, southwest corner of Walnut Lane
1690, et seq.

The original portion of the house known as Wyck was built beginning in 1690 and is the oldest structure in Germantown. A second house was built,

8 *Wyck*

and the two houses were bridged at the second story, leaving a carriageway, which was filled in by William Strickland in 1824 when he was hired to remodel the house.

The garden of Wyck was planted by the house's onetime owners Reuben and Jane Haines, who were founders of the Pennsylvania Horticultural Society in 1827. It was they who hired Strickland to remodel the house, and here the Haineses, hardly alone among the Philadelphians of their time, entertained the Marquis de Lafayette, who seems never to have needed to worry about where his next meal would come from. Anyway, the rose garden, which contains thirty-seven varieties, is one of the marvels of Philadelphia, being one of the country's oldest gardens still growing according to its original plan.

Continuing north on Germantown Avenue from the Green Tree Tavern and Wyck, you will soon come to West Tulpehocken Street. Detour to the left to see the:

9 EBENEZER MAXWELL HOUSE
200 West Tulpehocken Street
1859, Joseph C. Hoxie (probably)

Germantown's days as a quiet village were doomed by the arrival of the railroad in 1832, and the graystone Quaker tradition was supplemented by that of the gaudy suburban villa. An outstanding example of the new mode is this eclectic monstrosity (I mean that in a kind way) that was almost unconscionably pulled down in the 1960s but was saved by local preservationists and thousands of hours of volunteer work, and turned into a museum. There's a high tower, high chimneys, Flemish gables, a plethora of mansards, and, just for good measure, some Gothic arches. Inside and out it's virtually an encyclopedia of Victorian design tics, including faux details. The displays within explain Victorian decor and also how the house was saved and renovated.

Go back to Germantown Avenue, take a left and continue north to:

10 UPSALA

6430 Germantown Avenue, north of Johnson Street
1755, 1797–1801

Upsala was built in the 1750s but remodeled in the late 1790s in the Federal style. It is simpler and more graceful than the mid-Georgian Cliveden across the street. The façade is Wissahickon schist with marble trim. There are six-over-six, small-paned, double-hung windows with splayed lintels, and a pedimented, distyle porch with slender Doric columns.

A man named John Johnson (no connection that I know of with the great lawyer and art collector John Johnson) bought the house in 1766, and

9 *Ebenezer Maxwell House*

his descendants lived here until 1941. The Johnsons named it after the Swedish city to which they had some connection.

11 CLIVEDEN

6401 Germantown Avenue, near Upsal Street
1763–67

The lawyer Benjamin Chew (1722–1810) built himself a superb pattern-book country house, a full-blown Gibbs-Palladian job in local schist. The front is picture-perfect: the low stoop; the shallow, pedimented, and columned entrance; the profusion of nine-over-nine, small-paned, double-hung windows; the splayed lintels; the crowning pediment of the central section; the dormered, hipped roof with its broad end gables; not to mention all those urns on the roof—if it's not executed with quite the panache of Captain MacPherson's Mount Pleasant, it's nonetheless a rich and robust Georgian country house of great quality.

Cliveden now occupies grounds of about six acres, or a tenth of Benjamin Chew's estate at its high point. Chew was a Maryland-born Quaker who apprenticed with the renowned Philadelphia lawyer Andrew Hamilton before attending the Middle Temple in London. Chew became one of

10 *Upsala*

11   Cliveden

Pennsylvania's most prominent lawyers, at one time chief justice of Pennsylvania, as well as an ardent Loyalist whose house, during his Revolutionary incarceration, became a British redoubt. Chew had to sell Cliveden in 1779, though he reacquired it eighteen years later, after which the house remained in the Chew family until 1972. At that time, it was given to the National Trust for Historic Preservation, whose guides are knowledgeable and will tell you much about Germantown besides Cliveden, the interiors of which are well stocked not only with the ghosts but with the excellent furniture of old Philadelphia.

Of particular note among the furniture are some chairs and a sofa by Thomas Affleck (1740–95). Affleck was born in Aberdeen—a little more than a century before Alexander Milne Calder was born in that city. Thus, like so many of Philadelphia's builders, Affleck was a Scotsman. He was the foremost eighteenth-century furniture maker in Philadelphia. He arrived here in 1763 at the age of twenty-three, following periods of training in Edinburgh and London. A Quaker, he enjoyed the patronage of many of the city's leading Quaker families. His furniture is richly and sometimes extravagantly carved, and lushly upholstered in sometimes surprising colors. It is anything but Quaker-plain.

For me, one of the best things at Cliveden is a painting, one of the most mesmerizing portraits I have ever seen. It is of one of the Chew women and was painted by George Cochran Lambdin (1830-96), one of the best and most overlooked of the Philadelphia painters. He lived in Germantown and specialized in still lifes of flowers picked from his own garden. As a flower painter, he is the peer of Fantin-Latour. The portrait of which I speak is as much a flower painting as a portrait: she recedes behind the bunch of flowers she holds in her hands. Thus does Lambdin so exquisitely capture youthful, diffident femininity.

Cliveden is open Tuesday to Saturday from 10:00 A.M. to 4:00 P.M., and Sunday from 1:00 to 4:00 P.M. (215) 848–1777.

Right around the corner from Cliveden on Johnson Street is a typical Germantown street of old, sturdy stone houses. This particular block is well-maintained, and seems to me to be exactly the sort of Germantown street John Lukacs had in mind when he wrote of "snowy afternoons [around 1950] in Germantown before Christmas, with yellow lights shining serenely out of the gray-stone Quaker houses, with all of the promises of decency and of the sentimental warmth of an American small town."

CHAPTER 14

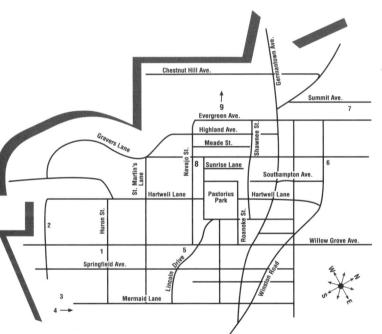

Chestnut Hill Ave.

Germantown Ave.

Summit Ave.

7

↑
9

Evergreen Ave.

Highland Ave.

Gravers Lane

Meade St.

Shawnee St.

Navajo St.

St. Martin's Lane

8 Sunrise Lane

Southampton Ave.

6

Hartwell Lane

Pastorius Park

Hartwell Lane

Huron St.

Roanoke St.

2

Willow Grove Ave.

1

5

Lincoln Drive

Winston Road

Springfield Ave.

3

Mermaid Lane

4 →

W N
S E

CHESTNUT HILL

CHAPTER 14

CHESTNUT HILL

HENRY HOWARD HOUSTON'S CHESTNUT HILL

Henry Howard Houston was an executive with the Pennsylvania Railroad when he conceived the idea of an upper-class suburb on three thousand acres of farmland just north of Germantown in the 1870s. This land was about eleven miles north and slightly to the west of Center City and was part of the village of Chestnut Hill, which had been annexed by Philadelphia in 1854 but was still quite rural by the 1870s. Houston was able to get the Pennsylvania Railroad to run a new branch line through his Chestnut Hill property, thus vastly increasing its value. Chestnut Hill, a remote rural area, was now within half an hour's train ride from Center City.

Houston hired the architects G. W. and W. D. Hewitt to design most of the early buildings of "Wissahickon Heights," as Houston originally called his new community. The first buildings that Houston and the Hewitts put up were the resort hotel called the Wissahickon Inn, the Episcopal Church of St. Martin in the Fields, and the Philadelphia Cricket Club. These, Houston felt, were just the things to lure Philadelphia's patricians and upper bourgeoisie to Chestnut Hill. And he was right. Where nearby Germantown had deep Quaker roots, Chestnut Hill would be the bastion of the Episcopalian elite.

1 WISSAHICKON INN
500 West Willow Grove Avenue
1884, G. W. and W. D. Hewitt

Houston built his 250-room inn as a rural retreat for city dwellers, whom he hoped would then see and buy the houses he was putting up in the area. The marketing strategy worked. With its shingled roofs, half-timbered gables, and generous porches, the Queen Anne style is similar to that of the Houston-Sauveur house (*see* page 260), though at a vastly larger scale. In 1898, after only fourteen years as an inn, the building became the Chestnut Hill Academy, a well-known private "prep school."

Across the street is the:

CHURCH OF ST. MARTIN IN THE FIELDS (EPISCOPAL)
Willow Grove Avenue and St. Martin's Lane
1888, G. W. and W. D. Hewitt

Odd that a church of that name should be in the Gothic style. It is situated next to the playing fields of the Philadelphia Cricket Club.

HOUSTON-SAUVEUR HOUSE
8205 Seminole Avenue
1885, G. W. and W. D. Hewitt

Houston built this house and, after it was completed, sold it to a man named Louis Sauveur. Queen Anne: the steeply pitched, shingled roof with the eyelid dormer; the half-timbered gable; the second-floor quasi-Palladian window topped by a scrolled pediment; the gorgeous double porch with an additional balcony on the top floor—this is a picture-perfect suburban house.

2 DRUIM MOIR
West Willow Grove Avenue
1885–86, G. W. and W. D. Hewitt
Gardens: 1921, Robert Rodes McGoodwin
Renovated in early 1940s, Robert Rodes McGoodwin
Renovated in 1982, DACP Associates

"Great crag" (Scots Gaelic). McGoodwin simplified the Hewitts' design by removing turrets and gables. Thus, as wildly picturesque as the house now appears, it is but a shadow of its original craggy self. Yet much of what must have been its original power remains, particularly in the sense it gives off of being some sort of natural outcropping of Wissahickon schist that's been winsomely dressed up. McGoodwin also designed the lovely garden that the house overlooks. When Houston built the house for himself, it stood amid fifty acres of virgin woods. About half the estate has been subdivided for new residential development, while Druim Moir itself was renovated in the early 1980s into three separate dwellings, with little effect on its external appearance. In all, the remodeling and the new development appear to have been sensitively done.

1b   *Church of St. Martin in the Fields*

1c   *Houston-Sauveur House*

Next door is:

BRINKWOOD
West Willow Grove Avenue
1887, G. W. and W. D. Hewitt

Houston built the less-imposing, cedar-shingled Brinkwood for his son.

At Lincoln Drive and Harvey Street, a few blocks west of Germantown Avenue at a little eastern spur of Fairmount Park in Germantown, is a good bronze statue of frock-coated Henry Howard Houston and his dog by John Massey Rhind from 1900. The location was chosen because this land was donated by Houston to the Fairmount Park Commission.

THE WOODWARD DEVELOPMENTS

Henry Howard Houston died in 1895, at which time his son-in-law Dr. George Woodward took over Chestnut Hill's development. Woodward was more the idealist than his father-in-law. Though he continued to develop Chestnut Hill largely as an upper-middle-class and upper-class enclave, he did so with a few twists. He had seen and been deeply impressed by Raymond Unwin's designs for Hampstead Garden Suburb in London. Unwin had rebelled against the uniformity and monotony of conventional suburban design and used a variety of housing types, from freestanding villas to terrace houses to clusters of small cottages to houses grouped around courtyards. This created visual variety and varied housing for a more diverse population. Woodward wished to do the same thing at Chestnut Hill.

Woodward was a reformer and president of Philadelphia's Octavia Hill Association, the purpose of which was to create model tenements for the working class. The reform-minded doctor was influenced by John Ruskin (Octavia Hill's mentor), the Arts and Crafts movement, and the Garden City movement begun in England by Ebenezer Howard and touted by Woodward well before that movement's foremost American spokesman, Lewis Mumford, came on the scene. Much of Chestnut Hill—about 180 houses—was built between 1910 and 1930 according to Dr. Woodward's precepts and those of his architects, Robert Rodes McGoodwin (1885–1967), Herman Louis Duhring, and Edmund B. Gilchrist (1885–1953). The area was developed as a kind of garden suburb with careful planning to ensure a high quality in the design of houses and, *à la* Unwin, the avoidance of suburban monotony.

Woodward's houses were not sold but rented. This was as true for the

large houses for well-to-do established families as for the smaller houses for young families just starting out. The reason for this was that Woodward wished to retain as much aesthetic control over his developments as possible. Under Woodward, Chestnut Hill became a more diverse community through the 1910s and 1920s. Woodward marketed some of his houses to young families. He also hired numerous emigrant Italian masons to build his houses, which are all constructed of the local schist and are exceptionally well crafted. Many of these masons then settled in Chestnut Hill, violating somewhat the rather purebred Episcopalian character Henry Howard Houston had attempted to cultivate.

The natural topographical features of the area enhance its attractiveness: the hilly terrain, the ragged edge of vast Fairmount Park forming the west edge of the district, and so on, obscuring the condition that Chestnut Hill was laid out (by the Hewitts) almost entirely as an extension of Penn's Center City gridiron.

3 KRISHEIM
McCallum Street and Mermaid Lane
1910, Peabody & Stearns

The distinguished Boston architects Peabody & Stearns designed Dr. Woodward's own house, a half-timbered and multi-gabled affair not unlike the multitude of houses erected by the father-in-law. This is just to the north, across a spur of park, from Woodward's later French Village.

4 FRENCH VILLAGE
West of Allens Lane, from Elbow Lane to Emlen Street
1925–28, Robert Rodes McGoodwin

McGoodwin was an École des Beaux-Arts man, hired by Woodward to create an ensemble of eight commodious houses along a trio of private lanes near the point where the Lincoln Drive segues east at Allens Lane to Germantown Avenue. It is called French Village because Dr. Woodward was inspired by the Norman hamlets that he toured on a trip to France. McGoodwin's houses are picturesque compositions of swooping gables and overhanging eaves, high chimneys, local fieldstone walls, and lots of shingling. They have landscape-hugging contours that recall not only their ostensible models but also seventeenth-century Dutch colonial farmhouses and twentieth-century houses by Frank Lloyd Wright but with a childlike winsomeness all their own.

In the chapter on the year 1922 in his wonderful book *A Thread of Years,* the historian John Lukacs puts it so much better than I can when he writes of

> . . . a wafting of spirit, extant and now present even in solid, near-somnolent, provincial Philadelphia. . . . One consequence of that spirit is how some Philadelphians will be inspired when they realize that northern Italian stonemasons now in their city are able to fashion beautiful stuccowork on their new houses and ceilings. In the 1920s the Museum of Art had been long overdue. It will be built finally, about fifty years after New York's and at least thirty after Boston's and even Chicago's. But in 1922 George Woodward, an old Pennsylvanian and an eccentric Progressive, is planning and building his French Village, that cluster of such wonderfully done up small Normandy houses in the green bowers of Mount Airy. . . . There was a temporary breeze of beauty in the air then, in the houses and gardens, something freshening the vision of even some of the stuffiest of citizens and brightening the eyes of their wives. Nothing like this happened in Europe at that time (or in England). (John Lukacs, *A Thread of Years,* New Haven: Yale University Press, 1998, p. 174.)

This "wafting of spirit," this "temporary breeze of beauty in the air" was present elsewhere in America, really beginning around 1910: that's when Dr. Woodward began his work in Chestnut Hill, work which hit its stride in the mid-1920s. Those are the same dates that the work of Margaret Olivia Slocum Sage, Grosvenor Atterbury, and Frederick Law Olmsted Jr. began and hit its stride at Forest Hills, New York. There are other examples from around the country: Mary D. Emery and John Nolen's Mariemont, near Cincinnati (with houses designed by Philadelphia's Cret, Eyre, McGoodwin, and Gilchrist and New York's Atterbury), Electus D. Litchfield's Yorkship Village in New Jersey, and so on.

5 LINCOLN DRIVE DEVELOPMENT

Lincoln Drive, from Springfield Avenue to Pastorius Park, just south of the intersection of Germantown and West Willow Grove Avenues 1906–31, Robert Rodes McGoodwin, Herman Louis Duhring, and Edmund B. Gilchrist (with their associated firms)

Woodward wanted a mix of housing types so that both middle- and upper-income residents would be accommodated here. So there are some large freestanding houses, row houses (Gilchrist's Linden Court is an example), courtyard housing (Duhring's Half Moon Houses and McGoodwin's 131–35 West Willow Grove Avenue are examples), and so on. Most of the development is still owned by the Woodward family. At 7620 Lincoln Drive is the house McGoodwin designed for himself (1916).

Here's the breakdown by architect (the dates are Teitelman and Longstreth's):

Robert McGoodwin:
7700 Lincoln Drive, 1916
7924 Lincoln Drive, 1917
224 West Willow Grove Avenue, 1916
131–35 West Willow Grove Avenue, 1915
300 West Hartwell Lane, 1928
8004 Lincoln Drive, 1920
8008 Lincoln Drive, 1917
8010 Lincoln Drive, 1928
8014 Crefeld Avenue, 1916
56–58 West Willow Grove Avenue, 1910

Louis Duhring:
7800-18 Lincoln Drive, 1906

7900-06 Lincoln Drive, 1914–25
This was the studio of the Willet Stained Glass Company, where the important neo-medievalist Charles Connick got his start (he had previously been a newspaper cartoonist).

7922 Lincoln Drive, 1917

20 West Willow Grove Avenue (Sulgrave Manor), 1927 (apparently, the house was moved to this development)
George Washington's ancestral home in England was re-created by Duhring (is this really true?) for the Sesquicentennial Exposition in 1926, following which the house was *moved* here.

7919–25 Lincoln Drive (the Half Moon Houses), 1917
42–52 West Willow Grove Avenue, 1915
8014–28 Roanoke Street, 1931

Edmund Gilchrist:
8005–19 Navajo Street, 1917
116–8 West Abington Avenue, 1914
8008–12 Crefeld Avenue, 1921
8001–13 Crefeld Avenue, 1913
8000 Crefeld Avenue, 1916
103–13 West Willow Grove Avenue (Linden Court), 1916
101 West Springfield Avenue, 1912

Some other houses by Woodward:

100–102 WEST MERMAID LANE
South of Crefeld Street, east of Pastorius Park
1909, Wilson Eyre

WINSTON ROAD DEVELOPMENT
Winston Road, Benezet Street, and Springfield Avenue, just north of Germantown Avenue and east of Willow Grove Avenue
1910–25

WINSTON COURT
7821–7909 Winston Road
1925, Herman Louis Duhring

7830–32 WINSTON ROAD
22–32 EAST SPRINGFIELD AVENUE
1920, Robert Rodes McGoodwin

5a   *Winston Road Development*

5b   *Benezet Street Houses*

BENEZET STREET HOUSES
28–34 Benezet Street and 25–33 Springfield Avenue
1910–16, Duhring, Okie & Zeigler

GERMANTOWN AVENUE
From Germantown, with its curious mix of urban devastation and beautiful historic houses, Germantown Avenue passes through the area known as Mount Airy. The avenue takes on a more kempt appearance in this largely middle-class, racially integrated community with some remarkable architecture of its own. Dr. Woodward's French Village, for example, which is just to the west off Germantown Avenue at West Allens Lane, is technically in Mount Airy, not Chestnut Hill. As Germantown Avenue moves from Mount Airy into Chestnut Hill, the change is at first subtle, until one realizes one is in an affluent neighborhood with a shopping strip lined with elegant and expensive stores. Interspersed with chain stores such as Talbots are several independent stores that are quite venerable, including the Philadelphia Print Shop, a well-known dealer in old prints and a treasure trove of Philadelphiana. There is also a large and well-stocked outpost of the Borders bookstore chain and many restaurants and cafés (including the inevitable Starbucks).

6 GRAVERS LANE STATION
Gravers Lane, near Stenton Avenue
1883, Frank Furness

This is my favorite work by Furness. The Reading Railroad, of which this was a station, came to Chestnut Hill in the 1880s. Many of the line's commuter stations were designed by Furness. Alas, only Gravers Lane remains, but it's hard to think it wasn't among the best. It's a thrillingly picturesque

6   *Gravers Lane Station*

composition of gables, but the kicker is in how the broad bracketed porch sweeps downhill from the fanciful round and multi-gabled tower, with a bow to the varied topography that makes the whole structure look like it sprouted from the earth, growing a new gable every hundred years or so.

Near Gravers Lane Station is:

7 ANGLECOT

Prospect Street, northeast corner of Evergreen Avenue
1883–1910, Wilson Eyre
Renovated in 1993, Greg Woodring & Associates

Begun in the same year as Gravers Lane Station, this house apparently started life as a relatively sober country house in the shingle tradition, but was remodeled as many as six times by Eyre, with each new bit lending greater whimsicality. It's a studiously asymmetrical composition with the large-gabled end separated from the small-gabled end by the main block of the house, with its porch, bay window, and broad shingled roof with an eyelid dormer. Each of the gabled ends is in its turn asymmetrical, and in the large-gabled (west) end there's a sundial set into the wall. It's all extremely self-conscious, though also fairly subtle—it does not at first attempt to knock you over with its kookiness. Instead, it's a good neighbor. Note, for example, the rather grand neo-Georgian house diagonally across Evergreen Avenue: it is such piquant yet well-mannered juxtapositions that make Chestnut Hill so much more engaging than most other suburbs (than *any* other suburb?).

8 VANNA VENTURI HOUSE
8330 Millman Street at Sunrise Lane
1962, Venturi & Rauch

There's a country song with the line "Mommas, don't let your babies grow up to be cowboys." Change "cowboys" to "architects," and you probably capture how many architects' parents come to feel. The Vanna Venturi house is a sterling example of how the young architect gets to stretch his wings, indulge his theories and fancies—at his poor parents' expense. Now, I like and respect Robert Venturi, and think he's grown to be nearly as engaging a designer as he is a writer and theoretician. But early on, some of his buildings, as here, were intellectually quite pretentious. I suppose that at the end of the day this is no worse than any number of other modern houses in Philadelphia or elsewhere, but its "allusions" to traditional elements of

7 *Anglecot*

design, divorced from any ideal of making a house that is beautiful or even good-looking, is fairly galling. You've got your "allusions" to Shingle Style gables, to arches, to Baroque décolletage, and whatnot, and to what end? It is all merely to say, See what a clever boy I am, mommy!

9 HIGH HOLLOW

101 West Hampton Road at Crefeld Avenue, just south of Bells Mill Road
1914, George Howe

Howe designed High Hollow for himself when he was still a student at the École des Beaux-Arts, though he did not build it until some years later. It's a lovely structure, looking a bit like a French country tollhouse. With its steeply pitched, shingled, and dormered roof; local fieldstone walls accented by red-brick stringcourses, door frames, and voussoirs; and shingled-thimble turret, the house blends into the landscape in the prescribed Chestnut Hill manner and overlooks Fairmount Park. This is seventeen years before Howe teamed with the Swiss Lescaze to design the PSFS Building on Market Street.

GEORGE HOWE (1886–1955)

George Howe attended Groton and Harvard before going to the École des Beaux-Arts, where he was trained in the atelier of Victor Laloux (as was Edgar Seeler), architect of the Gare d'Orsay. When Howe came to Philadelphia in 1913, he worked for Furness, Evans & Co., then Mellor & Meigs, a firm renowned for its country houses for affluent clients. Howe excelled at these but was himself perhaps too fashion-conscious not to hanker for the approval of the cultural progressives. As such, he did not realize that his early houses, including his own High Hollow, were far superior as works of architecture to most of what he did later on, even including his much-lauded PSFS skyscraper. Dismissing his earlier works with the sourly sardonic phrase "Wall Street Pastoral" (and what is wrong with *that,* one might ask), he soon was concocting such eyesores as the Wasserman house in Whitemarsh—in the style, Tom Wolfe might say, of an insecticide refinery.

BIBLIOGRAPHY

This is, I think, a complete list of the books I consulted in the writing of the present volume. I have commented on the books where I felt it appropriate.

Bach, Penny Balkin. *Public Art in Philadelphia*. Philadelphia: Temple University Press, 1992. An excellent, copiously illustrated reference on the many treasures of public art in the city.

Bacon, Edmund N. *Design of Cities*. New York: Penguin Books, 1976. Straight from the horse's mouth.

Baigell, Matthew. *Dictionary of American Art*. New York: Harper & Row, 1979.

Baltzell, E. Digby. *Puritan Boston and Quaker Philadelphia*. New York: Free Press, 1979. Seldom is so much information so genially conveyed as by E. Digby Baltzell, and seldom is any work of academic sociology such a pleasure to read. This book is a treasure trove of Philadelphiana. It is a bit like a cross between Max Weber and Ward McAllister.

Bissinger, Buzz. *A Prayer for the City*. New York: Random House, 1997. A look at the life of Mayor Edward Rendell, and a disturbing look at the enormous problems besetting Philadelphia as it continues to lose population, jobs, and money to its fast-developing hinterland.

Brooks, Michael W. *John Ruskin and Victorian Architecture*. New Brunswick, New Jersey: Rutgers University Press, 1987.

Burt, Nathaniel. *Palaces for the People: A Social History of the American Art Museum*. Boston: Little, Brown and Company, 1977. A genial general history of the American art museum, with a great deal of material on Philadelphia's museums.

Chappell, Sally A. Kitt. *Architecture and Planning of Graham, Anderson, Probst & White 1912–1936*. Chicago: University of Chicago Press, 1992.

Edel, Leon. *Henry James: The Conquest of London, 1870–1881*. New York: J.B. Lippincott Company, 1962.

———. *Henry James: The Middle Years, 1882–1895*. New York: J.B. Lippincott Company, 1962.

———. *Henry James: The Treacherous Years, 1895–1901*. New York: J.B. Lippincott Company, 1969.

———. *Henry James: The Master, 1901–1916*. New York: J.B. Lippincott Company, 1972.

Finkel, Kenneth, editor. *Philadelphia Almanac and Citizens' Manual*. Philadelphia: The Library Company of Philadelphia, 1993.

Finkel, Kenneth. *Philadelphia Then and Now*. New York: Dover Publications, 1988. Like many essays in "rephotography," absolutely riveting.

Fletcher, Sir Banister. *A History of Architecture*. 18th edition, revised by J. C. Palmes. New York: Scribner's, 1975.

Gallery, John Andrew, ed. *Philadelphia Architecture: A Guide to the City*. Second edition. Philadelphia: The Foundation for Architecture, 1994. An excellent, beautifully designed handbook of Philadelphia architecture, much different in scope, style, and purpose from the present volume, and indispensable.

Hines, Thomas S. *Burnham of Chicago: Architect and Planner*. Chicago: University of Chicago Press, 1979.

Jacobs, Jane. *The Death and Life of Great American Cities*. New York: Random House, 1961. Though this brilliant and influential urbanist's critique of modern planning orthodoxies is drawn from Mrs. Jacobs's experience of her own New York, there are several fascinating sidelights about other cities, including Philadelphia.

Jordy, William H. *American Buildings and Their Architects. Volume 5, The Impact of European Modernism in the Mid-Twentieth Century*. Garden City, New York: Doubleday & Company, 1972; New York: Oxford University Press, 1986. Contains outstanding extended treatments of the PSFS Building and the Richards Medical Research Building.

Kuklick, Bruce. *To Every Thing a Season: Shibe Park and Urban Philadelphia, 1909–1976*. Princeton: Princeton University Press, 1991.

Lukacs, John. *A Thread of Years*. New Haven: Yale University Press, 1998.

———. *Philadelphia: Patricians & Philistines, 1900–1950*. New York: Farrar Straus Giroux, 1981. A beautiful book profiling several eminent Philadelphians—including Owen Wister, Agnes Repplier, and Albert C. Barnes—of the first half of the twentieth century. Each of these figures is presented by the author—one of the greatest of American historians—as being in some significant manner characteristic of Philadelphia. There may be no better written or more compulsively readable book about Philadelphia ever published.

Marion, John Francis. *Bicentennial City: Walking Tours of Historic Philadelphia.* Princeton: The Pyne Press, 1974. One of the great urban guidebooks of all time, with remarkably detailed strolls through the principal historic neighborhoods.

Morrone, Francis. *The Architectural Guidebook to New York City.* Second edition, revised and enlarged. Salt Lake City: Gibbs Smith, Publisher, 1998.

Nairn, Ian. *The American Landscape: A Critical View.* New York: Random House, 1965. The English architectural critic and theorist of the "townscape" movement toured the United States in the early sixties. He mostly hated what he saw, including Independence Park.

O'Gorman, James F. *The Architecture of Frank Furness.* Philadelphia: Philadelphia Museum of Art, 1973.

Pevsner, Sir Nikolaus. *A History of Building Types.* Princeton: Princeton University Press, 1976.

Philadelphia Museum of Art. *Philadelphia: Three Centuries of American Art.* Philadelphia: Philadelphia Museum of Art, 1976. An encyclopedic catalog for a mammoth exhibition at the Philadelphia Museum of Art in the year of the Bicentennial. Nowhere else will you find between two covers so vast and detailed a survey of the remarkable artistic heritage of this city.

Pierson, William H., Jr. *American Buildings and Their Architects. Volume 1, The Colonial and Neoclassical Styles.* Garden City, New York: Doubleday & Company, 1970; New York: Oxford University Press, 1986.

———. *American Buildings and Their Architects. Volume 2, Technology and the Picturesque, the Corporate and the Early Gothic Styles.* Garden City, New York: Doubleday & Company, 1978; New York: Oxford University Press, 1986.

Pierson is the best. Volume 1 includes excellent material on Independence Hall, Girard College, and other Philadelphia buildings of the Colonial, Federal, and Greek Revival styles. Volume 2 is equally excellent on the Gothic Revival, including matchless assessments of St. Mark's and St. James the Less.

Reed, Henry Hope. *The Golden City.* New York: Doubleday, 1959. Descended from an old Philadelphia family, Reed is our leading defender of the classical as a living tradition and continuing source of inspiration for modern designers. This book is highly polemical and utterly convincing, and draws on its author's love of Philadelphia.

Repplier, Agnes. *Philadelphia: The Place and the People.* New York, 1898. "The Jane Austin of the essay," John Lukacs called her. Agnes Repplier was once one of the most popular writers in America, though she's little known today. It's a pity; her writings, not least about the city in which she lived her entire life, are marvelous.

Roth, Leland M. *McKim, Mead & White: Architects.* New York: Harper and Row, 1983.

Rybczynski, Witold. *City Life: Urban Expectations in a New World.* New York: Scribner, 1995. Brilliant essays on the peculiar history and prospects of American cities, with many examples drawn from Philadelphia.

———. "Moving the Bell." *The Atlantic Monthly,* June 1998.

Stokes, George Stewart. *Agnes Repplier: Lady of Letters.* Philadelphia: University of Pennsylvania Press, 1949.

Tatum, George B. *Penn's Great Town: 250 Years of Philadelphia Architecture.* New Haven: Yale University Press, 1975.

Teitelman, Edward, and Richard W. Longstreth. *Architecture in Philadelphia: A Guide.* Cambridge: MIT Press, 1974. A pioneering architectural guidebook. Very useful, and much broader in scope than either the Foundation for Architecture's guide or my own. It is also a remarkable testament of period prejudices.

Weigley, Russel F., editor. *Philadelphia: A 300-Year History.* New York: W.W. Norton and Company, 1982.

Whiffen, Marcus. *American Architecture Since 1780: A Guide to the Styles.* Cambridge: MIT Press, 1981.

Wolf, Edwin, II. *Philadelphia: Portrait of an American City.* Philadelphia: Camino Books and the Library Company of Philadelphia, 1990. A bright, beautifully illustrated history of the city.

Wurman, Richard Saul. *Philadelphia Access.* New York: Access Press, 1994. A remarkable and at times brilliant attempt to represent between two covers the physical city. Part of a long series of such attempts by the master designer Wurman.

———, and John Andrew Gallery. *Man-Made Philadelphia: A Guide to the Physical and Cultural Environment.* Cambridge: MIT Press, 1972.

INDEX FOR SPECIALISTS

This appendix serves two purposes. First, it is an effort to *recontextualize,* if you will, the material that appears in the fourteen chapters of the book. Second, there are many noteworthy buildings in Philadelphia that do not fit into the geographical compass of the fourteen chapters. Some of these buildings seem to me to be so noteworthy that I have included some information about them in this appendix. I have also, the reader will notice, included other useful or quirky information that could not appropriately be accommodated in the fourteen chapters. Entries are followed by page numbers.

Clearfield Street and Hunting Park Avenue a bit east of Laurel Hill Cemetery (p. 237), in a part of North Philadelphia that is outside the geographical compass of the fourteen chapters of this book. It is, however, worth seeking out as an important example of the Ecclesiological Gothic of which Notman's St. Mark's (p. 152) is a slightly later example. St. James the Less was built by a Philadelphia merchant named Robert Ralston, who oversaw the contractor, John E. Carver. The church was built from drawings sent to Philadelphia from the Cambridge Camden Society, and the builders of St. James corresponded directly with such luminaries of English Ecclesiology as Benjamin Webb and William Butterfield. St. James the Less is thus one of the most perfectly realized examples of Ecclesiological Gothic in the United States. For a detailed discussion of St. James the Less, I recommend William H. Pierson, Jr., American Buildings and Their Architects, Volume 2: Technology and the Picturesque, the Corporate and the Early Gothic Styles (1978), Chapter IV.

The Church of the Gesù is located at 18th and Stiles Streets in North Philadelphia. It is one of the most beautiful buildings in Philadelphia. It was built in 1879–88 and designed by the too little known Edwin F. Durang. The exterior was sparklingly restored in 1991 by one of our best contemporary architects, John Blatteau. As its name suggests, the church was built by the Jesuit fathers of St. Joseph's College, in the Jesuit style: Baroque. Durang based his design on Giacomo da Vignola's and Giacomo della Porta's sixteenth-century Baroque masterpiece, the Gesù in Rome. The interior is magnificent. The barrel-vaulted nave moves to a crescendo in the domed apse. Throughout are

and very expensive restaurants in operation. Le Bec Fin, on Walnut Street between 15th and 16th Streets, is on everyone's list of the ten best restaurants in the United States; if you go there, be prepared to spend about a month's salary. Di Lullo Centro (Locust Street between Broad and 15th Streets), La Truffe (Front Street between Market and Chestnut Streets), and Ciboulette (in the Bellevue, Broad and 15th Streets) are considered among the city's (very expensive) standouts. For moderately priced, cheerily Italian repast in a bright setting, I like Marabella's, at 17th Street and the Benjamin Franklin Parkway. Below are the restaurants that for one or another reason are mentioned in the text. For a full survey, there is a Zagat guide to Philadelphia restaurants available in any bookstore.

Bookbinders Seafood House (renowned for snapper soup and fried oysters served with cold chicken salad; moderate to expensive), 27

Dante's and Luigi's (Southern Italian; moderate), 137

Famous Delicatessen (Jewish deli, but renowned for chocolate chip cookies and chocolate malteds; inexpensive), 133

Geno's (cheese steaks; inexpensive), 138

Italian Market, 136

Jim's Steaks (cheese steaks; inexpensive), 132

Pat's (cheese steaks; inexpensive), 138

Ray's Café (Chinese, but renowned for coffee; inexpensive), 120

Reading Terminal Market (great for inexpensive meals and snacks), 119

ROBERT SMITH

(1722–77)

*Smith was in his late twenties when he emigrated from his native Scotland to Philadelphia, the first of the numerous Scotsmen to leave his imprint on the cityscape of this city. He was a carpenter and more what we would call a **builder** than an **architect**: his expertise was in interpreting and executing designs from **pattern books** or **copy books** sent to the colonies from London. (It is well not to underestimate the skill that this required.) He owned his own copies of such leading pattern-books as those of the arch-Palladians Colen Campbell (Vitruvius Britannicus, published 1714) and Isaac Ware. Smith was a prominent member of the Carpenters' Company, whose headquarters (Carpenters' Hall) he designed, and whose closely guarded Rule Book he helped to write. Among his non-Philadelphia works is the lovely Nassau Hall (1754–56) at Princeton University in New Jersey.*

Carpenters' Hall, 69

Christ Church (Episcopal), 102

Old Pine Street Church (Presbyterian), 90

St. Peter's Church (Episcopal), 93

WILLIAM STRICKLAND

(1788–1854)

(See p. 66 for a brief biographical sketch.)

Merchants' Exchange, 57

Second Bank of the United States, 65

St. Paul's Church (Episcopal), 84

St. Stephen's Church (Episcopal), 124

United States Naval Asylum, Gray's Ferry Avenue and Bainbridge Street, South Philadelphia, 1827–33, 1844. *Not in text.*

Some important works by Strickland *not* in Philadelphia:

College of Charleston [South Carolina], Main Building, 1828–29.

Mint Museum, Charlotte, North Carolina, 1835–40.

Athenaeum, Benefit Street, Providence, Rhode Island, 1837–38.

Tennessee State Capitol, Nashville, 1845–59.

Downtown Presbyterian Church, Nashville, Tennessee, 1849–51.

JOHN HAVILAND

(1792–1852)

Haviland was the son of a Sussex (England) country squire, and traveled to Russia before immigrating to Philadelphia. He authored The Builder's Assistant (three volumes, 1818–21), one of the first American pattern-books to illustrate Greek architecture. Though he went bankrupt in 1829 and had his reputation tarnished by being accused of misappropriating federal funds in a building project, he retained and even increased his renown as a prison architect.

Atwater Kent Museum (former Franklin Institute), 126

Eastern State Penitentiary, 217

University of the Arts/Pennsylvania Institution for the Deaf and Dumb (east building), 34

Walnut Street Theater, 49

THOMAS USTICK WALTER

(1804–87)

After apprenticing with Strickland, Walter, age twenty-six, established, in 1830, his own Philadelphia practice. He designed the Moyamensing Prison (1832, demolished 1968), at Reed and 10th Streets in South Philadelphia, in Gothic Revival (he also designed the prison's addition in 1835, in Egyptian Revival), but made his name with his ill-fated design, with much interference from Nicholas Biddle, for Founders' Hall at Girard College, for which Walter won a competition in 1833 (edging out his mentor Strickland). What Walter, one of the greatest of American architects, will best be remembered for, however, is none of his Philadelphia buildings, but his magnificent work on the Capitol in Washington: he designed the Senate and House wings and the dome. Obviously expert at monumental works, Walter consulted on the design of Broad Street's City Hall, designed by McArthur, who had apprenticed with Walter as Walter had with Strickland (and Strickland with Latrobe).

Walter taught, with Strickland and Haviland, at the Franklin Institute, and was a founder and the second president (he succeeded New York's Richard Upjohn) of the American Institute of Architects.

Founders' Hall, Girard College, 219
Philadelphia Contributionship for Insuring Houses from Loss by Fire, 81
Philadelphia Saving Fund Society (Walnut and 3rd streets), 59
Portico Row, 53
Society Hill Synagogue, 418

Spruce Street, 1829–30. *Not in text.*

Some important works by Walter *not* in Philadelphia:

Andalusia, Bucks County. Walter's extensive 1836 remodeling for Nicholas Biddle of his 1798 country house.
St. James's Episcopal Church, Wilmington, North Carolina, 1839. Gothic Revival.
Hibernian Hall, Charleston, South Carolina, 1839–40. Greek Revival.
Old First Baptist Church, Richmond, Virginia, 1839–41. Greek Revival.
Old Norfolk Academy, Norfolk, Virginia, 1840. Greek Revival.
Freemason Street Baptist Church, Norfolk, Virginia, 1848–50. Gothic Revival.

JOHN NOTMAN
(1810–65)
(See p. 153 for a brief biographical sketch.)

Athenaeum of Philadelphia, 38
Cathedral of Saints Peter and Paul (R.C.), 193
Holy Trinity Church (Episcopal), 149
Laurel Hill Cemetery, 237
St. Clement's Church (Episcopal), 168
St. Mark's Church (Episcopal), 152

JOSEPH C. HOXIE
(1814–70)
Hoxie was born in Rhode Island and in his thirties formed a practice in Philadelphia with his brother-in-law, Stephen Decatur Button (1813–97); the partnership lasted for four years. Hoxie specialized in churches and train stations, and did a great deal of work in small cities in Pennsylvania and Ohio. There is not a style

he did not employ, and creditably.

Arch Street Presbyterian Church, 166
Ebenezer Maxwell house, 252
Elliott and Leland Buildings, 111

NAPOLEON LEBRUN
(1821–1901)
(See p. 32 for a brief biographical sketch.)

Academy of Music, 30
Cathedral of Saints Peter and Paul (R.C.), 193
St. Augustine's Church (R.C.), 108

FRANK FURNESS
(1839–1912)
(See p. 7 for a brief biographical sketch.)

Furness & Hewitt:
Pennsylvania Academy of the Fine Arts, 3
Thomas Hockley house, 157
University of the Arts/Pennsylvania Institution for the Deaf and Dumb (west building), 34

Frank Furness on his own:
Centennial Bank, 32nd and Market streets, 1876. *Not in text.*
Kensington National Bank, Frankford and Girard avenues, 1877. *Not in text.*
William H. Rhawn house, 8001 Verree Road (way northeast), 1879–81. *Not in text.*

Furness, Evans & Co.:
First Unitarian Church, 158
Furness Library, University of Pennsylvania, 178

G.W. AND W.D. HEWITT

George Watson Hewitt
(1841–1916)
George Watson Hewitt, born in Burlington, New Jersey, trained under John Notman before

*partnering with John Fraser
and Frank Furness as Fraser,
Furness & Hewitt in 1867. In
1876, after co-designing the
Pennsylvania Academy of the
Fine Arts with Furness, Hewitt
formed his own firm, shortly
thereafter bringing in his
brother William as partner.
The brothers had one of
Philadelphia's most prolific and
varied practices, and if they
produced no masterpieces, there
is a uniformly high quality to
their works, and they certainly
deserve to be better known.*

Wilson Eyre
(1858–1944)

*Eyre was born in Florence to
American parents: a good start.
He studied under Henry Van
Brunt at M.I.T. and from
1877 to 1881 worked in
Philadelphia for James P. Sims
(the architect who in 1881
added the pediment to Thomas
U. Walter's Philadelphia Saving Fund Society building of
1839 at 306 Walnut Street).
Eyre moved from Queen Anne
to a simpler Shingle Style, always with a heavy Arts-and-
Crafts flavor. There is a flair
and originality to his picturesque suburban houses that I
suppose makes comparisons
with his close contemporary
Frank Lloyd Wright (1869–
1959) inevitable.*

HORACE TRUMBAUER
(1868–1938)

*Trumbauer is hands down my
favorite Philadelphia architect.
Yet when the drum roll sounds
and Philadelphia's architectural greats are introduced, you
will hear the names of
Strickland, Walter, Notman,
Furness, Eyre, Cret, Howe,
Kahn, Giurgola, and Venturi.
Likelier than not, Trumbauer
will be left off the list. He was
one of America's best Beaux-
Arts architects, which is I suppose the undoing of his reputation. Ironically, as in the case
of Stanford White and Cass
Gilbert and a few other so-
called Beaux-Arts architects,
Trumbauer never actually attended the École des Beaux-
Arts. Indeed, Trumbauer appears to have had little formal
education of any kind, a lack
that exacerbated his painful
shyness and insecurity. But just
as his lack of formal schooling
renders his architectural ac-
complishment all the more impressive, so his shrinking-violet
personality seems not to have
hindered his remarkable abil-
ity to get commissions from
many of the richest parvenus in
Philadelphia and elsewhere.*

*This salesman's son, born in
Philadelphia, worked first as a
messenger then as a draftsman
for George W. Hewitt from
1884 to 1892. Trumbauer's
first major commission was to
design Grey Towers (1893–98),
the William Welsh Harrison
house that is now part of Beaver College, in Glenside, Pennsylvania. The spectacular country house would become a
Trumbauer specialty. He designed the 150-room Whitemarsh Hall (1916–21), with
grounds by Jacques Gréber, for
Edward T. Stotesbury of Drexel
& Co., in Wyndmoor, Pennsylvania. One of the most spectacular houses ever built in the
United States, Whitemarsh
Hall was demolished in 1980.
For an unparalleled discussion
of this house, see James T.
Maher's excellent book* The
Twilight of Splendor: Chron-
icles of the Age of American
Palaces *(Boston: Little, Brown,
1975). Trumbauer also became
the favored architect of James
B. Duke of tobacco fame, designing his palatial house
(1909–12) on Fifth Avenue in
New York, and the campus
(1928–30) of Duke University
in Durham, North Carolina.
(The Duke house in New York
was renovated into New York
University's prestigious Institute
of Fine Arts in 1958 by
Philadelphia's Robert Venturi
and John Rauch's firm of Cope
& Lippincott.) Trumbauer designed The Elms (1899–1901)
on Bellevue Avenue in Newport
for Edward J. Berwind.*

*Much of the credit for
Trumbauer's later works must
go to his excellent assistant
Julian Francis Abele. Abele was
a young African American
working in Trumbauer's office
when, courtesy of Trumbauer,*

he attended the École des Beaux-Arts, something Trumbauer himself had been unable to do. (It recalls how Stanford White paid the way of Frederick MacMonnies to the École, and how Daniel H. Burnham, who also never attended the École, had attempted to pay the way of young Frank Lloyd Wright.)

Trumbauer never overcame his painful shyness; became an alcoholic; and died, a childless widower, of cirrhosis of the liver.

PAUL PHILIPPE CRET
(1876–1945)
Cret was an anomaly: a Beaux-Arts-trained Frenchman working in America. Born in Lyons, he was called to the University of Pennsylvania in 1903 at the age of twenty-seven. He was one of the twentieth century's most versatile designers. He designed city plans and intimate parks, large office buildings and small museums, country houses and suspension bridges. There was, in short, nothing Cret could not and did not design, and better than just about anyone else in his time. The very versatility may work against his reputation: Is it so much of a sin to suggest that Cret excelled

Frank Lloyd Wright as a designer?

Some of Cret's best buildings are not in Philadelphia:

In Philadelphia:

(VERUS T.) RITTER (1883–1942) & HOWELL LEWIS) SHAY (1885–1975)

ADDISON HUTTON

(EHRMAN) MITCHELL (1924–) & (ROMALDO) GIURGOLA (1920–)

ROBERT VENTURI
(1925–)
(See p. 241 for a brief biographical sketch.)

Venturi & Rauch:

Venturi, Rauch & (Denise) Scott Brown (1931–):

BEFORE 1776

INDEX

Index

Index

Index

Index

Index

Index

Index

Index

Index

Index

Index

Index

Index

Index

Index

Index

Index

Index

Index

Index

Index

Index

Index

Index

Index

Index

Index

Index

Index

Index

Index

Index

Index

Index

Index

Index

Index

Index